Best Wishes,

[signature]

WENONAH'S STORY
a Memoir of a Chickasaw Family

J. WENONAH PAUL GUNNING'S memoir
as told through ROBIN GUNNING

ISBN: 978-1-935684-34-3

Cover & Book Design: Corey Fetters

Chickasaw Press
PO Box 1548
Ada, Oklahoma 74821

www.chickasawpress.com

To my beloved brother Willie.
- James Wenonah Paul Gunning

To my mother, Wenonah, who taught me to appreciate my family.
- Robin Gunning

- Table of Contents -

- Acknowledgments -

There's no way I can thank my mother, Wenonah Gunning, enough—not just for being my inspiration and for providing most of the information contained in this book, but also for the love and support she and my father, Donald Gunning, gave me over the years. They deserve credit for everything that I have achieved and for none of my failures.

All of my mother's family had pride in their heritage, but the person who instilled that pride was my grandmother, Victoria May Rosser Paul. She taught her children to value the history of their ancestors, and she saved the documents, pictures, and mementos that provided the background for the early part of this book.

Other than my mother, the person who did the most to learn and to compile information about our family was my uncle Haskell. He traveled to California, North Carolina, and even to Scotland, collecting documents and pictures and locating family members. He also recorded information about the early history of Pauls Valley and the early settlers from conversations with Grandmother and with Uncle Buck, Smith Whealton Paul, my grandfather's brother.

I want to thank my wife, Sarah, who for years has put up with my preoccupation with this project. Without her love and support, I would never have been able to complete it.

Steven McLean, my cousin and best friend through the years, has done the most to encourage me. He and his brother Homer have both shared their memories with me, and they were both a source of company and cheer for my mother during the years after my father died.

The other person who helped me tremendously, reading my notes and making additions and corrections, was my cousin Tom Paul, or "Little Tom," as he is called in the book. Tom, a talented writer himself, was fourteen years older than me and witnessed events that neither Wenonah nor I knew about. Unfortunately, Tom passed away in 2007, three years before my mother.

I also want to thank my cousin Christine Paul Swinney, who shared her memories, gave me encouragement, and who loved my grandmother.

Adrienne Grimmett, of the Pauls Valley Historical Society, has been most helpful in sharing her time and her extensive knowledge of Pauls Valley history and has helped me locate documents and pictures from the Pauls Valley Depot Museum and from the Nora Sparks Warren Memorial Library in Pauls Valley.

Finally, I owe a debt of gratitude to Wiley Barnes of the Chickasaw Press, who saw enough value in my manuscript to give me the chance to develop it into a book and to my editors, Suzanne Mackey and Stanley Nelson, also of the Chickasaw Press, who patiently worked with me to knock the rough edges off my manuscript and taught me a lot about writing.

- *Preface* -

Wenonah's Story is a joint effort by my mother, James Wenonah Paul Gunning, and me, to tell her family's story. Though I wrote the stories, they are hers, taken from conversations and taped interviews during the last ten years of her life. I've also spent many hours of research in an effort to provide documentation and background for her stories. When there was a discrepancy about facts, I used the version that she told me.

Because the stories are hers, I chose to write *Wenonah's Story* as a memoir in her voice. This has allowed me to transmit some of my mother's personality and to tell things from her perspective.

Wenonah and I first discussed writing a book in 2005, but the truth is, *Wenonah's Story* has been in the making much longer than that. My mother spent her life saving keepsakes, pictures, letters, and newspaper articles about our family. She taught me at an early age that I was part Chickasaw Indian, that the town of Pauls Valley, Oklahoma, was named after my great-great-grandfather, that my great-grandfather had been a member of the Chickasaw Lighthorse police force and a senator in the Chickasaw Nation before statehood, that my grandfather had built some of the important buildings in Pauls Valley, and that my uncle, Homer Paul, had been a member of the Oklahoma State Legislature.

I think Wenonah learned pride in her heritage from her mother, Victoria Paul. Grandmother's house was like a museum. Every piece of furniture, every picture, and every plant in her yard had a story to tell. There were water buffalo horns on the wall that she had bought in Galveston in 1913, a pendulum clock that had been a wedding present in 1898, and a sidesaddle she had ridden when my grandfather had been a rancher. Grandmother sat with me on her porch swing when I was little and told me stories about Indian Territory, about her childhood on the frontier, and about her children.

Growing up in the Paul family was a wonderful experience. When my aunts and uncles and cousins gathered in Pauls Valley, Grandmother's old house came alive. They would gather around the big dining room table and laugh and talk about old times. The Pauls were passionate and volatile. Everyone's problems were discussed, especially if they weren't there, and there was always a new story to tell. The Pauls knew how to make a little boy feel special, too. Grandmother taught me to paint with oils, Aunt Kaliteyo ate cookies and milk with me after school, Uncle Tom taught me to box, and Uncle Haskell took me to his farm, explained how the windmill worked, and let me ride on the tractor.

The summer after my senior year in high school, Wenonah took the money she had saved from her grocery budget and paid for a family vacation for us through the South. We visited Georgia, where her mother's family had lived before the Civil War, and we toured the Chickasaw homeland in Mississippi, where her father's people had lived before the Removal, when the federal government forced the Chickasaws to move from their homeland to what is now Oklahoma.

After I graduated from college and left home, I became involved in my work as a geriatrician and with my own family, but Wenonah continued working to preserve our family's history. She saved newspaper clippings about family and friends, and when Grandmother passed away, she saved many of her keepsakes. Later, Wenonah was appointed to the board of directors for the Chickasaw Historical Society. She donated books, documents, and pictures to the Chickasaw Archives, as well as the museums at Pauls Valley and Wynnewood. She and my father attended tribal gatherings. She became reacquainted with some of the women she had gone to school with, and many other Chickasaws with whom she shared a common heritage. She told me that during that time she felt more at home than at any time since she was a child.

When my father passed away in 2000, Wenonah was left alone. Since we were separated by the six hundred miles between Denver and Oklahoma City, I started calling her regularly to make sure she was okay.

At first she was frightened and unsure of herself. She had never before had to manage her own finances, the maintenance and repairs of the house and the cars, but she talked to the lawyer, the accountant, and the banker, and soon she had everything organized. She had lists of bills, calendars with doctor's appointments, and so forth. Within a year she had a routine and had regained her confidence.

It was amazing to me to see how Wenonah adapted to her new life. She woke up early, about 6 a.m., and did her exercises. I set my alarm one morning just to watch her. She worked out vigorously for thirty minutes, walking briskly around the room, doing leg and arm exercises with two-pound weights, and doing modified push-ups and sit-ups on the floor. I couldn't believe it! She was ninety years old!

She would take me shopping, driving the car herself, at the speed limit. I asked her to read the street signs to prove to me that she could see them. Her routine was to go to the post office, to the gas station, to the grocery store, the pharmacy, and of course, the used book store, to exchange the books she had finished for new ones. She knew the clerks at the stores, the gas station attendant, the pharmacist, and of course, the lady who owned the bookstore. She chatted with them, asked about their families, and everywhere she went, she left people smiling.

We carried on our regular phone conversations for almost ten years, and I visited her as often as I could. We not only talked about family history, but also current events, the books she was reading, her health problems, and the loneliness and isolation she felt. In turn, I told her about my work with the elderly and about my love for the mountains. This time we had together was a blessing for us both. We got to relate to each other as friends, not just as mother and son, and I learned to appreciate her in different ways than I ever had before.

During our conversations, she told me stories about her life, her relatives, and her childhood in Pauls Valley. As we talked, I regained my fascination with our family's history, and I started piecing together the stories she told me. Her memory was astonishing. The more questions I had for her, the more details she filled in.

Talking to my mother made me curious about the history of the times our ancestors lived in and what life was like in Indian Territory before statehood, when sixty miles was a two-day trip, when food was stored without refrigeration, and when every fever might turn into a life-threatening illness. As I read history books, I started finding references to members of our family. Wenonah and I shared the excitement of these discoveries, and we worked together to put them into the context of her memories and the stories that had been handed down in the family.

We found a map of Fort Arbuckle in 1859, with Smith Paul's farm clearly marked, together with the homes of several other Chickasaw families. One of the homes belonged to the family of Susan Garvin, whom Wenonah knew as a child. There was a story in the same book about a Comanche raid on the little community, during which the Chickasaw settlers took refuge in the fort.

There was a lot of information about Wenonah's grandfather Sam Paul, who was sent to jail in 1883 for killing a white horse thief in his capacity as an Indian policeman. He was later pardoned by the president of the United States, in response to a petition by the Chickasaw Legislature. We found a copy of his pardon and also the transcript of his trial. The most interesting part of the transcript was the testimony of a cowboy who had tracked the horse thieves and reported their location to Sam Paul. My mother and I sat at her kitchen table and read his testimony together, fascinated as he described tracking the stolen horse for miles, identifying it only by a missing shoe.

There weren't many surprises in the family's more recent history because of Wenonah's phenomenal memory, but we did clarify one mystery. When Wenonah was six, her parents moved the family to San Antonio, Texas, where her father joined his cousin selling real estate in Mexico. The business failed, and the family had to return after less than a year. Wenonah couldn't tell me why, but after studying the history of the area, I discovered that Pancho Villa was terrorizing the countryside about that time, making it clear why no one was interested in buying Mexican real estate.

Wenonah was never easy to please, and working with her on this book was no different. She was especially concerned that I made it clear that her parents were educated and cultured, even though they grew up on the frontier. She saved me from some embarrassing mistakes too, like when I read a letter from her grandfather that referred to "good ol' sorghum molasses," and concluded that he meant it tasted good. Wenonah laughed and informed me that they used sorghum as medicine and that it tasted terrible. She also helped me with my writing style, telling me over and over to "just tell the story, don't embellish it." After a while, she started calling me her "biographer."

As I helped Wenonah put together her memories, I got insights into what she was like as a mischievous little girl, as a popular teenager, and as a strong, assertive young woman. I learned about her dreams and ambitions, about her values, and about the events that had molded her character. I began to understand her loyalty and devotion to her family and her dedication to preserving their memory.

When I started writing the stories, I was never quite satisfied with the way they sounded. Something was missing. Something didn't seem quite right. Then one day, it occurred to me—these aren't my stories. They're Wenonah's, her joys and disappointments, her triumphs and failures, the deepest feelings of her heart, and she should tell them herself. So I rewrote them from her perspective, like she told them to me. My mother had a gift for expressing herself anyway, like all the members of her family, and the narrative always sounded better when she told it.

Unfortunately, Wenonah passed away before this book was finished, but it is hers, the story of a remarkable woman and the result of a lifetime of dedication to helping her family and to preserving its history.

CHAPTER 1
- Roots -

J. Wenonah Paul Gunning: In the summer of 1922, I was eight years old and confused. So much had changed in Pauls Valley since we left three years before. The Harkreader family had moved into our big house in town, and we were living out at the farm, cramped up in the old house where Papa was born. It's a good thing it was summertime, because the roof leaked and there were big cracks in the walls. There was no indoor plumbing like we had in town, and we had to use an outhouse and draw our water from a well. Mama no longer had a maid and had to do all the housework herself. She worked outside too, helping my oldest brother, Willie, tend the animals and plant a few crops. Papa didn't have a job or a car, but every morning he'd get dressed in a suit and tie anyway, hitch up one of the horses, and drive the buggy into town.

I blamed Papa for our troubles, probably because Mama told me it was his fault. She used me and my six-year-old brother Bob to blow off steam. We'd sit in the kitchen, and while we watched her cook and do the dishes, she'd tell us how our lives had been ruined by Papa's drinking. "Your damned old daddy," she'd call him. He hated to be called "daddy."

While I always took Mama's side, not everything she said made sense. After all, it was Mama's idea to leave Pauls Valley in the first place, and the jobs Papa had tried since then were her idea, too. Sometimes Papa didn't come home at night, but we didn't see him drunk. My brothers and sister were divided on who was to blame. Bob, like me, sided with Mama, but Haskell and Kaliteyo sided with Papa. They said everything was fine until Mama talked him into leaving Pauls Valley. If Snip had an opinion, he kept it to himself. Besides, he was too busy cooking up schemes to make money. My sweet brother Willie never took sides. He just did what he could to help out the family and to keep the peace.

We didn't get much company that summer until Uncle Tom came to visit us. I'd never seen my mother's older brother before. He was tall and slender, his hands rough and his face ruddy from working out in the sun. He walked with a limp because he wore an artificial leg. He didn't talk much, but once he got started, he could tell some good stories. He had a thick Southern drawl, like Grandpa.

Mama was working in the kitchen the day Uncle Tom arrived. She kept staring out of the window, trying to make out who it was, until suddenly she screamed at the top of her lungs, burst out of the door, and ran down the road to meet him.

For a while, everyone was happy. Mama and Papa took Uncle Tom around to see our friends and relatives. There were a few people who still remembered him from when Mama's family had come to Indian Territory as settlers thirty years before, and of course, he went down to Ardmore to visit Grandpa in the old soldiers' home.

Uncle Tom spent about a month with us, and it made Mama so happy to be with him. They would sit together and talk until late into the night about their childhoods, about their family's long migration from Georgia to Indian Territory after the Civil War, and about living in a log cabin and tilling the fields with a hand plow pulled by an ox. They told us stories about the big "*lobo*" wolves that howled at night and sometimes tried to get at the livestock, about the old bachelor who used to visit them and play the fiddle, and about their mother teaching them all to read and teaching the little girls to sew. Uncle Tom told Mama about his farm on the banks of the Mississippi River, how he had to fight the tobacco worms, how some years the river would flood and he would make rafts for himself and his horses, and how he made annual trips to Hot Springs, Arkansas, to have the malaria "boiled" out of him. When Papa wasn't around, Mama would confide in her brother about her troubles and about how we had come to be in our present depressing state of affairs.

In my eight-year-old mind, I had decided all our troubles were the result of Mama and Papa's marriage, and since Uncle Tom was Mama's older brother, I figured he should know all about it. After all, he had been with her when she came to Indian Territory, when she started courting Papa, and when they got married. All month long I screwed up my courage, and finally one day I asked him. He was drawing water from the well. "Why did you let Mama marry Papa?" I blurted out. He looked right down into my eyes and replied—I'll never forget it—"We did everything we could to stop Vick from marrying your father, but she was headstrong."

Mama's family came from the deep South. Grandpa and my grandmother Emily were born in Georgia, where their parents owned plantations. They didn't consider most people their equals, especially people of color, and although they had to compromise in Indian Territory, where the prominent citizens were all Indians and most of the whites were "low class," they certainly didn't approve of their daughter marrying Papa, a Chickasaw.

I never knew my grandmother, Emily Bass Rosser. She died of a tumor soon after the family came to Indian Territory. But Grandpa lived with us when I was little. I was named after him. I was supposed to be a boy. His name was James Thomas Rosser, and I was named James Wenonah Paul. Everyone called me Jamie when I was little, and later, Jim. As much as I loved Grandpa, I hated having a boy's name. Mama did give me a feminine middle name, Wenonah, although most people still called me Jim until I was grown. She got Wenonah from Longfellow's poem, *The Song of Hiawatha*. She spelled it wrong—Winona—but after I was old enough to read the poem myself, I started spelling my name like Longfellow spelled it.

It's a beautiful poem:

> *By the shores of Gitche Gumee,*
> *By the shining Big-Sea-Water,*
> *Stood the wigwam of Nokomis,*
> *Daughter of the Moon, Nokomis. ...*
> *Fair Nokomis bore a daughter.*
> *And she called her name Wenonah,*
> *As the first-born of her daughters.*
> *And the daughter of Nokomis*
> *Grew up like the prairie lilies,*
> *Grew a tall and slender maiden,*
> *With the beauty of the moonlight,*
> *With the beauty of the starlight.*[1]

The Song of Hiawatha tells how the beautiful Wenonah was swept off her feet, so to speak, by the West Wind, by whom she bore a son named Hiawatha. In spite of his lofty stature among the gods, the West Wind turned out to be a deadbeat dad. He deserted Wenonah and left her to die of a broken heart. So as you see, Wenonah was quite a romantic figure, not at all like me.

As a member of the Southern aristocracy, my grandmother Emily was raised to be a lady, to know how to dress appropriately for any occasion, how to entertain guests and join in polite conversation, how to grow beautiful flowers, and how to prepare tasty *hors d'oeuvres* and desserts. Grandpa grew up on a neighboring plantation, learning the corresponding behavior and skills appropriate for a gentleman.

When the Civil War broke out, Grandpa joined the Confederate Army. He attended a military school as a boy, and even when I knew him he still stood ramrod-straight, like a soldier at attention. I don't think he saw much action. Mama ordered his military records when she applied for membership in the United Daughters of the Confederacy. They showed he enlisted as a private in May of 1862 and was reported as "sick in hospital" on the next muster call.[2] He doesn't appear in the records again until August of 1863 when he re-enlisted, this time as a sergeant. He married my grandmother Emily in the meantime.[3] Six months later, Grandpa resigned from the army for good.[4] I don't really think his heart was in it. He always said the war was caused by "a bunch of hotheads."

James and Emily's world was turned upside down by the Civil War. Not only was much of their family's wealth destroyed, there was looting and chaos, and a poorly functioning government. With the support of some freed slaves, opportunists from the North, known as "carpetbaggers" for the luggage they brought with them, took over many government positions. The hostility between those newcomers and the Southern whites led to the encounter that forced Grandpa and Emily to flee their home in Georgia.

Emily had just delivered their first baby, Cora Lee. There was an election coming up in Cedartown, and Grandpa was trying to convince the family's former slaves not to vote for the carpetbaggers. While he was making his case to an ex-slave, a carpetbagger came walking by. The man accused Grandpa of trying to influence the black man's vote, and there was a fight. The man fell, his head hit a rock, and he didn't get up.

There was no time to lose. Southern whites had virtually no influence at the time, and Grandpa was facing a long jail sentence, at the least. I'm not sure if the man died or not, but Grandpa couldn't afford to wait around to find out. That night he and Emily took their baby Cora, and whatever they could pack in a wagon, and fled west. They kept going until they got to Alabama, where they felt safe enough to settle down for a while. Thus began the family's twenty-two-year journey to Indian Territory.

Grandpa was headed for Texas to join his brother Ed, but he took his time. In each new community he would rent some land and a cabin. He would stay long enough to make a few harvests and build up a little stake before moving again. Sometimes they would stay in the same place for several years. Times were tough for a while,[5] but Grandpa became fairly prosperous for a pioneer. He was able to hire teachers for the children, and he and Emily even had some semblance of a social life. By the time Mama was born, Grandpa had become known as "Captain Rosser"—he probably exaggerated his role in the Civil War—and in one community he was even elected magistrate.

Four more children were born while the family crossed Alabama: two sons, Thomas and Luther,[6] and two daughters, Kittie and Lillie.[7] Mama was born later in Calhoun County, Mississippi, on March 31, 1877, sixteen years after her parents had fled from Georgia. Years later, I found a note that Mama had written: "I was born in Calhoun County, Mississippi, just three miles from the Yellow Bushy Swamp."[8] The Yalobusha River runs through Calhoun County and means "tadpole place" in Chickasaw. So, ironically, Mama was born in the heart of the old Chickasaw homeland.

The same year Mama was born, the family was struck by their first tragedy. Her brother "Lutha" died—with her Southern accent, Mama always reversed her "a's" and her "er's." He had lived seven years, seven months, and twenty-seven days.[9]

In 1880, Mama's family moved again. Her younger sister, Ada, was born that year. Mama was three.[10] This time they settled in the little community of Palmer Station, Arkansas, just twenty-five miles west of the Mississippi River, where Mama spent her childhood.

Mama loved Arkansas. She loved the rolling hills, the forests and streams, and the beautiful wildflowers and birds. She told us about seeing flocks of passenger pigeons so dense they blocked out the light of the sun. Mama's mother Emily taught her to read there. Her sisters Kittie and Lillie got to go to a school in nearby Hyde Park, but Emily told Mama she was too young.

Mama learned a little about farming from Grandpa. She learned the right time to plant onions, sweet potatoes, corn, and strawberries, and which wild plants were good to eat, and which had medicinal uses—knowledge that would come in handy later, during hard times. She also learned practical lessons about living on the frontier, like the value of the giant king snake, which would keep the area clear of rattlers, and the danger of wolves which roamed the forest at night. Grandpa always plowed a few furrows around the cabin to protect it from fire, but beyond this small clearing was the forest. The girls played there during the daytime, picking the wildflowers and eating the pawpaws, always guarded by their faithful dog, Watch.

Watch was a huge Great Dane. The little girls put dresses on him and harnessed him to their wagon. Ada was small enough to ride him. Watch patiently tolerated the abuse heaped on him by his little mistresses, but he knew his duty.

Emily warned Mama and her sisters to play close to the house and not to stay out past dark, but one evening the girls were late coming in. They hadn't noticed the sun sinking over the horizon until Watch began to growl. They knew immediately they were in danger. They couldn't see the wolves, but they knew they were there. The little girls started running toward the house, and as they ran, they heard Watch growl menacingly behind them as he faced the wolves. When the girls got to the cabin and opened the door for Watch to follow, they saw the wolves behind him in the clearing.

After the Rossers had lived in Palmer Station for two years, another daughter was born—Sister Eula, or "Euler," as Mama said it. Eula died before she was a year old.[11] The little girls believed that when their brother Luther and their sister Eula died, they took their place among the stars. Afterward, on some evenings, the girls would lie out on the grass, look up at the sky, and try to find their brother and sister. A star that shone a little brighter than the others would be Luther, watching after his little sister Eula, twinkling next to him.

In 1888, Grandpa decided it was time to move again. The children were growing up. Sister Cora was married,[12] and Sister Kittie was already fourteen. It had been twenty-two years since the family had left Georgia, and they still had another five hundred miles to go before they could join Uncle Ed in Texas.

About that time a Chickasaw named Sam Paul visited Palmer Station.[13] Mr. Paul didn't match Grandpa's image of an Indian at all. He was dark-skinned, all right, but he dressed neatly in a suit and spoke eloquently. Mr. Paul visited all the farms in the area and invited everyone to come to a meeting to learn about the opportunities for white settlers in Indian Territory. Grandpa decided to go.

James Rosser, Grandpa

Sam Paul was a good salesman. He knew how to make a speech and knew about farming. He described how his father, Smith Paul, came to the territory with the Chickasaws and married his mother, Ela-teecha, a full-blood Chickasaw woman. He told how they became the first settlers in the fertile Washita River valley around Pauls Valley, a town named for his father.[14] He said the Indians who controlled the land there were eager to lease it out and a white settler could farm all the land he wanted, simply by buying a five-dollar permit.[15] Mr. Paul told them the Santa Fe Railroad completed a line through the area the year before[16] and there was a train depot right there at Pauls Valley. Farmers could sell everything they could produce. Mr. Paul's vision for the future was that Indian Territory would be developed through the cooperation of Indians and whites and before long it would become a state of the Union.

It sounded almost too good to be true, but Grandpa went to check it out anyway. He was gone about a month. When he got back, he was excited. He said the Indian communities were civilized, even more so than some white communities in Arkansas. He found the Indians warm and accommodating and the land just as rich as Mr. Paul said, better than any he would find in Texas. It was a place where they could finally settle down. Grandpa told his family to pack. They were moving to Indian Territory.

Mama was eleven in 1888 when she came to the Chickasaw Nation. It must have been exciting for her. I'm sure she imagined seeing vast herds of buffalo, bands of "wild Indians" dressed in colorful costumes, and desperadoes hiding by the roadside, but what she found was entirely different. The country was settled by Chickasaw farmers, and they were not wild at all. Their skin was dark, but they dressed like white men, lived in houses, and were quite hospitable. She described her family's journey years later in an interview:

> I remember people telling my father that he would have to be on the lookout for horse thieves. We had some trouble while crossing Arkansas, but after we crossed into the Indian Territory we never were bothered by anyone. My father would buy feed from the Indians, and they were the most accommodating people I ever met. We came through Muskogee, but there wasn't much of a town there then. At that time there were but few roads, and at times it looked as if it would be impossible to go any farther. After several months of traveling over rough country, we located at Pauls Valley. My father traded the ox team, a tent, and a few horses to Mr. John Burks for a

lease that had a two-room log house on it. This lease had never been worked, but there was a plowed furrow around it. My father and brother began putting this prairie land in cultivation. There was open range at that time, and you could have all the hogs and cattle you wanted to own, but you had to have your brand and mark on them.[17]

The first Indians the Rossers met might have been "accommodating," but they soon found out the Chickasaws were sharply divided in their attitudes toward whites.

On the one hand, the mixed-blood Chickasaws like Sam Paul, the man who had talked Grandpa into coming to Indian Territory, welcomed the white settlers. They believed that integration with whites was their best chance for survival as an independent Indian state, and also they were making a profit by renting them land. On the other hand, there were the full-bloods, who controlled the Chickasaw legislature. They had seen their homeland in Mississippi taken away by white settlers fifty years earlier, and now they saw it happening again.

By the time the Rossers arrived in Indian Territory, the Chickasaw Legislature had passed a law providing that only citizens with Indian blood could vote, giving the full-blood party a majority in the next governor's election. After the election, Sam Paul led an armed revolt against the full-blood-controlled legislature.[18] Grandpa must have wondered just what he had gotten his family into, but it was too late. He had sunk everything he had into the new farm.

Luckily the Rossers' neighbors were mainly white or mixed-blood Chickasaws, so they were welcomed into the little community of Klondike, near Pauls Valley. After Grandpa and Uncle Tom got the crops planted and Emily and the girls made their little cabin livable, Mama and Aunt Ada were sent to school in Pauls Valley. That's where they met Papa, William Hiram Paul, the son of Sam Paul and the grandson of Smith Paul, the town's founder.

Sam Paul might have been a prominent politician, but he led a wanton personal life. It was said that after Papa was born, in March of 1876, he spent the next month on a drunken spree with one of his girlfriends.[19]

Papa's mother, Sarah Lambert Paul, probably got a little help with her new baby from Sam's family, but for the most part she was on her own. She not only had her new baby, Billie, to care for, but also his brothers. Buck was two and Joe, Sam's son from a previous marriage, was seven.

Mrs. Paul—that's what we called our grandmother—was a timid woman. She lived across the street from us when I was little, so I knew her pretty well. Mama used to say Mrs. Paul was scared of her own shadow, but it was understandable. She had been through a lot.

Her life with Sam must have been hell. He went out with other women constantly, and when he came home he was usually drunk. He even brought his women friends home with him, and if Mrs. Paul complained, he would tell her that if she didn't like it, she could leave. He once even threatened to kill her.[20]

Sam could be cruel and ruthless. Mrs. Paul guessed he had killed as many as fifteen men. Such was his reputation that when she finally did try to leave him, her father wouldn't let her in the door. He told her that it was better for her to be killed than the whole family.[21]

So Papa and Uncle Buck grew up kind of like wild turkeys. Their father was rarely at home, and when he was, he didn't pay much attention to them. I don't think they relied that much on their mother, either. They didn't even call her Mama. She was always just "Sis."

If Papa and Uncle Buck got any supervision, it was from their aunts and uncles. Sam may have been wild, but he was part of a close-knit family, and Chickasaw families took responsibility for their children. His sisters, Kathrine and Sippie, and his brother, Tecumseh, all lived nearby, and had large families.

When Papa was six, his father was sent to prison. Sam was an officer in the Chickasaw Lighthorse police, and he was convicted of manslaughter for killing a prisoner. According to Sam, the man went for his gun, but the prisoner was a white man, and Indian police had no authority over white men, so the federal marshal decided to make an example of him.

In spite of his shameless personal behavior, Sam had killed the man in the course of his duty as a police officer, and he was from a prominent family, so the Chickasaw Legislature applied for and was granted a presidential pardon for him. He was released after about a year in prison.

After returning home, Sam divorced Mrs. Paul—he thought she had an affair—and took custody of Papa and his brothers. As a white woman, Mrs. Paul had no right to custody of her Indian children. Sam remarried and sent his boys off to school. Joe went to college in Sherman, Texas, and Uncle Buck and Papa went to a boarding school in Whitebead, about five miles west of Pauls Valley.

Mama at age fifteen

Sam wasn't a very strict father, and young Chickasaw boys weren't physically punished, anyway—they were shamed, instead—so Papa didn't get much discipline. That doesn't mean their father was lenient, though. The first time he took Papa and Buck to school, they ran away. Papa said they were exhausted when they got home, hungry and thirsty, and afraid they'd get a whipping. Sam didn't scold them, though. He just walked out to the barn, hitched up the buggy, and took them back.

Sam also demanded his sons be treated with respect. One of Papa's teachers at the boarding school was prejudiced against Indians and had the habit of calling his students "little Indian pups." When word of this got back to Sam, he rode out one evening and accosted the teacher while he was riding home. He pulled the man down from his buggy and horse-whipped him.

After a couple of years in boarding school, Sam enrolled his boys in a subscription school[22] at home in Pauls Valley, the school where Mama and Papa met. Billie was outgoing and smart and immediately attracted to Vickie Rosser, the pretty, vivacious white girl with the Southern accent. He admired her skill at playing the melodeon her family had brought all the way from Georgia, and she admired his skills in riding and roping.

In the meantime, Billie's father became more prominent. Sam seemed to turn over a new leaf after his time in prison. He remained faithful to his new wife, Jennie. His enthusiasm was undiminished, but he changed his focus from law enforcement to politics. He ran for the office of senator and won, representing Pickens County in the Chickasaw Legislature.[23]

Sam Paul hung out a shingle advertising himself as a lawyer.[24] According to Uncle Buck, Sam attended a military school for two years, but had only gotten through the third reader,[25] so he was essentially self-taught. But he was brilliant. Buck said he could speak the languages of all the Five Civilized Tribes, as well as Caddo, Wichita, and Comanche. He was an eloquent speaker and was familiar with Chickasaw law, so he had everything he needed. Soon he bought two newspapers, the *Chickasaw Enterprise* in Pauls Valley and the *Chickasaw Chieftain* in Ardmore, and before long he became the Progressive Party's candidate for Chickasaw governor.

Sam gave speeches all over the Chickasaw Nation and even traveled to Washington, D.C., to make a case before the U.S. House of Representatives' Committee on Indian Affairs for an end to the old tradition of communal land ownership and for the integration of whites into tribal governments. At home he faced hostile crowds, and during one speech he even dodged a bullet.

Then, suddenly, Papa lost his father. One evening, while Sam was dining in a restaurant in downtown Pauls Valley, his oldest son Joe walked in, leveled a double-barrel shotgun at his father, and pulled the trigger. Sam died instantly.

Joe and his father never got along, and since Sam's return from prison, their relationship had gone from bad to worse. I don't know what their issues were, but on two other occasions they apparently exchanged gunshots. At the time of his assassination, Sam was considered by many to be a traitor to his people because of his opposition to the Chickasaw tradition of communal land ownership. Papa always said it was the full-blood party who talked Joe into killing Sam.

Papa and Uncle Buck never blamed their brother for what he did. It's not that they didn't love their father, but they loved their brother, too. Papa said there were times during Sam's absences when they would have starved if it weren't for Joe.

Papa was fifteen when his father was killed, and it was about that time he decided to court Mama. Papa used to tell us about it. He would ride up to the Rossers' front door and knock. Grandpa wouldn't exactly run him off, but instead he'd make excuses, like: "Vick can't come to the door," or "Vick's not feeling well." So Papa would get back on his horse and wait outside.

I can just imagine the arguments that went on inside the house. Grandpa would have tried to reason with Mama: "Now Vick, you may think Billie is a nice boy, but look at the people he comes from. Not only is he an Indian, but his father was a womanizer and a murderer!"

Mama would have defended Papa. "Billie has always been a perfect gentleman, and he's nothing like his father. He's smart and popular and the rest of his family are fine people, too. And you have no reason to look down on Indians. They are head and shoulders above most of the white people in this town. They are honest and generous and they take care of their own."

Papa was persistent. He just kept coming back and sitting outside on his horse until Grandpa finally let him in.

CHAPTER 2
- Mama and Papa's Courtship -

Some of my earliest memories are of Grandpa. I can remember him holding me on his lap like it was yesterday, rocking me back and forth and singing old Negro spirituals. I can still hear his voice. "Eighteen hunnerd and fawty one," he would sing with his thick Southern drawl, "Jesus' works have just begun."

Grandpa came to live with us when I was about four, the perfect age for me to enjoy my loving grandfather, and vice versa. He had a routine. Every morning, he would get dressed, eat one or two of Mama's biscuits, and then look for his hat. He never seemed to know where it was, even though it was always in the punch bowl where he had tossed it the day before. Then he would walk downtown, about three blocks from our house, buy a newspaper and a package of chewing tobacco, and sit in the shade on one of the benches on the courthouse lawn while he chatted with his cronies.

Our main meal was at noontime, and Grandpa was never late. I can remember standing at the door, watching for him to walk back from town. He'd holler at Mama as he walked through the door, "Hi Vick, what's for supper?" and then he'd toss his hat back into the punch bowl and sit down at the table with us to eat.

In the afternoons I would play next to Grandpa's chair as he read his newspaper and chewed his tobacco. Every once in a while he'd spit tobacco juice into the spittoon on the floor next to his chair. He always gave me the little red donkey off his tobacco wrappers. I saved them in a special box. After a while he'd lay down his paper, pick me up, and set me on his knee, groaning as he lifted me. I'd say, "Grandpa, why do you groan like that?" "Because it helps my rheumatism," he'd say.

I think it must have been a big help to Mama to have Grandpa there with her. I remember he always had some pins stuck in his lapel that he had picked up off the floor so we wouldn't step on them, and she must have counted on him to watch us while she did her work. Grandpa had a calming effect on Mama, too. She was always high-strung. I can still hear him say to her, "Now, settle down, child."

Grandpa was such a gentle soul. I can just imagine him, in his quiet way, trying to deal with Mama's budding love affair with Papa. Mama's mother died in 1893, not long after Mama and Papa started courting, and Mama and her younger sister Ada were the only two Rosser children left at home. Uncle Tom made the land run of 1893 into the Cherokee Strip and was busy farming his homestead. Mama's older sisters Kittie, Lillie, and Cora left home, too. Sister Kittie and Sister Lillie—Mama always included "Sister" in their names—both lived in Pauls Valley. They married brothers, Charles and George Brooks. The Brooks brothers were brokers in real estate, and quite prosperous, according to Mama.

Sister Cora married a man named Morris in Arkansas, but divorced him some time later and followed the family to the Chickasaw Nation. She owned and operated a millinery shop in Wynnewood, just seven miles south of Pauls Valley. After their mother died, Cora invited the two younger girls to live with her. "Old Sis" as Mama called her—she always used "old" to describe someone she didn't like—was fourteen years older than Mama, so she was more like an aunt than a sister. Cora must have come down pretty hard on Mama about seeing Papa, because their relationship gradually deteriorated to the point that she and Mama were hardly speaking.

After Sam Paul's death, the Chickasaw court assigned Papa and Uncle Buck a guardian, even though their mother lived right there in Pauls Valley. The guardian was one of Sam Paul's business partners. Mama hated him. She said he gambled away most of the boys' inheritance. "He'd bet on whether or not he could shoot a rooster off a fence post," she told us. Anyway, he sent Papa and Uncle Buck away to school in Sherman, Texas, making it even harder for Papa and Mama to continue their love affair.

By the time Papa came of age in 1895, four years after his father's death, he had apparently decided to give up on Mama, because he married Abbie McClure,[1] his uncle Tecumseh's daughter.

Papa on Old Deck, 1892

Meanwhile, the drama and conflict in his family continued. Later in 1895, Joe, who still hadn't stood trial for murdering his father, was thrown into jail for drunk and disorderly conduct. The next day, his uncle Tecumseh bailed him out of jail and was giving him a lecture on his behavior when, according to the story reported around town, Joe slapped him. Tecumseh didn't say another word. He just turned around and walked away. Two months later, Tecumseh's son Jennison emptied his shotgun into Joe's chest.

Over the next year or so, the relationship between Papa and the McClures must have gotten worse and worse. On a cold morning in February of 1897, Jennison's body was found on the railroad tracks just south of Pauls Valley. The body was badly mutilated by the train, but it was rumored that bullet holes were found. Papa and Uncle Buck were the prime suspects. They were questioned, but charges were never brought.[2]

Papa started seeing Mama again while he was still married to Abbie McClure, and his divorce from her wasn't final until a month before his marriage to Mama. I didn't find out about Papa's previous marriage until years and years later, after I moved away from home and was married, myself. I was stunned. I had no idea.

Mama's determination to be with Papa must have terrified the Rossers. The recent murders only confirmed their opinion of Papa's family, and of him, too, so in desperation they sent Mama to Georgia to visit Grandpa's mother. Grandpa's father had died during the Civil War, and his mother had married a man named Lumpkin. Maybe Grandma Lumpkin could talk some sense into her.

Much to Mama's relief, Grandma Lumpkin supported her relationship with Papa. According to the story handed down in the family, her only question to Mama was, "Does he have any money, honey?" and when the answer was "yes," she was satisfied. Whether the story is true or not, Papa did inherit a lot of property, so he was wealthy, even if his guardian had spent most of the money.

Mama had a wonderful time in Georgia. Grandma Lumpkin was a spry old lady, and she was fascinated by her pioneer granddaughter. She showed her off to all her neighbors around Cedartown, and introduced her to a "passel" of kinfolk that Mama had no idea existed. Mama eagerly told them stories about the Wild West, and about her Indian friends, and was a big hit with everyone. She amazed Grandma Lumpkin with her skill in playing the melodeon and in quilting, and they found they shared a love of flowers.

It must have frustrated Mama's family when she came back from Georgia full of excitement about her upcoming wedding. Mama's relationship with "Old Sis" was so bad at this point, Mama had moved out of her house. I'm not sure where she stayed, probably with one of her other sisters. She and Papa were together almost constantly. They were busy making plans for their wedding, their honeymoon, and their life together. Mama was hurrying to finish the quilt she started in Georgia to put into her hope chest.

Mama and Papa were married on November 30, 1898, in the home of Sam and Susan Garvin, old family friends. It was a double wedding. The Garvins' daughter Bird, Mama's best friend, and Buss Mays, Papa's best friend, were married at the same time. Sam Garvin was the wealthiest man in the county, and his wife, Susan, came from a prominent Choctaw family. Both the Pauls and the Garvins were well known in the community, so I imagine there was a big crowd at the wedding.

After Emily died, Grandpa sold his livestock and his farming equipment—he couldn't own the land, of course—and moved to Emet, a small town down by Tishomingo, the Chickasaw capital, where he opened up a store.

Over the years, Mama's sisters moved away from Pauls Valley. Sister Cora married a doctor and moved to Idaho. Sister Lillie moved to Texas, and Sister Kittie and Sister Ada ended up in California. Uncle Tom, of course, moved back to Arkansas, where he bought a farm on the banks of the Mississippi River, but Grandpa stayed in Indian Territory. After a few years, he moved back to Pauls Valley, opened another store there, and eventually moved in with us.

I don't know for sure why Grandpa stayed close to Mama instead of going to live with one of his other children, but I always suspected he was trying to protect her, the headstrong little daughter who married an Indian. Maybe something happened that scared him. I don't know—it was before my time—but Mama was grateful. I know when he finally moved away in 1921, to live in the old soldiers' home in Ardmore, she cried like a baby.

CHAPTER 3
- Newlyweds -

Our house in Pauls Valley had a large, screened-in back porch. Mama used to do her washing back there, but most of it was just used for storage. There were boxes of canned goods, lumber, rolls of barbed wire, fence posts, garden tools, farm equipment, and back in a corner was a lady's sidesaddle.

It was Mama's, from the early days of her marriage. Back in those days it wasn't considered ladylike to straddle a horse, so their saddles were engineered to be sat on sideways, so that a lady's skirts could cover her ankles. The old saddle was dusty and weathered, but still kind of pretty, with ornamental stitching on the leather and red fabric covering the seat. There was a curved rod extending from the left side for a lady to brace her leg on. I always wondered how she could ride a horse in such an uncomfortable position.

I used to imagine Papa taking Mama riding, back when they were young, in love, and full of hope for the future. Mama would have ridden sitting on her side saddle, wearing a frilly dress with a full skirt and a bonnet. She would have packed a lunch for them, and they would have stopped by a stream, spread out a cloth, and eaten in the shade of a big cottonwood tree.

Papa's first job after he and Mama married was as foreman of the Byars Ranch on the banks of the Canadian River, the northern boundary of the Chickasaw Nation. Papa planned to become a farmer and rancher like his father and grandfather before him.

After their wedding, my parents took a short honeymoon trip to Sulphur, then loaded a wagon with two big trunks full of clothes, a couple of pieces of furniture, and the pendulum clock the Garvins gave them as a wedding present, and headed north. The ranch was about fifty miles from Pauls Valley, a long day's ride in a wagon.

The Byars, Bill and Juda, were friendly, hospitable people. After Mama and Papa unpacked and got a good night's sleep, Mr. Byars gave them a tour of the ranch and took Papa out on the range to meet the ranch hands, leaving Mama and Mrs. Byars at their house to get acquainted. Mrs. Byars was a busy housewife with seven rambunctious children. Mama liked her right away. They talked a little more, and then Mrs. Byars left to get back to her chores, leaving Mama to clean up the little house where she and Papa would be staying.

Soon they established a routine. Papa and Mr. Byars would be gone during the day, and since Mrs. Byars was busy too, Mama was left pretty much to her own devices. In the evenings though, the two couples would sit together on the Byars' big porch, looking out at the stars and exchanging stories.

When he had time, Papa would take Mama riding. They rode down to the river and out to the pastures. He taught her a little bit about ranching and about horses. She used to tell us that quarter horses were the best for working cattle. "They're smart, quick, and agile," she'd say. Papa also taught her to shoot a rifle. I remember him bragging about what a good shot she was. In later years she always kept her old shotgun in the hall closet. The boys used to take it hunting.

In 1898, the same year Mama and Papa were married, Congress passed the Curtis Act, which provided for the division of tribal lands into individual allotments and the end of tribal governments, so Sam Paul's dream, the integration of whites and Indians into the state of Oklahoma, would soon come to pass.

Papa's idea was to use his and Mama's allotments to start his own farm. He started out by buying cattle from Mr. Byars and branding them with "VP," for Victoria Paul, his new bride. When I was little, Mama still had her old branding iron. She kept it in the kitchen and used it to wedge against the door of the stove, which had a broken latch.

Mama soon got bored sitting at home alone, so one day Papa brought her an orphaned baby raccoon. Mama named him Jim and kept him in the bedroom. She fed him from a baby bottle at first, but Jim grew fast,

Papa with other cowboys, about 1899

and soon he was eating leftovers. He also became more active. Jim loved to climb. He could climb almost anywhere and get into almost anything. Raccoons' paws are more like hands, so they can open drawers and cabinets. Soon little Jim was getting into the cabinets in the kitchen, but he also got into other places. He would open Mama's dresser drawers during the night and pull her clothes out on the floor. When she got up the next morning, there he would be, lying asleep in the middle of the mess he made. Mama used to entertain us with stories about Jim the raccoon.

Mama loved her little pet in spite of his shenanigans. She let him ride on her shoulder while she went around the house doing her chores, and she would take him over to the Byars' for the children to play with.

As Jim grew older, he started slipping out of the window in the evenings to go exploring, but he was always back in his box by the next morning. One morning when Mama awoke, Jim wasn't there. Papa consoled her. "He just found himself a little girl raccoon to pal around with," he said. Mama was upset about losing her pet, but she convinced herself that Jim was happier where he was. Then she found out what really happened. Some of the ranch hands had shot Jim and cooked him on their campfire. Mama was furious when she found out. "They knew that he was my pet," she cried. "It was just a big joke to them."

After the death of little Jim, Mama started spending her afternoons with Mrs. Byars. She would help with the children, and they would chat. Mama was pregnant by that time, and Mrs. Byars had plenty of experience to share about what to expect with the new baby. She went through her old chests and gave Mama hand-me-downs.

Papa's work was strenuous and dangerous. The prairie was open range in most areas, and it was a full-time job for the ranch hands to keep track of the stock. Cattle had to be herded from one pasture to another. Strays had to be roped, calves branded, and new horses broken. Papa fit right in with the Chickasaw cowboys who worked on the ranch. He had become an expert rider and roper as a boy, riding with his father on the range and on the annual cattle drives to Kansas City.

In those days there were no events comparable to the modern rodeo, but the cowboys did compete among themselves. On special occasions they held roping contests, which Papa entered and sometimes won.

Every spring there was a big roping contest in Oklahoma City, about sixty miles north of the ranch. Mr. Byars went every year and took his whole family. In 1899, the year after Mama and Papa moved out to the ranch, the Byars invited them to go. Papa decided to enter.

On the day they were to leave, Papa and Mr. Byars loaded their luggage onto the wagon along with Papa's ropes and saddle. The children would ride in the wagon while the Byars, Mama, and Papa rode in a buggy. Papa tied his horse, Old Deck, to the back of the wagon. A few of the ranch hands went, too. Some of them would enter the contest, and others just went along to celebrate the holiday.

Everyone dressed up for the trip, even the children. They would stay in a hotel and eat in restaurants. Oklahoma City, although only ten years old, had already become a city of fifteen thousand. Mama and Papa were excited.

After they checked into the hotel, Papa left Mama with the Byars, saddled up Old Deck, and rode over to the corral where the contest would be held. Other contestants were there, chatting and practicing their roping. Papa knew several of the other cowboys. I have a picture of him sitting on his horse holding his lariat rope, along with four other contestants. One of them was Jesse Chisholm, a descendant of the frontier trader after whom the Chisholm Trail was named.

The next day there was a big crowd down at the corral. Although bleachers had been set up for spectators, there weren't enough seats for everyone, so most people just stood along the fence. Mama and the Byars family had seats in the bleachers and when Papa's turn came to ride they stood up, cheered, and waved. Papa looked up, saw them, and tipped his hat. Then his calf was released. As it took out running across the arena, Old Deck, knowing what to do, galloped after it while Papa twirled his lariat over his head, aiming for the calf's hind leg. Then—I don't know exactly how it happened, maybe Papa's saddle was loose—he fell off his horse and landed on the turf. The same thing had happened countless times before, but this time Papa didn't get up. Mama screamed as she fought her way through the crowd down into the arena. By the time she got to him Papa had regained consciousness, but he couldn't move his legs.

Mr. Byars got a wagon, and they carried Papa to the doctor in Oklahoma City. The doctor said he couldn't be sure, but he thought Papa's neck might be broken. If it was, he would never walk again. In the meantime, there was nothing to do but apply poultices, and wait.

Mama took Papa home to the ranch. She applied the poultices like the doctor directed, and she prayed, but the next day there was no improvement. The Byars were kind and supportive. Mrs. Byars would come over every

23

day, bring food, and sit with Mama, but there was no consoling her. There she was, pregnant with her first child, and Papa, her only support, might never walk again. A week went by, then two. Finally the Byars called in a chiropractor. He examined Papa, made an adjustment to his neck, and slowly but surely, Papa began to get some feeling back in his legs, and then, movement. In another couple of weeks he could walk with crutches, and after a month he threw them away. It was a miracle.

After a month, Papa's neck was still stiff and his legs were still weak, and it became clear he would never be able to return to the rough work he had done before. He and Mama bid the Byars farewell and returned to Pauls Valley, where they moved in with Papa's mother, Mrs. Paul.

That's when Mama got acquainted with Uncle Buck, Papa's older brother, who also lived with Mrs. Paul. Papa and Uncle Buck were close. It seemed to me like they were always together, but they were different as night and day. They were both dark-skinned, but Papa was overweight and Buck was thin. Papa was outgoing and talkative, while Buck hardly ever said anything—Indian-like—except to Papa. They would talk in Chickasaw. Uncle Buck even walked like an Indian. It fascinated me. He'd pick up his feet and then plant them down carefully, like he was stalking a deer. They were both smart. Papa was good with people, selling, and wheeling and dealing, but Buck was good with figures, and he never forgot anything. He could remember everyone who ever lived around Pauls Valley, where they lived, and what became of them. And there was one other difference. Uncle Buck didn't drink.

While Papa continued to recover from his injury, he and Uncle Buck spent a lot of time together. Buck ran their father's newspaper, but it wasn't very profitable, so he looked for another business to get into. Papa still owned stock on the Byars ranch, so he and Mama had an income for the time being.

Meanwhile, Mrs. Paul kept Mama company while she planned for the arrival of the new baby. They knitted booties and sweaters. They sewed little dresses and quilts. Mama bought a crib and a baby buggy. Mama's sisters Kittie, Lillie, and Ada lived in Pauls Valley, too. Sister Cora was nearby in Wynnewood, and Aunt Sippie and the Garvins were in Whitebead, just five miles up the road, so Mama had a lot of visitors and a lot of gifts for the new baby.

My oldest brother, Samuel Garvin Paul, was born on October 24, 1899. He was named after Sam Garvin, not Papa's father. It wasn't that Papa didn't love his father, but there had been so much turmoil in Sam Paul's life maybe Papa just didn't want to be reminded of it. Sam and Susan Garvin had a stable, loving home, and they were kind to Papa and Mama, so it made sense to name their first child after him.

Little Samuel, as he was known, was a tiny, sickly baby, and he died of pneumonia after only a month. They buried him out at the Old Cemetery in Pauls Valley, overlooking Rush Creek, next to the graves of Ela-Teecha, Smith Paul, Sam Paul, Joe Paul, and Jennison McClure. There he lay among the old pioneers, the gunslingers who died over forgotten disagreements, and the early Chickasaw and Choctaw settlers, buried under traditional rock mounds with the weapons and supplies they would need in the land of the spirits. But to Mama there was only one grave, her Little Samuel's.

Dr. Branham assured Mama that losing Little Samuel didn't mean she couldn't have strong, healthy babies, so she and Papa were still optimistic about having a family.

They decided to move to Whitebead, about five miles northwest of Pauls Valley. It wasn't a hard decision to make. Because of the railroad, Pauls Valley became a bustling trade center. The Santa Fe Railroad brought business, but also attracted a lot of unsavory characters, and bars, fights, and shootings. Whitebead was more of a family town and a better place to raise children. By the time Mama and Papa settled there, Mama was pregnant again.

CHAPTER 4
- Willie and Victoria -

When Mama and Papa moved to Whitebead in 1900, it was actually bigger than Pauls Valley. The people who lived there were mainly old settlers, or their descendants, and most of them were Chickasaw or Choctaw. The Garvins lived there, as did Papa's Aunt Sippie and her family.

I remember Aunt Sippie well from when I was a little girl. She was dark like Papa, and she had a round, gentle face, with high cheekbones and laughing eyes. She used to come into Pauls Valley from Whitebead every two or three months and stay with us for a week or so. By that time, her husband had died and her children were grown. Papa handled her business affairs.

Aunt Sippie's visits were special occasions. She would chat with Mama during the days, and in the evenings we would all gather around, and Papa would get her to tell stories about the old days when the Plains Indians roamed the prairie.

I loved listening to Aunt Sippie tell about when she was a girl, living on her father Smith Paul's farm next to Fort Arbuckle. She told of the great herds of buffalo which migrated across the plains, the deer, the wild turkey and grouse, and the occasional bear. There were always bands of friendly Wichita, Osage, Caddo, and even Comanche camped near the fort to trade with the soldiers and to obtain rations. Smith Paul supplied them with corn in exchange for meat. Aunt Sippie described the beautiful beadwork and colorful dresses, shawls, and headdresses the Plains Indians wore during their ceremonies. I used to imagine sitting under the stars with her, listening to the drums beat, and watching them dance around the fire.

Bob and I used to find old flint arrowheads out by Rush Creek, and when we did, we would remember Aunt Sippie's stories and imagine ourselves stalking a deer in the forest. Sippie and her brothers, Jessie and our grandfather Sam, actually grew up with the young Plains Indian children, fishing, hunting, and riding ponies. Jessie and Sam learned to track, to shoot a bow and arrow, and they could even speak some of the languages.

Not all the Plains tribes were friendly. Aunt Sippie told us about hiding in the corn from hostile bands of Cheyenne or Comanche who raided the farm to steal horses, or just to terrorize the Chickasaw settlers, and she told us a story about one day when her mother, Ela-Teecha, bravely invited a band of Comanches into the house and fixed them a meal. Ela-Teecha told her children that when she was a girl, some of the Chickasaw braves were almost as wild as the Comanches, just boys full of energy and meanness.

I remember one story Aunt Sippie told us about our grandfather, Sam Paul. She said that after the Civil War, when the army was rounding up the Plains Indians to force them onto reservations, they asked for volunteers from among the Chickasaws to serve as interpreters and scouts. Sam could speak Comanche, and he was also a good tracker, so he volunteered. Several months later, the family got word that Sam was near death. It wasn't an arrow or a bullet that had taken him down, but smallpox. Hearing that, his father, Smith Paul, got on his horse, rode out to where the army was camped, and took care of Sam until he was healthy enough to ride home.

Aunt Sippie's stories were not only entertaining, they filled me with pride—pride in our heritage and pride in our family, how they survived, and how they built a community in a primitive and sometimes hostile land.

Mama and Aunt Sippie got to be friends while she and Papa lived in Whitebead. Mama must have been as fascinated as we were by her stories. She learned practical things from Sippie, too. She learned how to store vegetables and fruit in a haystack to keep them from spoiling. She learned about the wild plants, those that were good for cooking and those that could be used for medicinal purposes. Mama was always interested in plants.

During the time Mama and Papa lived in Whitebead, Papa was a member of the Chickasaw Legislature, and they made frequent trips down to Tishomingo, the Chickasaw capital. Tish, as they called it, was fifty miles south of Whitebead, a trip that took two days in a horse and buggy. Election days were especially exciting. Citizens from all over the Chickasaw Nation would travel to Tish to vote. Mama said that Papa and the other men would laugh and talk in Chickasaw, while she would sit with the other wives. Usually she could find someone who spoke English.

By that time, the process of breaking up the Indian nations was well under way. The land had been surveyed, and tribal rolls were being compiled for the assignment of allotments. To most of the full-bloods, this whole process was unthinkable. To them, the land should be like the water and the air, for each to use as he needed, and so they protested, first by refusing to talk to the government agents, then by voting against the treaty, and finally by refusing to apply for allotments. Papa and other leaders went out into the countryside, visiting the Chickasaw families and explaining to the full-bloods that the only way they could keep their homes and support their families was to be included on the rolls. As a result, most of the tribe received allotments.

The other problem which faced the Chickasaws was the thousands of greedy white men who falsely claimed Chickasaw citizenship to get land. Everyone knew of someone who had made a fraudulent claim. There was an old man who lived down the street from us, a "good" Episcopalian. He had married a Chickasaw girl in order to become an intermarried citizen and then left her the morning after their wedding. Mama hated him.

My brother Willie was born at Whitebead on November 28, 1900, as William George Paul. He was named William after Papa, and George after Sister Lillie's husband, George Brooks. Willie would grow up to become Mama's rock in the troubled times ahead, a model for the older boys, and a father figure for us younger children. Willie was a healthy baby, and he grew strong and fast. He was already walking by July 21, 1902, when my oldest sister, Victoria Sue Paul, was born. Victoria was pretty and sweet, and Papa named her after Mama and Susan Garvin. Victoria would become the light of both Mama's and Papa's lives.

During the time Mama and Papa lived in Whitebead, Papa went into the real estate business with his brother Buck. They had inherited several town lots from their father,[1] Papa had some cattle to sell for startup money, they both knew everybody in the county, and with the coming of allotment, real estate was becoming a booming business.

In 1904, Papa decided to move the family back to Pauls Valley to be nearer to his clients. By then Whitebead was dwindling in size, and thanks to the railroad, Pauls Valley had become the center of growth for the county. It was becoming more civilized, too. With the coming of statehood, the days of the "Wild West" were coming to an end.

William Hiram Paul, Papa

CHAPTER 5
- *From Prosperity to Polio* -

There was something different about my older siblings, except for Willie, of course. They had a self-confidence, an arrogance, that we younger children didn't have. It was as if we were from two different families. They were more active than we were in school functions, and it seemed like they were never at home, always off with friends or planning some project. Mama treated them differently, too. It's as if she expected more of them than she did of us. Part of the reason may have been her old-fashioned ideas about giving respect and authority to men, but she treated my older sister Kaliteyo special, too, fixing pretty dresses for her, teaching her to be ladylike, and sending her to parties.

We younger children, Bob and I, Teker and Tom, weren't as outgoing as our older brothers and sister. We spent most of our time at home with Mama, following her around the house when we were younger and reading or doing school work when we were older. We milked the cows, washed the dishes, plucked the chickens, peeled the potatoes, and didn't complain about it. We never thought we were special.

It's not that our older siblings didn't go through hardships. They did, but they never accepted our situation. I guess it's because when they were little Mama and Papa were prosperous and they thought of themselves as heirs to wealth and privilege. I just thought they were lazy and selfish.

My older brother Snip was born on August 4, 1904, just after Mama and

Papa moved back to Pauls Valley. Snip's given name was actually Homer. Mama named him after the ancient Greek poet, the author of *The Iliad* and *The Odyssey*. He got the nickname "Snip" because his baby picture had the corner snipped off of it. When Snip got older and more "distinguished," he went by his given name of Homer, but we always called him Snip. He was the last one of my siblings to get a Chickasaw allotment.

By the time Snip was born, Papa and Uncle Buck's real estate business was going strong, and they were making plenty of money. Papa bought Mama a nice home and beautiful clothes—people really dressed up in those days—and expensive jewelry. Papa was always buying Mama jewelry, even in later years when he couldn't afford it. Mama also hired a seamstress, Miss Mary Cochell, to keep her wardrobe in tune with the latest fashions.

With a new baby and two toddlers underfoot, Mama was busy, but Papa hired a maid, Ruth, to help her with the cooking and the housework, so Mama was able to get out and socialize.

In the evenings, Mama and Papa would either go out visiting, or they would entertain at home. There were also certain days when Mama would go calling. On those days she would get in the buggy and drive to a neighbor's house where she would present her card. I saved some of her calling cards. They read simply, "Mrs. Victoria M. Paul." If the lady was receiving visitors that day, she would have the maid show Mama into the parlor, where the ladies would have refreshments and visit. On other days, the process was reversed and Mama would receive visitors.

It's hard to imagine these social practices occurring in Indian Territory, but they did. Many of the white settlers were from wealthy Southern families and were well educated, and so were the Indians. These pioneers, both Indian and white, wanted to create an atmosphere of culture and refinement in their new home.

Mama bought beautiful furniture for the house, also drapes and carpeting, and she started building a library. Mama and Papa both loved to read. They bought an encyclopedia, history books—Mama's mother's people were French and she loved French history—the classics, poetry, and children's books. Mama had a set of books called *The Children's Hour*, inspired by the Longfellow poem of the same name:

> *Between the dark and the daylight,*
> *When the night is beginning to lower,*
> *Comes a pause in the day's occupations,*
> *That is known as the Children's Hour.*

Mama, Snip, Willie, and Victoria at Seven Falls
in Colorado

We loved those books. They had all the fairy tales: Grimm's, Hans Christian Andersen, and Aesop's fables. Mama used to read them to us, and it gave us all a love for reading.

Mama loved poetry, too, and she was one of the charter members of the Pauls Valley Poetry Society. Once each month, the ladies of the Poetry Society gathered to read poetry, some by famous poets, and some that they had written themselves. Mama also joined the Alternate Saturday Club, organized in 1897 "to promote social, intellectual and moral culture."[1]

Papa was an important man in the community back then, and he always practiced the Chickasaw tradition of generosity. Ed Lowe, a prominent banker in Pauls Valley during my childhood, had gotten his stake from Papa, and he was always Papa's loyal friend. A lot of people would come to Papa when they needed money. Harve Williams told me that Papa had given land to his brother when he was struggling to make ends meet. Later, when times were hard for us, Mama used to complain that if she had all the money Papa had paid on other people's notes, she'd be a wealthy woman.

By that time, Mama's sister, Cora, had married again and moved to Idaho, but Sister Lillie and Sister Kittie and their families were still living in Pauls Valley, and they visited with Mama and Papa often. Grandpa had moved back to Pauls Valley, too, and had opened his little store there.

When I was little, the only traveling we did was to Wynnewood or Sulphur, and that was just when someone offered us a ride. But when my older brothers and sisters were young, they went to Hot Springs, Heber Springs, and Eureka Springs in Arkansas. Those places were resorts back then, and people came from all over the country, even from Europe, to bathe in their healing mineral waters.

In 1905, Aunt Ada and her husband moved to Colorado Springs, Colorado, so for a couple of summers Mama took Willie, Homer, and Victoria to spend the warm months there. Papa would ride out with them on the train, and then come back home to run his business. I remember Aunt Ada. She used to visit Mama when I was a child. She had pretty auburn hair and she wore beautiful clothes. She gave Mama a blue robe that was decorated with feathers. Mama kept it in her armoire, although she never wore it.

Mama had a photo taken of the family at Seven Falls near Colorado Springs. Later she had it enlarged, and ever since I can remember, it hung on our living room wall. Willie, Homer, and Victoria are sitting on a burro at the base of the falls, and Mama is standing behind them dressed in a long frilly dress wearing a bonnet. They look so happy!

My older siblings were also witnesses to important events in state history. After allotments were assigned to citizens of the Indian Nations, Congress took up the issue of statehood for Indian Territory and Oklahoma Territory, the portion of land that had been opened up to settlement by whites. Although their governments were scheduled to be dissolved in March of 1907, the Indians made one more attempt to retain some degree of independence. They assembled in the town of Muskogee and wrote a constitution for a separate Indian state, which would have been called Sequoyah. Papa was a delegate, and he was elected assistant secretary of the convention.[2]

As it turned out, Congress decided to admit the two territories together as the state of Oklahoma. Even though the Sequoyah movement failed, ironically, its leaders became the leaders of the new state. William H. Murray, who represented the Chickasaw Nation at the Sequoyah Convention, was elected chairman of Oklahoma's Constitutional Convention, and Charles N. Haskell, who had represented the Creek Nation, became the state's first governor. Papa knew them both, of course.

Oklahoma became a state on November 16, 1907, and when Charles Haskell ran for governor, Papa was one of his staunch supporters. In fact, he was so confident Mr. Haskell would win, he named my brother after him, Haskell Paul, even though he was born on February 11, seven months before the election. Luckily, Mr. Haskell did win. Later, Mr. Haskell told my brother that he was the only baby named for him before he was elected governor.

Unfortunately, prosperity didn't protect our family from trouble. Soon after Haskell was born, our family was faced with a crisis. Snip came down with polio. In those days, childhood was a dangerous time. Every sore throat brought the fear of scarlet fever or rheumatic fever, every cough could be the start of pneumonia, and every headache, meningitis. Antibiotics weren't available until after I graduated from college, and the only vaccine was for smallpox. When one of us got sick, Mama would try to isolate us from our brothers and sisters by moving us into her bedroom. She made sure we didn't eat or drink from the same utensils, she tried to protect us from getting chilled, and she applied the tonics, balms, and purgatives recommended as treatments.

Dr. James Callaway was Mama's support. He often had little to offer, but he came anyway, no matter what the weather, no matter what the hour. We all loved Dr. Callaway. He was always cheerful, and he always had some

Life Savers candies in his pocket to give us. When one of us was seriously ill, he'd come by every evening and just sit with Mama for a while. Dr. Callaway died in 1928 of influenza. I know he went straight up to Heaven.

In those days, polio was one of the most feared diseases. It was called "infantile paralysis" because of its propensity to strike babies. Polio is contagious, and at that time, when anyone got a contagious disease, a large red sign was placed on the family's door designating their house as quarantined. I remember running as fast as I could past any house with that dreaded red sign.

Polio starts with weakness in the legs, and Snip was a toddler at the time, so Mama would have known right away what he had. Everyone knew the symptoms of infantile paralysis. The paralysis slowly works its way up through the body over a month or more, and if it reaches the lungs, the victim can suffocate. Snip had polio before the "iron lung" was invented, so there would have been no hope for him if his breathing had been affected. The suspense must have been unbearable.

It was a lot of work keeping Snip clean and turning him so he wouldn't develop bed sores. Haskell was just a baby, and Mama didn't want him to catch the disease, so she depended on Ruth to do most of Snip's care. That was when Mama grew to love Ruth. Incredibly, no one else in the family got polio, and Snip survived.

During his convalescence, Mama got help from an unexpected source. There was a little girl named Dixie Taylor who lived with her aunt across the street from us in one of Papa's rent houses, and every day she would come over and sit with Snip. Dixie was about six or seven at the time. After that, we just thought of Dixie as part of our family. Even later, when I was old enough to remember, Dixie spent as much time at our house as she did at her own, and whenever we went anywhere, we always took Dixie with us.

Snip walked funny after having polio; his right shoe wore out before his left, and he was always asking us to do things for him. We just thought he was lazy, but now I realize that the weakness from his bout with polio is probably what made him that way.

CHAPTER 6
- Death and Change -

If Mama and Papa had a favorite child, it would have been Victoria, hands down.

Her picture always hung over Mama's bed. She looked a lot like Kaliteyo. Mama would talk about her sometimes, especially when we went out to the cemetery. With tears in her eyes, Mama would tell us how pretty and how sweet she was, and how she missed her. She died years before I was born, but I loved Victoria, too, or at least the picture of her I had in my mind. I remember stroking the little lamb on her tombstone while Mama tended her grave.

Victoria's death was sudden. Maybe that's the reason it hit Mama and Papa so hard. When Mama told the story of her illness, it always started the day before she got sick. She had done something naughty, and Mama punished her by locking her in the hall closet. Victoria was only six, and the experience terrified her. When Mama opened the closet door to let her out, she was huddled in the corner, trembling. Mama knew instantly that she had made a mistake, and the sight of Victoria trembling in that closet always haunted her.

The next morning Mama woke up in a cold sweat. She had dreamed that there were bugs crawling all over her. It was a sign. Something terrible was going to happen. After supper—we always had our big meal at midday—Mama got Willie back off to school, and Victoria begged to go outside. Even though it was February, it was pretty out, so Mama dressed her warmly in her union suit and overalls and let her go out in the yard to play. Mama and Ruth chatted while Ruth cleaned up the kitchen, and then Mama got busy with the babies, Homer and Haskell. Time passed by quickly.

Papa decided to come home early that afternoon, and as he walked up to the gate he saw Victoria lying on the grass. He called out to her, "Hi there, Vickie. Come give Papa a kiss," but she didn't move. Papa ran over to her and lifted up her head. She barely opened her eyes. He picked her up and carried her inside. Mama felt Victoria's forehead and said, "She's burning up with a fever!" Papa called old Dr. Callaway and he came right over. "Is it diphtheria?" Mama asked. Mrs. Bradley's daughter had diphtheria, and Victoria had been playing with her. No. The news was even worse. It was meningitis. By the next morning Victoria was gone.

The *Pauls Valley Enterprise* printed a brief obituary:

Little Victoria
Another precious jewel was added to the crown of glory in Heaven when the soul of little Victoria Sue Paul, the 6-year-old daughter of Mr. and Mrs. W. H. Paul, took flight Tuesday morning…every effort was used to keep her on earth; but she was needed Up There

Victoria was buried at Mount Olivet, on the other side of Jackson Hill from where Little Samuel lay. The cemetery was new then, and Victoria's was the second grave there. Papa had her tombstone imported from Italy.

After her death, Mama became despondent. Both she and Papa were devastated, but it almost killed her. She went to bed and stayed there for days, while Ruth watched after the children. Dr. Callaway examined her and told Papa she had a weak heart, and the strain of Victoria's death had been too much for her. It was a long time before she left home again, and then only to visit little Victoria's grave. Papa bought her presents. He even offered to build her a house across the road from the cemetery so she could be nearer to Victoria, but nothing would console her.

As time went on, she remained withdrawn. She rarely left home. Her sisters and a few close friends came to visit, but for the most part she devoted herself to her children.

That's how she dealt with the loss of Victoria, and in the process she pushed Papa away. He couldn't deal with Mama's depression. I think he loved Victoria as much as she did, but he had a different way of dealing with her loss, and that was to escape. He stopped coming home in the evenings, instead staying in town with his friends, and drinking.

Mama and Papa had been through a lot during their marriage—Little Samuel's death, Papa's fall from the horse, and Snip's bout with polio—and their troubles always brought them closer together. But somehow, Victoria's death was just too much.

On November 10, 1909, nine months later, Mama and Papa received a gift that brought them together again, at least for a while—the birth of my older sister, Kaliteyo Mahota Paul. Mama and Papa were thrilled. It was as if little Victoria had been reincarnated. Papa named her after Kaliteyo Maytubby, Ela-teecha's sister. Kaliteyo means "clear, running water" in Chickasaw. I called her "muddy water" when I was mad at her.

Kaliteyo's middle name, Mahota, was suggested by Mama's good friend, Jesse Moore.[1] Mrs. Moore was Chickasaw, and she and her husband, E. M. Moore, were married the same year as Mama and Papa. They were neighbors for years.

Kaliteyo was a frail little thing. Mama told us she carried her around on a pillow for the first six months of her life. Again, Mama relied on Ruth to look after the boys.

In May of 1910, Papa bought the house where I grew up. It was on the corner of Pine and Grant, the road going out of town toward Whitebead. He bought it from one of his Waite cousins, J. C. Eliott, who had taken a job at the state capitol in Oklahoma City. Papa wanted to build a brick house in the Garvin addition, a more affluent neighborhood at the time, but Mama said the little boys liked the house on Pine better.

Our house was wood frame, two stories tall, with an ornamental wire fence around the yard. It was built during the horse-and-buggy days, so there was a hitching post out front and steps for climbing up into a buggy. We had a big front porch with a porch swing that faced the sidewalk, a screened-in porch in back that Mama used for washing and storage, and a cistern where we collected water to wash our hair.

Out back there was a servants' quarters, a barn, and a chicken coop. We always had a cow and some chickens. We owned the whole block, so there was plenty of room for the cow to graze and for Mama to plant a garden. Plumbing was installed by the time I was born in 1913, and the garage would have been built around that time, too, because that was when Papa bought a car. The house was wired for electricity, but the current wasn't

Victoria Sue Paul, age 6, 1910

very dependable. Mama kept coal oil lamps in all the rooms to use when the power was out. After we moved there, Papa built a house across the street for our grandmother, Mrs. Paul.

For the next few years, things were better. The birth of Kaliteyo gave Mama and Papa a new lease on life. Mama still devoted herself to her children, Papa started coming home early again, and he and Mama entertained friends like they used to do during the earlier years. But things would never be the same again. Something in their marriage had been broken.

Papa still went out with his friends, and when he came home, Mama would harangue him about his drinking. There were fights, too, sometimes physical—none when I can remember, but back when Kaliteyo was a baby.

Willie was protective of Mama, and one time he tried to stand up to Papa. He must have been nine or ten. Anyway, Papa started whipping Willie with his belt. Mama pleaded with him to stop, but he wouldn't. He had lost control. Finally, Mama got the shotgun and leveled it at Papa. He stopped. He knew she would use it. That was about the time Grandpa moved in with us. I think he was afraid for Mama's safety.

Through it all, Mama and Papa never stopped loving each other. I truly believe that. Papa never went out with other women, and as long as her body would let her, Mama kept having more babies. Mama continued to fuss at Papa about his drinking, but behind it all I think she was just afraid for him—afraid for what he was doing to his body.

Papa was a handsome man, and he took pride in his appearance. He always wore a suit and tie, and he liked jewelry. He had some beautiful black diamond cufflinks that were stolen from him while he was on one of his drinking sprees, or toots, as Mama called them. Because of his Indian heritage, Papa's skin was smooth. His few facial hairs he plucked out with tweezers.

Mama and Papa were both jealous when it came to each other. I remember one time when I was little, Mrs. Garvin's daughter-in-law got a crush on Papa. One day, she gave Kaliteyo a message to give to him, and Mama found it. She got her quirt, went over to the woman's house, and told her that if she didn't stay away from her husband, she would use it on her, and that was the end of that.

Papa was the same way. He was a Presbyterian, like most of the Chickasaws, but Mama was an Episcopalian. She started going to the Episcopal Church after Snip's bout with polio because during that time the

Willie at about age 10, 1910

Episcopal priest would come by the house to pray with her. Papa certainly hadn't been any help. He dealt with trouble by avoiding it. Anyway, Papa got jealous of the priest, and for a while Mama had to stop going to church.

In the spring of 1913, Mama got pregnant with me. She was happy about having another child, of course—Mama always loved babies—and since she was happy, Papa was happy too. He decided to take the family down to Galveston, Texas, on a vacation.

Papa had just bought a Model T Ford. It was one of the first in town, and it was a fancy one, too—a four-seater with isinglass windows and a top that rolled down. Papa loved that car. Even years later, when I was old enough to remember, he'd go out every morning, start it up, and race the motor just to hear it roar.

So, early in the summer of 1913, Mama, Papa, and the kids, Willie, Snip, Haskell, and Kaliteyo, all piled into that Model T Ford and drove down to Galveston, leaving Grandpa at home to watch the house. In 1900, Galveston had been destroyed by a devastating hurricane, so much of the city had been rebuilt, along with a seawall to protect the town from flooding again.

The vacation was a great success. The children enjoyed swimming at the beach, and Mama enjoyed seeing the beautiful mansions that overlooked the waterfront. They brought home a pair of water buffalo horns from the Philippines as a souvenir. Those horns hung in our living room over the door to the hallway all my life. Just after they left, another big hurricane hit Galveston. If they had been there a week later, they would have been caught in it. Perhaps it was omen, a sign that bad times were coming for our family.

CHAPTER 7
- I Am Born -

I was born in 1913 on statehood day, November 16, and the name on my birth certificate read simply, "Baby Girl." Kaliteyo's said the same thing. Dr. Branum wasn't a very good record keeper.

I think I was kind of a disappointment to Mama and Papa, or at least an anticlimax, since they had planned on me being a boy. Of course, Grandpa was proud of his little namesake, James Wenonah, and Mama was always happy when she had a baby to worry over, but I think Papa must have felt a little left out. I was healthy and strong, but that first year I did have pneumonia, so Mama was busy with me as well as with Kaliteyo, who had just turned four and was still puny. Papa continued to drink and come home late, or not at all.

The year I was born, Papa sent Willie off to the Western Military Academy in Alton, Illinois. I don't know if it had anything to do with the conflict they had over Mama, but I doubt it. Papa had gone to boarding schools, and it was a common practice back then. He just wanted Willie to get a good education. Willie's best friend, Preston Burch, was going there, too, so he was eager to go.

That first year at Western must have been hard on Willie. I have one of Mama's letters to him from that year. She was trying to explain to him why he couldn't come home during the Easter break:

Pauls Valley Oklahoma, March 30, 1914

Dear Willie.

I received your letter today. You must stay there. I have bin trying to get your Pap to write a nice letter to Mr. Jakson for you but I donot think that he ever did. he is to lazy to do anything. you must stay there and behave yourself. don't go to town by yourself & be verry careful to not get hurt. I will be oneasy about you until school starts. I will be afraid that something will happen to you. the children are all sick here and I am to nothing here but confusion…

you tell your Principal or whoever you ought to tell that you are to stay until school is out. It is two expensive for you to come Home for so short a stay. I will close there is so much noise I dont think there is any sense to this Letter. be a good boy and don't get hurt.

Your Loving Mother Victoria Paul

In the letter, Mama reminds Willie not to get hurt. It might have been the year that Willie broke his collarbone playing football. They played without pads back then, and it was really rough. After he got hurt, Mama wouldn't give her permission for him to play anymore. Willie was all man, but he was gentle and sensitive, too, not rough like my other brothers. He liked to read, and he also played the violin. He took lessons from old Professor Bruin, a sweet old man who had immigrated to Pauls Valley from Belgium. They investigated him during World War I for fear he might be working for the Germans, but nothing ever came of it.

Willie went to Western for three years, until he graduated from high school. He made good grades and wrote home often. Mama saved his letters in a red leather binder, but it got lost over the years. I only have one of his letters, but it illustrates what a kind, sweet person he was. It's addressed to Kaliteyo:

Western Military Acad, Alton Ill. Jan 16, 1916

Dear Kaliteo:

How are you getting along? I am well and feel fine. Have you gotten out of bed yet if not are you still having fevor. How is Papa getting along with his rheumatism. How is Mama and Grandpa and the rest of you all getting.

[Willie said his grades were] an average of 93 1/2 that will give

9th place on the Upper ten if I just keep it up. I am learning how to box now and when I come home I will teach you and then you can whip Homer and Haskell. I havent seen a little girl here at school since Xmas. If I do see some I don't think that they will be as pretty as you...

I want you to wear that watch I gave you to Sunday school and when you go to any entertainment. Have you ever found your muff or your furs since I left. I hope that you find it or some one gives it to you. If you will be a good girl at school and at home I will send you a box of candy Easter. I would send you a box now but they wont let you sent any thing away if they know it and I don't want to take any risk.

There is going to be a dance here February twenty second and I wish that it was in the afternoon instead of the evening. Write soon.

Your Brother, Willie Paul

A lot of changes took place while Willie was away at school. I was still a baby at the time, so I got most of my information later from Kaliteyo.

First of all, Uncle Buck got married. That was a big surprise to Mrs. Paul. I guess she didn't think he'd ever leave home, and on top of that, he married Mollie Travis, a widow with six children. Mrs. Paul got mad at Mama for introducing them, but Mama said she didn't even know Aunt Mollie until she married Buck. Anyway, Buck and Mollie did just fine in spite of Mrs. Paul's disapproval; they had a long and happy marriage, and they had another six children together.

Uncle Buck also quit the real estate business about that time. Papa probably didn't think Buck would ever leave him, either. They had been together all their lives, except when Mama and Papa lived on the Byars' ranch. But Buck wasn't outgoing like Papa, and I don't suppose he enjoyed haggling over property and making deals, so he took a job as a mail carrier. It didn't change things that much, though. It seemed to me like they were always together, anyway.

Another big change that happened while I was a baby was that Mama's sisters Lillie and Kittie moved away.

Sister Ada and Sister Cora were already gone. Ada was in Colorado Springs, where Mama used to visit her before Victoria's death, and Cora married a second time, to a doctor, and they moved to Idaho. She opened a flower shop there. They didn't correspond much that I can remember. I don't think Mama ever forgave her for opposing her marriage to Papa.

Sister Lillie was the next to go. She was closest to Mama in age, and from their pictures, I thought she looked the most like Mama, although I never saw her in person. Lillie was married to George Brooks, the brother of Kittie's husband, and after Mama and Papa were married, he and Papa became good friends. My brother Willie was named after him, William George Paul.

Sister Lillie and her husband moved down to Texas while I was a baby, and it may have been partly because of a fight she had with Mama. Mama had a terrible temper.

Aunt Lillie had a daughter named Alma Sue, or "Punkin" for short. Punkin was about Kaliteyo's age, and when the two families visited, they would play together. One day something happened between them. I don't know what it was, but it caused a big fight, and Mama stopped speaking to Aunt Lillie. I don't know that they ever saw each other again.

Sister Kittie moved away about that time to Georgia. Her first husband, Charles Brooks, had died of a bleeding ulcer. He's buried out at the Old Cemetery. I remember Mama getting letters from her and from her daughter Lucille.

Mama lost Ruth about that time, too, all because of Papa's temper. Everyone cooked on wood-burning stoves back then. In fact, we didn't have a gas stove until I was twelve. One morning the boys were eating breakfast, and Willie asked Ruth for more bacon. It was summertime, and hot in the kitchen, and Ruth had already let the wood burn down. She told Willie that she was done cooking and wasn't going to rekindle the stove just to fix him one more slice of bacon. Anyway, that set Papa off. He fired Ruth on the spot.

My brother and playmate, Robert Edward Lee Paul, was born May 20, 1915. He was named after the Confederate general and after Uncle Ed, the brother Grandpa had planned to join in Texas after the Civil War.

Bob was another baby for Mama to love, but I'm sure his birth put more of a burden on Papa. According to Kaliteyo, his toots started lasting longer, sometimes for several days, after which either Mama or Uncle Buck would get a call saying he was stranded somewhere and out of money. Sometimes things were stolen. He would come home without his tie or his coat. One time he lost an expensive jeweled tie pin.

Kaliteyo liked to tell a story about one time Mama had gone to Oklahoma City to get Papa after one of his toots. She had left Snip at home in charge of the children. Snip had everything under control except for Bob, who was the baby at the time. He had changed him and fed him, walked with him, and rocked him. He even tried singing to him, but nothing seemed to work. Bob just wanted Mama. Finally, Snip got an idea. He put on Mama's robe. I remember it was a pretty orange silk kimono she always wore. And after that, Bob settled right down. Kaliteyo said that kimono made Snip look just like Mama.

When Willie graduated from Western, he and his friend Preston went off to seek their fortunes. Mama suspected something was up when he stopped writing letters home. Anyway, after school was out and Willie didn't come home, Mama and Papa really got worried. Papa talked to Preston's father and found out he hadn't shown up, either. It was a long month before Papa and Mr. Burch got letters from the boys asking for money to come home. They were in Texas, broke, and hungry for their mothers' cooking.

I don't blame Willie for not wanting to come home, with the tension and uncertainty of our situation, but his little escapade may have done some good, at least temporarily, because as soon as he got home, Mama and Papa decided to do something about their problems.

Mama had always blamed Papa's drinking on the bad influence of his friends. She reasoned that if she could just get him away from them, away from Pauls Valley, then he would no longer be tempted to drink. Papa didn't want to take responsibility for his drinking, anyway, so he was happy to go along with her. He kept his eyes open, and when the drugstore in the plush Skirvin Hotel in Oklahoma City was put up for sale, he bought it and went into the drugstore business with Willie as his partner.

Mama was ecstatic. The new venture would get us out of Pauls Valley and get Papa away from his cronies, but it was a big mistake, the first in a series of mistakes that would lead to the end of our family's prosperity, and it taught me a lesson. You can't run away from your troubles.

CHAPTER 8
- Oklahoma City -

One of the first things I remember is going to Oklahoma City with Mama and Papa in 1917. I was four. Papa went there to make arrangements to buy the Skirvin drugstore. We stayed in a fancy hotel, and I remember being fascinated by the elevator. There was a man inside who could make it go clear up to the top floor of the building.

During the day, Mama took us out to look around town, and she bought me a pinwheel and a balloon. I enjoyed waving the pinwheel around and making it spin, but I managed to pop the balloon. Mama bought Haskell and Snip a book that showed how to make shadow figures on the wall using your hands.

For some reason, Kaliteyo wasn't with us. She must have been sick. Haskell wrote her about the trip. You can tell he was disgusted with me for popping my balloon:

Dear Kaliteo

how are you gatting along I bought you a little automobill.

Mama bought Jim a bloom and Jim busted it last night and she said she was glad of it and Mama bought me and Homer a book of shadow pictures thing to make shadows on the wall That little automobill I was telling you about has got little wheels on it...

Haskell Paul

Left to right: Homer (Snip), Bob, Kaliteyo, and Haskell
Behind on porch: Wenonah

Haskell and Kaliteyo were close like Bob and I, but Kaliteyo always thought of me as a pest. Mama tried to get her to take me under her wing, but it didn't work out.

I remember going to Oklahoma City another time when Kaliteyo was with us. We were staying at the Skirvin Hotel, where Papa and Willie were setting up their business. We were all sitting in the Skirvin's fancy restaurant, waiting to eat, when I needed to go to the bathroom. Mama made Kaliteyo take me. She was embarrassed to walk out in front of all those people, and we had to go through the kitchen, too, where the cooks and waiters were busy preparing the food and getting it ready to serve. It was exciting to me, but Kaliteyo would hardly speak to me afterward.

Mama was happy in Oklahoma City. Our house was just off Classen Boulevard, right next to an Episcopal Church. She enjoyed socializing with the ladies at the church, and she also started to develop her artistic talent. One of her church friends was Nan Sheets, an accomplished artist and the wife of a prominent physician. Mrs. Sheets gave Mama lessons in charcoals and oils and got her started creating some of the beautiful pictures that later adorned our walls.

We just lived in Oklahoma City for a few months, and I don't remember too much, only bits and pieces. There was a crisis with Haskell. I remember that Mama bought him a pair of roller skates, and to try them out, he decided to skate out to Belle Isle Lake, about two and a half miles south of where we lived. By the time he got back, he was exhausted and weak. Mama took him to the doctor, who told her he had damaged his heart. Haskell was always athletic, though, so he must have gotten over it.

Papa took advantage of his heritage and sold Native American crafts in the store, an idea which would probably work now, but I guess it wasn't popular back then. The business failed. By the summer of 1918, we were back in Pauls Valley, where my little sister Oteka was born, on May 20. She and Bob had the same birthday.

Oteka's name came from a book that Mama and Mrs. Lydey were reading at the time. Mrs. Lydey was one of Mama's friends from the poetry club. It's supposed to mean "daughter of the moon," or that's what I've been told. It's not a Chickasaw word. Mama just thought it sounded pretty.

Kaliteyo was seven when Oteka was born, and she claimed her from the start. She played with her, she helped Mama bathe her, she dressed her up and fixed her hair, and when Oteka was older, Kaliteyo took her along when she went out with her friends. I was proud of Oteka, too, but I wasn't old enough to help take care of her. One time Mama let me push her in her stroller, and I accidentally dumped her out. After that, Kaliteyo told Mama I couldn't be trusted with her.

The United States entered World War I in 1917, and by the time we got back into our old house in Pauls Valley, there were thousands of our boys fighting in Europe. Papa was too old to go, and Willie was too young, but Mama supported the war effort by working with the Red Cross knitting weskits (vests) to send to the troops. Snip wanted to help so she taught him to knit, too. Mama saved a newspaper article which stated that she was named "production chairman" of the project.

While Snip was learning to knit weskits for the Red Cross, my brother Haskell was studying diligently in school. They were both industrious, always working part-time to make a little extra money, but other than that, they were as different as night and day. Haskell was shy and studious, and he always made good grades. Snip, on the other hand, was outgoing and popular, a born politician, president of his class, but usually flunking about half the time. It wasn't that he was dumb. Grades just didn't matter to him. Mama didn't think he'd ever graduate.

Snip was conniving, too. Mama and Papa would always put silver dollars into our stockings on Christmas morning, and Snip would talk Bob and me out of ours. Willie knew about it, but he never told on him.

Snip was always coming up with schemes to make money. One time Mama found out that he was fighting gamecocks, and she gave him a whipping. He yelled like she was killing him. After that, I heard him advise Haskell, "When Mama whips you, holler real loud, and she'll feel sorry for you and stop."

Snip loved animals. That was his saving grace. He had a little dog named Puppy that followed him around everywhere. He even had some white rats. Bob and I used to see brown rats with white spots on them when we played out in the barn. We figured they were descendants of Snip's rats.

Haskell was timid as a little boy. Unfortunately, he grew out of that. Mama used to call him her "angel boy." Once he was kept in after school and didn't come home until after dark. Papa went to the school the next day and talked with the superintendent. He found out that Haskell's teacher had labeled him a troublemaker and had even warned the other teachers about him.

The next day, Papa asked around town about the teacher and found out that he didn't like Indians. Papa went back to the school the next day and

Kaliteyo and Wenonah, 1917

demanded that Haskell be transferred to another class. It's a good thing for the teacher that Papa wasn't more like his father, Sam Paul. He might have ended up being horse-whipped, or worse. Anyway, Haskell was transferred into Mrs. McMurtry's class, and he never had any more trouble. In fact, at the end of the term, Mrs. McMurtry told Mama that Haskell was the nicest boy in her class.

In retrospect, it may have been Haskell's hearing that got him into trouble. He had a lot of ear infections as a child, and he was practically deaf by the time he was grown. Haskell probably couldn't hear, and the teacher thought he was ignoring him.

Kaliteyo was next to Haskell in age, and she tried to keep up with him, even though she was weak and sickly. One day, they were playing follow the leader and climbing the chinaberry trees that grew along the side of the house. Kaliteyo saw a pretty flower out at the end of a branch, leaned out to pick it, and slipped, falling to the ground, landing on a stick, and puncturing her bladder. She had trouble with bladder infections for the rest of her life.

Mama and Papa always toadied to Kaliteyo. We all did, because she was sick so much. Papa was always giving her presents. He would usually give me something at the same time, but I knew he was doing it for Kaliteyo. One time, he gave us both nice bracelets, and I chewed mine up. I was too young for that kind of a gift. Another time, Papa gave Kaliteyo a beautiful cedar chest to keep her things in. Mama told me it was for both of us, but I knew that it was really for Kaliteyo.

Papa would help Kaliteyo with her homework, too. That's the reason she was good in math. I guess Kaliteyo took Victoria's place in Papa's heart. She was the last one of us that he spent much time with.

In the fall of 1918, I started in the primer, or kindergarten, as it's known nowadays. Miss Ruby Perry was our teacher. She taught at Lee School for so long—first as a kindergarten teacher, and later as principal—that she thought of most of the people in town as her children. She also taught Sunday school. I have notes she wrote to Willie, Homer, and Haskell, reminding them to come to Sunday school.

Miss Perry had a little ritual she would put us through at the beginning and end of each school day. In the mornings, we would line up outside, and she would play music on a Victrola while we marched into class like soldiers. Once inside, we would sing a little song:

Good morning to you,
Good morning to you.
We're all in our places,
With clean shiny faces.
Oh, this is the way to start a new day.

She had another song we sang at the end of the day before marching out, again to the accompaniment of the Victrola:

Let us put our books away,
Study time is over.
Gaily tripping, homeward skipping,
Soon we'll be at play.

Actually, it wasn't as much fun as it sounds. Miss Perry was strict. I'll never forget her punishing me for drawing an eight by stacking two circles on top of each other. She had me hold both my hands out, palms up, while she slapped them with a ruler. I told Kaliteyo on her, so the next day Kaliteyo came into my class and tried to show me how to draw an eight on the blackboard. Miss Perry caught us, so then we were both in trouble.

Our mother was strict, too. She told us that if we got into trouble at school, we'd get a whipping when we got home. I don't know if it was that time or another, but one time when Kaliteyo was kept in after school, she slipped out the window when the teacher wasn't looking. She said she was more scared of Mama than she was of her teacher.

I remember Papa from those days. He was good-natured and fun to be around. He took us swimming down at the town of Sulphur one time. The pool there was fed by the spring that gave the town its name, and it had that rotten-eggs smell that comes from the sulfur in the water. We didn't mind, though. You get used to the smell after a while. I was just big enough to get into the water. I splashed around in the shallow end of the pool for a while, and then Papa picked me up and put me on his stomach while he paddled around the pool on his back.

Papa's drinking continued during this time, and Mama complained to him about it almost every night when he came home. I only remember one time that he came home drunk. We were all sick at the time, and he came in with a sack of goodies, sat down on the bed, and handed out candy and fruit to everyone. He was cheerful—you know how people are when they're drunk—and slurring his words. Mama was furious. She blew up at him for coming home drunk and made him leave. Kaliteyo used to say that when Papa was in a good mood, Mama was mad, and when Mama was in a good mood, Papa was mad. That's kind of the way it was during my childhood.

In the spring of 1918, Papa got a letter from San Antonio. A cousin of his, Merle Standish, was selling real estate down there, and he wanted Papa to come down and go into business with him. Mama was overjoyed. It was an answer to her prayers. Moving to San Antonio would get Papa away from his drinking buddies, and finally everything would be all right. Papa wrote back to his cousin and accepted the offer. Maybe he still bought into Mama's idea. His idea of opening a store hadn't worked out, but maybe this one would. Anyway, he gave way in the face of Mama's determination, and they started making arrangements for us to move to San Antonio.

It was the biggest mistake they ever made.

CHAPTER 9
- San Antonio -

We moved out of Pauls Valley in the spring of 1919, lock, stock, and barrel. Mama said she didn't want to leave anything behind that would draw us back. Papa sold our house and most of his property. Mama sorted through the accumulation of twenty years of marriage—furniture, clothing, books, tools, china, silverware, kitchen utensils, pictures, and keepsakes—packed it in boxes, and shipped it to San Antonio.

Nothing was stored. We left a few things in the house. Snip had a pretty cherry bedroom suite with a chest of drawers and a bed that could be folded up against the wall. Mama said it was too heavy to move. We also left Papa's big rolltop desk that I used to hide in. Luckily, Mama and Papa couldn't sell the farm, since it was Willie's allotment, and as things turned out, it came in handy later on.

Papa, Grandpa, and the boys drove the car down to San Antonio, while Kaliteyo and us little children rode with Mama on the train. Once we arrived and checked into the hotel, Mr. Standish took us on a tour of San Antonio. It took two cars to carry all of us—Mama, Papa, Grandpa, Willie, Homer, Haskell, Kaliteyo, Me, Bob, and little Oteka. We went to Breckenridge Park and to the zoo. I remember Papa driving the car across a stream in the park and the water splashing up around the tires. We also went downtown. We saw the Alamo and the Buckhorn Saloon, with its collection of mounted horns. It was late in the afternoon when we got back to the hotel.

The hotel was elegant. I remember big pillars inside the lobby encircled with benches covered with thick red velvet cushions. When we arrived, I promptly fainted and woke up on one of those pretty red cushions with everyone fawning over me. It was so embarrassing. It had been such a wonderful day. But I always reacted to stress that way. I was the fainter in the family.

Papa soon found us a house in a nice neighborhood called Beacon Hill. San Pedro Park was within walking distance. The house was a two-story buff brick with a red tile roof. There was a large wraparound porch with a swing in front. The front door opened into a little foyer. On the right was a door leading into the kitchen, which had a pretty blue-and-white tile floor; on the left was a stairway going up to the second floor, and straight ahead were the living and dining rooms. The ground floor was really spacious, with big rooms and high ceilings, just like our house in Pauls Valley. The bedrooms were upstairs, and Mama's and Willie's bedrooms had porches that overlooked the front yard. I loved to sit upstairs on the porch off of Willie's room and look out over the neighborhood.

Most of our things survived the move, but there were a few casualties. One was a picture of Aunt Sippie that used to hang in our living room. It had been taken out of the frame and rolled up for transport, and when Mama unrolled it in San Antonio, the paint had cracked and peeled off. We had most of the furniture we needed, but I remember Mama buying a big dining room table and a sideboard for dishes and linens.

Papa bought a rooming house downtown to start bringing in income until his real estate business got going. He and Willie ran it. Most of the roomers were soldiers. Papa gave each of them a packet with a little black cross inside and a printed prayer asking God for safety in battle. He gave me one of them, too. I didn't find out until years later that Pancho Villa was raiding the countryside at the time, and the soldiers had been sent down to defend the border.

I think Papa did stop drinking for a while in San Antonio, and we were happy there. He even gave me some attention. He taught me a poem from the second-grade reader that he would have me recite when he brought friends by the house. I can still remember it:

Oh, what shall we do
The long winter through?

The baby ferns cried
When the mother fern died.

The wind whistled bleak,
And the woodland was drear,
And on each baby cheek
There glistened a tear.[1]

Kaliteyo liked to take Oteka down to San Pedro Park to play in the wading pool. Mama would make her take me along, too, even though she didn't want to. When Mama wasn't listening, she would tell me that I wasn't really her sister. She said that Mama found me. She also told me that if I swallowed watermelon seeds, they would sprout in my stomach and grow out through my nose.

Kaliteyo was a daredevil. I guess it was because she was sickly and Mama was always protective of her. Mama bought Haskell a bicycle while we were in San Antonio, and Kaliteyo used to ride it. I remember her speeding down the hill in front of our house like a demon.

There was a man who would come through the neighborhood selling tamales, and they were really good. Mama bought them for us nearly every day, until one of her neighbors told her that one of the tamale man's children had tuberculosis. That was the end of our tamales.

Bob and I spent most of our days playing in the backyard. I remember figs, ants, cockroaches, and horny toads. There was a big fig bush in our yard, and when the figs got ripe we could pick and eat them. They were so good. There were also huge red ants—if you weren't careful, they would crawl into your pants and sting you—and the biggest cockroaches I ever saw in my life. We would capture the horny toads and tie strings around their necks so they couldn't get away. I liked to pretend that I was a little brownie small enough to ride on a horny toad's back. I imagined myself riding out to do battle with the ants and the cockroaches on my tiny toad.

The other thing I remember about San Antonio was airplanes. There was an air base outside of town, and every once in a while an airplane would fly over. There would be a roar above us and everybody would look up. It was the first time in my life that I saw an airplane.

One day Mama let Snip, Haskell, and Kaliteyo go downtown on the trolley. I begged to go, too, and Mama finally let me go with them, giving

Victoria May Rosser Paul, Mama

my brothers strict orders to watch me closely so I wouldn't wander off. When we got downtown, Snip, Haskell, and Kaliteyo got off the streetcar, and as it pulled away, they looked up and saw me still inside, waving out the window at them. Homer and Haskell had to run to the next stop to get me off. I had a great time, but the boys were in trouble with Mama when we got home. She didn't let them go to town alone again.

Since we were dark-complected, we were sometimes mistaken for Mexicans. That aggravated Mama. I remember her taking us downtown to buy shoes one day. When a Mexican clerk came over and spoke Spanish to us, Mama stood up to her full five feet three inches and commanded, indignantly, "Send me someone who speaks English."

Mama got Kaliteyo some pretty, white calf leather shoes that day, but Kaliteyo didn't like them. She said they weren't fashionable. Even at the age of nine, Kaliteyo was concerned about being stylish.

Papa also was embarrassed by his dark skin. As soon as we were settled, he and Mr. Standish made a trip down to Tampico, Mexico, to check out some properties on the Gulf coast. They spent about a week down there, and Papa came back a dark shade of brown. After he got home, he got in the bathtub and scrubbed and scrubbed to try and get the tan off his skin. Mama teased him about it, but it was a serious thing to him. People of color, whether black or brown, were looked down upon.

Willie, who had been managing the rooming house, got sick soon after Papa returned. His face would be swollen in the morning when he woke up, and during the day the swelling would work its way down into his feet. He got weak too. Finally Mama took him to a doctor who said Willie's kidneys were failing. He gave Mama some medicine and warned her to be careful in giving it to him. He said if it was taken incorrectly, it could act as a poison. Since Willie had to stay down at the rooming house to help out, it was up to Papa to give him his medicine. I remember Mama saying how proud she was of Papa for keeping track of Willie's medicine.

As soon as the summer was over, we started to school, except for Bob and Teker, who were still too young. I was in the first grade. They vaccinated us for smallpox, and mine didn't take and had to be done over again. The schools in San Antonio were good, and we learned fast.

Mama joined the Beacon Hill Baptist Church and had us all go to Sunday school there. Our Sunday school teacher was diligent, like Miss Perry in Pauls Valley, and she sent us postcards to urge us to come to class.

Papa and Mr. Standish had trouble getting their real estate business off the ground. If they had stopped to think, they might have realized that Mexican real estate wouldn't be very popular during a revolution, but in their defense, problems are easier to see in retrospect. Mama handled our finances, and I remember hearing her say to Papa, over and over again: "It costs us ten dollars a day just to live here." The income from the rooming house wasn't enough to support us. Mama and Papa discussed what to do. They even talked to Willie about selling his allotment, but he balked at that. Willie wanted to keep his land.

It was clear Mama and Papa had to come up with another plan, and again it was Mama who prevailed. Her solution was to buy a farm in Arkansas, the home of her childhood. She loved the rolling hills, the forests, and the wildflowers. Going back to Pauls Valley was still out of the question for her. She was certain that Papa would fall back in with his old drinking buddies there. Now, it seems foolish for a successful real estate broker to leave a large, growing city, regardless of Pancho Villa, for a small farm in Arkansas, but at the time it may not have been so unreasonable.

Farming was a booming business at the time, especially right after World War I, when Europe was depending on us for much of their food supply. Also, the introduction of tractors and other farm machinery enabled farmers to produce more. Mama's older brother Tom had been a successful farmer for years in eastern Arkansas, and of course, in Papa's family, farming had made both his father and his grandfather rich.

Mama chose Clarksville, Arkansas, as our next destination. There was a little college there, the College of the Ozarks, and she wanted Snip, now fourteen, to be able to continue his education. Willie went down first, to scout the area and find some good land for sale. Soon, he wrote back that he had found a place, so Mama left us with Grandpa, took Oteka, and rode the train to Clarksville to check it out.

By now Mama, at the age of forty-four, was pregnant again, but this would be her last baby. The trip must have been hard on her. She sent a postcard to Kaliteyo and me from Fort Smith:

> *Well Girls, We were tired and dirty when we got here we saw lots of mountains as we came but the cinders came in at the windows so bad that it kept us from seeing lots. We came through a tunnel. And crossed lots of bridges. We come through Ft Smith and Van Buren. It all one city divided by the Arkansas river. A lot of folks went out fishing from the Hotel this morning. They say that they catch nearly all kinds of fish in White river. You all be good and don't get sick.*
>
> *Your Mother.*

Willie met Mama and little Oteka at the train station in Clarksville and showed them around. The property he had located was at the base of Stillwell Mountain, just north of town. There was a nice little house there and forty-eight acres of land. Trees lined the fields, and a little stream wound its way along the edge of the mountain. The neighbors were nice, and there was a church and a school close by. Mama approved of everything, and she signed the papers agreeing to buy the farm. Pleased with herself, she bought a bottle of apple cider and packed it in her suitcase to bring back for us. Willie stayed in Arkansas for spring planting.

When Mama arrived back home in San Antonio, the apple cider had spilled out all over the inside of her suitcase. She made the best of the situation, though, and managed to salvage a few spoonfuls so everyone could get a taste.

On March 16, 1921, my baby brother, Thomas Smith Paul, was born. He was named Thomas after Uncle Tom, and Smith after our great-grandfather. After Mama took some time to recuperate from Tom's birth, she started packing again, getting us ready to move to Arkansas.

CHAPTER 10
- Clarksville, Arkansas -

Haskell didn't want to go to Arkansas with the rest of us. He was right in the middle of his last year of junior high school, and he didn't want to take a chance of being put back a grade. Besides, he had made friends in San Antonio. He even learned a little Spanish. So he asked if he could stay behind with Papa and Grandpa while they sold our house and ran the rooming house to keep some money coming in. Papa said it was fine with him, so Mama gave in and let Haskell stay.

I imagine Papa dreaded the move to Arkansas. He wasn't raised to be a farmer. His father owned a farm, but he didn't really do the work—he managed it. Papa had never done farm work, either, and he didn't aspire to be a farmer. After his brief stint in the ranching business, all he ever wanted to be was a businessman. Never in my life did I see my father dressed in work clothes.

As for Willie, I never saw him dressed in a suit, except when Snip graduated from high school, but that was a special occasion. Willie was as eager as Mama to move to Arkansas and to try his hand at farming. As soon as Mama signed the papers, he started to work on their little plot of land, and he wrote to Uncle Tom, asking for advice.

Uncle Tom had been a successful farmer in the Mississippi River basin for over twenty years, so he knew a lot about farming. Uncle Tom wrote back saying he'd had a bad cold, and the bayou had been flooded, so he couldn't fill Willie's order for seeds right away, but he said he'd send them as soon as he could—"Georgia Heavy" cotton, "the best in the world for up land." He also told Willie he was looking for farmhands; he was willing to pay them twenty dollars per month, and they could also make a share crop.

Snip went back to Pauls Valley. He told Mama he was homesick, arguing he could finish the school term there and stay with Willie's friend, Preston Burch. Mama was an easy mark as far as her sons were concerned, so she said yes. Of course, Snip had no intention of going to school. He just wanted to have some fun, and in the process, make a little money.

When time came for school to be out, Willie wrote a letter to Snip asking him to come to Clarksville to help him out on the farm. There was a lot of work to be done for just one person, and Willie was still having trouble with his kidneys. Snip sent the following amusing letter to his older brother, typed on stationery borrowed from an insurance company's office and addressed very formally to "The Right Honorable W.G. Paul, Esq., Clarksville, Arkansas, USA, North American Hemisphere."

May 25, 1921

Dear Bill:

Received your letter just awhile ago and was glad to hear from you. What made you sick; I guess you did not eat for a week or something like that. I am going to run a root beer BBL for Preston [Burch] and if I can't do that I will work in the hay for Mr. Johnson as he wants me to work for him all summer. Now Bill I don't believe you are sick if I thought you were I would come back and work but I don't believe you are; and I can make some good money here and I want to do it as there will be a time when I will need some money. You have not got but about twelve acres to work. The folks will be down there in about a week so there is no use of me coming down there. There is going to be a big rodeo here for three days starting Thursday. I will make a pot of money while it is in session as I am going to run a stand for Oscar Cobble or Preston one. I owe Hardy Russell $4 and fifteen cents and I will have to pay that before I come back. I bought a pair of work shoes for [from?] him. And a pair of socks also. In a month I will be pretty well hooked up but if I come back now I will only be looser and the gainer of nothing and as the folks are coming right on down there it is of no use for me to come. I had a dickens of a fight the other day. [My brothers took great pride *in their fighting prowess]*

If you are really sick I guess I will have to come back.

But I sure as Hell don't want to at all and I don't reckon I will unless you are about to die.

Snip

There is a handwritten note at the bottom of the page:

Bill Snip is a liar I have told him that he ought to come back but he won't listen to me. Press [Preston]

Willie really was sick. When we arrived at Clarksville, he picked us up at the train station in a buggy and drove us out to the farm. We were so excited to see him that we didn't notice anything wrong at first. We did tease him about how he had let himself go. He was dirty from working in the fields, and his clothes were worn. He hadn't been eating right, and he looked thin. His belt had broken, and he had cinched up his pants with a wire and a nail.

When Willie unhitched the horses, Kaliteyo and I ran up the hill to see the fields and the little stream that ran along the edge of our property next to the mountain. It was so exciting. Mama got busy straightening things up for us and making a list of things we would need. Our new neighbors, the Selfs, came over and brought some food and offered to help us get settled.

The next morning we got a shock. Willie's face was swollen. It wasn't until then Mama realized his kidney trouble had come back. She got him into the buggy right away and took him into town to see the doctor, who put him back on his medicine. Soon he started looking better.

We were all excited about living in the country, but the house was quite a bit smaller than the one we left in San Antonio. We were a little cramped, so Mama started having the little children sleep with her. She'd put Teker and Tom up next to her—one under each arm—with Bob and me down at the foot of her bed. Bob and I would fight, and Mama would kick us to make us settle down and go to sleep. There was another bed for Kaliteyo in Mama's room, and the boys, Willie, Homer, and Haskell—when they all got there—slept in the other bedroom.

Mama managed to keep us fed and comfortable until our furniture arrived, and then life started to seem more normal. She and Mrs. Self were soon fast friends. There was a little Baptist church down the road, and the parishioners there made us feel welcome. Mama bought a cow, a pig, and some chickens. Kaliteyo claimed Willie's horse when he wasn't using it for farm work, and she would ride it bareback. I can still see her long hair flowing in the wind as she raced across the pasture.

Back in San Antonio, Grandpa, at the age of seventy-nine, was suffering from his rheumatism. When Haskell's school was out, Grandpa took a break from house sitting and went down to Corpus Christi to lie in the warm seawater, but it didn't help much. He wrote to Mama:

> *July 8, 1921*
> *Dear Vick,*
>
> *I have been waiting to have something to write, hoping that the place would sell. There has been several hear to see it but not sold yet—we are keeping batch ["baching" is a slang for men living without a woman's help] getting along very well. I done a good job of cleaning it up stairs and down stairs looks nice know Bill [Papa] has been trying to sell it but has failed so far. I have gained four pounds in my weight I feel better hear than I felt at Corpus.*
>
> *Well Jim I must write you and Colly [Kaliteyo] a little. Write how you like Arkansas. If you have good water and a plenty of good old sorgum molasses if you have any chills where you live. I am doing very well all things considered. All write. Tell Haskell regards to all. [That must mean "Haskell sends his regards"]*
>
> *J T Rosser.*

We had good water from the well, I suppose, but the water in the stream was contaminated by copper—cupreous they called it. It gave the surface a golden sheen. We enjoyed splashing around in it, though, and we caught minnows and crawdads and made little boats to float down the "rapids." One day, Kaliteyo got the idea to dam up the stream to make us a swimming hole. She organized all the neighborhood children, including me, to work on her project. We worked hard for a couple of days, but every time we would create a little pool with our dam, the current would wash our rocks away.

Since Bob and I were too little to ride the horse, Mama got us a little burro. He was small enough to ride, but try as we would, we couldn't get him to walk. One of us would get on him, and the other would push. He was so stubborn he just refused to budge. We even picked up his legs to give him the idea of walking, but he would just put them back down where they had been. I can still hear him bray.

We had more luck climbing trees. There were trees lining the pasture that had muscadine vines growing on them. They were easy to climb, and the muscadine grapes tasted good.

I guess we city kids were curiosities to the locals. Of course, they were interested in our adventures in San Antonio, but they also took advantage of our ignorance to have a little fun at our expense. I remember some of the older kids taking us aside and warning us about the panthers that came down out of the mountains at night looking for little children to eat. The story caused us some trepidation on the way to the outhouse at night until we found out they were just pulling our legs.

Mama really seemed happy in Arkansas. The people were nice, and they did their best to make us feel at home. Everyone went to the same little church, and every few weeks they would hold a church social to raise money. Each family would bring a box supper, and after the service the suppers would be auctioned off. Then everyone would sit down together and eat, visit, and sample each other's cooking.

When fall came, Snip and Haskell joined us, and we all started back to school. The boys went to the high school, and Kaliteyo, Bob, and I went to the grade school. The grade school just had two classes, one for the older children and one for the younger ones. Kaliteyo was in the fifth grade so she was in the older group. We were all ahead of our age groups because of the good schools in San Antonio. I have a picture of Kaliteyo with her class in Clarksville. She's wearing one of the weskits Mama knitted for the soldiers during World War I.

Papa stayed a few months longer in San Antonio, running his boarding house and waiting for our house to be sold. He sent us money and bought things for us that we needed. A postcard he sent to me said:

> *Helo Jim*
> *Look in the coat pocket I sent Wille and get your little Lord Jesus.*
> *Write me. Love to all*
> *Papa*

I kept that little crucifix until Willie died.

By winter Papa had joined us. He finally sold the house in San Antonio and turned the rooming house over to his cousin Standish. Willie harvested the small amount of cotton he planted on Uncle Tom's advice, and with his profits and the money from the sale of our house, we had enough to keep us going for a while.

Grandpa didn't follow us to Arkansas. He ran off, as Mama described it, and moved to a home for Confederate veterans in Ardmore. She cried so hard you would have thought he died. I missed him, too. I missed sitting on his knee, listening to his stories and songs, but I suppose he was happier at the home. He and the other old veterans could reminisce about their lives before the Civil War. He even met an old lady in Ardmore and married her.

It wasn't long before something happened that changed our lives once again. This time it wasn't Papa's drinking, and it had nothing to do with money. Snip came home from school one day and announced that he was getting married!

I don't really know the details of Snip's situation. I was too little to understand, but Mama and Papa talked to Snip, and they talked to the girl and her parents, and before I knew what was happening, they had packed Snip off to Pauls Valley and were making plans for the rest of us to follow.

So after three years, Mama had come full circle and we were headed back to Pauls Valley, the place she had risked everything to leave.

CHAPTER 11
- Returning Home -

After five moves and three failed business ventures, our family ended up right back in Pauls Valley where we started, and what had it gained us? Nothing. We were ruined financially. We had spent everything we had moving from place to place—on houses, furniture, farm equipment, stock, and living expenses. Papa had given up his job and his position in the community. We children missed several months of school. We no longer had a car, or our house, for that matter. Mama pushed Papa into each move, thinking she could run away from trouble, but she was wrong, and we all paid for it.

We arrived in Pauls Valley on a cloudy day in the spring of 1922. Mrs. Campbell, one of Mama's old Chickasaw friends, met us at the train depot and took us to her house to stay for the time being. I remember being excited about returning home. I missed Mrs. Garvin, Aunt Sippie, and the children I started to school with. I ruined our warm welcome, though. As Mrs. Campbell drove her car into the garage I pushed the door open, anxious to get out, and broke one of the hinges. I don't remember if Mrs. Campbell was angry, but I got a stern reprimand from Mama.

Papa did the best he could to get our old house back, but it wasn't for sale; besides, he only had a little money left over from selling our house in San Antonio, so we ended up living out at the farm, on Willie's allotment, in Sam Paul's old house, the house where Papa was born.

As soon as our furniture arrived, we started moving in. It was the smallest house we ever lived in, and it was run down from years of disuse. There were holes in the roof and cracks in the walls. The little draft we got at night didn't bother us though, since it was springtime. Mama stuffed rags into the cracks. Willie patched the roof and replaced Mama's rags with caulking.

Willie was as excited as we children were about coming back to Pauls Valley. I suspect he was proud to be farming his own land. He bought two horses—we named them Mack and Maggie—and an old wagon on credit from Mr. Wiggins, as well as a pig, a cow, some chickens, and a pair of geese. The geese had three babies, and Mama named them Shadrach, Meshach, and Abednego, from the Bible story. She also managed to bring our little burro from Arkansas, but somebody stole him.

Willie and Mama sat down and decided what to plant, and before long we had a garden full of vegetables. We were so proud when Willie's strawberries and sweet potatoes were ripe. I don't remember what Willie planted in the fields, probably some hay, alfalfa, and corn. Papa eventually got back into the real estate business, but he was never successful again. He would sell a little property from time to time to supplement our income, and he had some rental property, too, but Willie's farm eventually became our main source of income. Papa supported Willie's farming venture, but he didn't help him. Every day, Papa would get dressed in his suit and drive the buggy downtown to his office, even though he would have been more useful helping Willie with the farm work. Soon he was drinking again.

Since we moved during the school year, we had to start to school as soon as we got back home. Snip was seventeen and should have been finishing his senior year, but he had missed so much school at that point, he didn't see any point in going back. He argued he would be more help to the family out working, but Mama made him go to school, anyway. She said he needed to graduate. Unlike Snip, Haskell was eager to go back to school, and he did fine, as always.

Kaliteyo did okay as far as I know, but I had trouble. When we left Arkansas, my class was just taking up long division, and when we got home, the third-grade class in Pauls Valley had already covered it. So since I couldn't do long division, I was put back into the second grade.

It was so embarrassing. Not only did I have to go to class with the second-graders, the third-graders all knew me. They were the same kids I started kindergarten with two years before, and they teased me unmercifully. I got so mad that I picked out the biggest girl in the third grade and started a fight with her. She was an Indian girl and more than a match for me. She was bigger and stronger, and I ended up having to bite her to get her off me.

Being put back into the second grade was the worst thing that ever happened to me in school. It haunted me until I graduated from high school, and I still can't do long division.

Soon after we settled into the house at the farm and were all back in school, the spring rains came. The land Sam Paul gave to the Santa Fe Railroad for the town of Pauls Valley back in 1887 was right in the fork between the Washita River and Rush Creek.[1] The area is relatively low, and every spring there was a flood. The flood of 1922 wasn't the worst in history, but it certainly was a memorable one for me.

The rain started one day while we were in school, and Mama was worried. We had to cross the Rush Creek bridge to get back out to the farm, and the water was starting to rise. Rush Creek was aptly named. Although usually placid, a downpour could quickly turn it into a raging torrent. Mama called Mrs. Trimmer, whose house was on our way, to ask her to keep us until Willie could check the bridge.

Haskell was walking Bob and me home from school when Mrs. Trimmer met us. She told us we could stay at her house until it was safe to cross Rush Creek. Snip and Kaliteyo weren't with us for some reason. Maybe they were home sick.

Mrs. Trimmer brought us inside and dried us off. She had already started planning for us to spend the night. The Trimmer children had a play room in the barn, which was warm and cozy, so Mrs. Trimmer decided to fix pallets out there for us. She was telling us about her plans when Willie came to the door. Mama had sent him with the wagon to pick us up. He said he had come across the bridge without any trouble, so he thought it would be okay to take us home.

Haskell, Bob, and I gathered up our school books and went outside with Willie. It had stopped raining, but the ground was muddy. I had some pretty, new shoes, and I remember worrying about getting them muddy. Willie stopped along the way to pick up Fred Snyder, a neighbor boy who also lived on the other side of Rush Creek, and then hurried to get back to the bridge before the water rose any higher.

When we got to the bridge, the little park next to Rush Creek was flooded, and the bridge, which had no railings, had disappeared under the water. There were men standing on either side of the creek to mark the location of the bridge for those wanting to cross.

Willie stopped and talked to the men. They assured him the bridge was only a couple of inches under water, and he would be fine. So he urged Mack and Maggie out onto the invisible bridge. As the horses slowly advanced, the wagon wheels sank in deeper and deeper, and Willie began to realize that the men had misjudged the depth of the water. The wagon started slipping sideways, and it was too late to turn back. I remember the men yelling, "Keep to the right! Keep to the right!" Willie was standing now, yelling at the horses, urging them on and pulling on the reins with all his strength to steer them to the right.

The wagon was made for hauling dirt or grain, and the boards in its bed were loose, so as the water rose around us, they just floated away. Suddenly I found myself in the water. As I looked around, I saw my six-year-old brother Bob clinging to Fred Snyder as Fred struggled to swim to the bank. It was a comical sight. Bob had his arms wrapped around Fred's head, covering his eyes so that he couldn't see. When I looked back toward the wagon, all I could see were the horses' ears above the water. It was just about then that I went under.

The next thing I knew, a hand grabbed me and pulled my head up out of the water. It was Haskell. I tried to fight him, but he was stronger, and he finally managed to get me to the bank. As we slogged through the mud, one of my new shoes came off. I turned to go back and get it, but Haskell wouldn't let me.

When everyone was safely out of the water, Willie took us over to the Bradley house on the far side of the creek and then went back to take care of the horses and see if he could salvage the wagon. Mrs. Bradley cleaned us up and put dry clothes on us, and Mr. Bradley drove us home to Mama. In later years, when I got on Haskell's nerves, I would remind him that it was his own fault because he saved me from drowning in Rush Creek.

That was the summer Mama's brother Tom visited us and I asked him why he let Mama marry Papa. As it turned out, I wasn't the only one following Uncle Tom around that summer. Haskell had questions for him too, just a different kind. He wanted to know about raising tobacco and cotton, about living on the Mississippi River, about the swamps, and the wildlife. Haskell had an unquenchable thirst for knowledge, even as a boy. So when Uncle Tom left, he asked Mama if Haskell could come home with him for the rest of the summer.

Mama said yes, of course. Haskell was a different boy after coming back from San Antonio. He was sullen and disrespectful of Mama, blaming her for all our troubles. Papa must have confided in him while they were living together. Mama probably thought it would be good for Haskell to spend some time with Uncle Tom, and maybe get a different perspective on her side of the family.

I doubt if the summer changed Haskell's opinion of our family troubles, but he certainly had a good time. Uncle Tom was probably glad to have his help, too. Haskell was tough, and he was a hard worker, not lazy like Snip. He came back with a deep tan and bigger muscles, which he was proud to show us, and with a great admiration for Uncle Tom.

As Haskell found out, Tom was a remarkable man. After leaving Indian Territory to farm along the Mississippi, he fought malaria, the periodic flooding of the river, and back-breaking labor to become a successful farmer. Then he faced two tragedies that would have broken most men.

First was the loss of his leg. It happened during one of Tom's trips to Hot Springs, where he went every summer to get the malaria "burned" out of him.

On the day he was to leave, he got a late start, arriving at the station just as his train was pulling away. He ran for the train, but when he leaped for the platform, his foot slipped and he fell under the wheels! He survived, but his right leg was severed just above the knee. He almost bled to death, and he spent several weeks in the hospital recovering. In the days before antibiotics and blood transfusions, it was a miracle he survived.

After being released from the hospital, Tom faced the second tragedy. He learned that his bank had failed. In those days there was no deposit insurance, so it meant he had to start all over again, and with only one leg. At the time of his visit in 1922, Uncle Tom had recovered his losses and, according to Haskell, he still worked as hard as any of his hands.

When Haskell got home he begged Papa for some land of his own. He had always been jealous of Willie and Snip anyway, because they were old enough to get allotments. Somehow Papa managed to buy him a little plot of land out west of town. Haskell appreciated it, too. In later years, he kept some cows out there and planted hay, corn, and peanuts. He played at farming for the rest of his life.

During that first summer back in Pauls Valley, all our relatives and friends came by to visit. We told them about our adventures and caught up on their news. I could tell Papa was happy to see Uncle Buck and Mrs. Paul. Uncle Buck and Aunt Molly had added a couple of babies to their already large brood of children. Mama seemed happy to see her lady friends too, especially Mrs. Garvin, and we went over to Whitebead to visit Aunt Sippie. Her sons had moved out to California, so she asked Papa to manage her business affairs.

After I almost drowned in Rush Creek, Mama was anxious to move into town. Luckily, the Harkreader family, who had bought our house, decided to move about that time. They weren't planning to leave until the end of the summer, though, and that wasn't soon enough for Mama, so Papa arranged for us to move into Dr. Johnson's old house. Dr. Johnson lived right across the street from us, next door to Mrs. Paul, but while we were gone, he built a new house on his lot and moved his old house down the street a couple of blocks. The old house was still vacant, and that's where we lived for the rest of the summer.

After our furniture was brought in from the farm, we moved into the house. Mama and Kaliteyo got busy cleaning and straightening up inside, while Bob and I went out to get reacquainted with the kids in the neighborhood.

It wasn't long before we had another scare, and I'll bet Mama was grateful we were back in Pauls Valley, so she could call old Dr. Callaway.

One day three-year-old Oteka was sitting on the floor playing with her toys while Kaliteyo was sweeping the floor. When Kaliteyo got to the corner of the room where Teker was sitting, she just pushed her aside with her broom. As she did, Teker let out a blood-curdling scream. A splinter from the floor had been driven up into her little bottom. The splinter was huge, and it broke off inside her. Mama couldn't get it out, so she sent Kaliteyo to get Dr. Callaway. He came right over. The old doctor had Mama hold Teker across her lap while he worked to get the splinter out. I can still hear Teker scream. The splinter left a big hole where it went in, and Mama spent several days putting coal oil in the wound to keep Teker from getting lockjaw. Mama kept that splinter in a fruit jar on the window sill in the kitchen for years. It must have been three inches long.

It was a happy day when we finally moved back into our old house. The Harkreaders sold the lot at the end of the block to the Ashhurst family, so we no longer owned the whole block, but the Ashhursts were good neighbors. Their daughter Vera and I were the same age, and we got to be close friends.

The Harkreader children made one improvement to our property that we appreciated. They hung a swing from a tree on the far edge of our lot next to the Ashursts's fence. We could stand on the fence, swing out over our yard, and let go, dropping four or five feet to the ground. We got to swing on it for several days before Mama saw what we were doing and made Willie cut it down.

By the time school started again, we were almost back to normal.

CHAPTER 12
- Back in Pauls Valley -

It wasn't long before Mama got back to normal, too. She started going to the Alternate Saturday Club meetings again, and of course, the poetry club. She also joined the women's auxiliary of the Woodmen of the World, an organization that sponsored social and charitable projects, but the organization she was most passionate about was the U.D.C., the United Daughters of the Confederacy. She was a charter member of Pauls Valley's Jefferson Davis Chapter and their perennial president. It was her way of honoring Grandpa.

The tiny, but enthusiastic, congregation of St. Mary's, Pauls Valley's little Episcopal church, still hung in there. The minister Papa was jealous of had moved on, so Mama didn't have to contend with that. She started taking us to church again, although Papa didn't come with us.

Once we were back in our old house, Kaliteyo and the older boys slept upstairs, while Teker, Tom, Bob, and I still slept downstairs with Mama. Papa had started drinking again, and sometimes he'd be gone for days. When he was home, he'd sleep in one of the upstairs rooms.

Papa was kind of a curiosity to me. I remember watching him get dressed in the morning. He slept in long-handled underwear. The first thing he'd do every morning was bend down and touch his toes. That was his exercise. Then he'd go into the bathroom, get cleaned up and dressed, and walk downtown, usually after having one or two of Mama's biscuits.

Papa's isolation from the family must have irritated him, and I think Mama must have been afraid of him sometimes, especially since Grandpa wasn't with us anymore. One night in particular, I remember Papa coming home late. He was drunk, and Mama told us to hide under her bed. Papa didn't see anyone around, so he started going from room to room looking for us. Finally, he opened the door into Mama's room. We children were told to be quiet, so there was no sound, until Teker's little voice pierced the silence: "Don't come in here, Papa, because we're in here." Papa started to laugh, and then everything was okay.

Mama brought the cow, the geese, and some chickens in from the farm, and she also kept a little banty rooster as a pet. She called him Chanticleer, after a rooster she had read about in a poem. We all played with him, and sometimes we would bring him into the house. After a while, my little brother Tom started having trouble breathing. Mama called Dr. Callaway. He told her that Tom had asthma, and he got it from playing with Chanticleer.

I guess there wasn't much treatment for asthma back then. Dr. Callaway just told Mama to keep Chanticleer out of the house and warned her that if Tom started having an asthma attack she was under no circumstances to hold him in her arms. I guess he thought it would restrict Tom's breathing, but that was a tall order for Mama. I remember Kaliteyo running to Mama and throwing her arms around her to keep her from picking Tom up.

Even after Chanticleer was banished from the house, he continued to get our attention every morning by crowing to wake us up. One morning we didn't hear him crow, and he didn't show up later to be fed with the other chickens. After several days, we found him in the cistern. He had flown in there and couldn't get out. He had caught cold and lost his voice. Gradually, Chanticleer regained his health, but his voice was never quite the same. Every morning he would still try to crow, but all he could manage was a kind of croak. Years later, Oteka found a cuckoo clock in Germany that reminded her of Chanticleer. I heard it, and sure enough, it sounded just like him.

The winter of 1922-23 was especially severe, and one night Mama dreamed about muddy water. It was another foreboding. That night our pipes froze, as they often did during the winters. The crawlspace under our house was about four feet high—when Bob and I were little, we could stand up straight under there—so the pipes were exposed to the cold air.

The next morning, Mama sent Kaliteyo over to Mrs. Paul's house to get water, and on the way back, she spilled some on herself. Mama got her dried off and sat her by the fireplace, but by afternoon she was coughing. That night she woke us all up screaming. Mama ran upstairs to check on her and found her burning up with a fever. Dr. Callaway came out the next morning and diagnosed her with pneumonia.

There were no antibiotics in those days. Dr. Callaway prescribed poultices, to apply to Kaliteyo's chest, and purgatives, the remedies they had back then. There wasn't really much he could do, but every evening after he finished seeing patients, he would come by anyway and sit with Mama and Kaliteyo for a while. He always had some Life Savers in his pocket for us, too. We all loved old Dr. Callaway, and we looked forward to his visits. He reminded me of Grandpa.

Kaliteyo was sick for a long time. Mama kept her in her room and sat by her bedside most of the time. Mama was scared to death we'd get sick, too, so she moved Bob and me upstairs. I used to cough a lot at night, and Mama would come upstairs when she heard me to make sure I hadn't kicked off my covers. Then she would put some sugar in a spoon with a drop of coal oil and give it to me for my cough.

Anytime one of us got sick, Mama moved us into her bedroom and made sure our clothes and dishes were washed separately. She soaked our cuts in coal oil to prevent infection. Mama was always afraid we'd get chilled and catch pneumonia. She'd come around at night to make sure our covers were pulled up around us, and if we were sick, she'd heat up a brick, wrap a towel around it, and put it under the covers to keep us warm.

Mama was fanatical about preventing infection. She never let us use the same utensils twice, and she never let us touch each other's food. Once, Miss Mary Cochel, Mama's seamstress and friend, was visiting us, and Haskell asked her to pass him a biscuit. Miss Mary just picked up a biscuit and handed it to him. Mama gave Miss Mary a look, then stood up, took the biscuit from Haskell, and threw it away. Then she handed Haskell the bread tray.

In spite of her fear of contagion, Mama always helped out when someone in the community was sick. Mrs. Johnson, Dr. Johnson's wife, told me years later how grateful she was to Mama for bringing in custards and other food for her children when they had typhoid fever and no one else would come around her.

Kaliteyo couldn't sleep and she wouldn't eat. She lost weight. Dr. Callaway said if she could just get through the crisis she would make it. I was Mama's errand girl, and she would send me down to Mr. Tether, the pharmacist, to pick up Kaliteyo's medicine.

One day, Kaliteyo saw icicles hanging from the eves of the house, and asked Mama if she could have one to suck on. Mama asked Dr. Callaway that evening when he came by, and he said it would be all right, it might even help bring down her fever. So Mama started letting her have icicles. One day, I was in the kitchen washing dishes and Mama came in crying. She said that Kaliteyo had bitten the thermometer, thinking it was an icicle, and broke the glass in her mouth. She had been delirious with fever. Mama was beside herself. She said, "Jim, I tried to clean the glass out of Kaliteyo's mouth, but I don't know if I got it all." She asked me to go in and sit with Kaliteyo while she got herself together.

I went into Mama's room and held Kaliteyo's hand. She was so still. As I sat there, I remembered all my evil thoughts about her and started to feel guilty. It seemed like forever before Mama came back into the room.

Lucky for me, Kaliteyo didn't die, so I soon got over my guilt. Everyone pampered her during her convalescence. Willie bought her some silk stockings—Kaliteyo was always vain about her pretty legs—and Papa brought her candy. Every day Mama took her down to Dr. Callaway's office—I got to go, too—so he could paint her throat with mercurochrome to keep her from getting consumption.

When spring came I took my turn at causing a fuss. I was swinging as high as I could on the swing at school, trying to go over the top, and fell out. I broke my finger and hurt my side. Kaliteyo told me I would never be able to dance because I was going to have a crooked finger. I did have trouble with my side after that, but my finger healed straight.

Mama and Papa were struggling financially at that time, even though we children weren't aware of it. Papa and Uncle Buck's rent houses brought in the little income we had. Willie's farm kept us fed, but it didn't make much money. The farm boom following World War I had petered out, and the mechanization that enabled farmers to increase their production led to lower prices that just made it harder for small farmers to survive. Willie, like most farmers at the time, lived from one mortgage to another. The payments from the Chickasaw fund came in from time to time, and Mama said that when they did, the first person she would pay was Dr. Callaway.

That fall, Willie butchered a hog from the farm. Snip and Haskell helped him. I remember Mama boiling water to scald the hide to remove the bristles. She made sausage and sauce meat and put the rest in the smoke house. We had sausage all winter long.

CHAPTER 13
- Me and Bob -

I was always a tomboy. I don't remember ever owning a doll. Kaliteyo told me if I kissed my elbow I could turn myself into a boy, so for years I struggled to stretch my lips out that far, but I never could do it. Bob was two years younger than me, and we were constant companions during most of our childhood. I think he wished I was a boy, too.

Bob and I played together, but we didn't always get along. We fought when we were sleeping at the foot of Mama's bed. We fought inside the house, and we fought outside. We even fought when we were sick. Bob and I had mumps at the same time, and our jaws were swollen. Mama put us together at first, away from our brothers and sisters, but we fought so much she had to separate us. When we had the measles, Mama just moved Bob down to her bedroom. He was really sicker than me. That's when Mama taught me to crochet, to occupy my time. I got bored without Bob there to fight.

Bob and I got a whipping practically every day. When we were little, Mama would hold our heads between her knees to keep us still while she spanked our bottoms with her hands. As we got older, she used switches. She would have us pick switches for each other. I would get a little switch for Bob, and he would bring back a tree limb for me. If Mama was really serious, she'd get out her ironing cord. It was the ironing cord that really put the fear of God into us.

Bob had a little dog named Ring who dearly loved him, and when Mama would start in whipping Bob, Ring would jump up and try to take the switch away from her. He'd bark and run back and forth. Pretty soon she would get the switch tangled up in her apron, get tickled, and stop.

Since I was older, I usually won our fights, so Bob was always trying to get even. He would hit me and run out the back door, slamming it behind him to slow me down. Slamming the door sometimes broke the glass. Mama would yell, "Don't slam the door," but fear would get the better of Bob, and he would slam it, anyway. So the glass in the back door was broken most of the time. One day, during a desperate attempt to defend himself, Bob picked up a bone Mama had saved for the dog and hit me across the eye with it. I still have the scar. I could whip him until he got to junior high and started getting stronger. Also, he learned how to cheat. He'd hit me in the stomach.

Bob and I didn't fight all the time. We climbed the trees, and we climbed on the roof of the house. I'm afraid of heights now, but as a child I was never afraid. The windows to our bedrooms upstairs were set into gables, so we could climb directly out onto the roof. We liked to play in a little fenced area at the top of the roof called the widow's porch.

Mama always had chores for us to do, and when we were little, we had to wash the dishes. I would wash and Bob would dry. Bob wasn't a willing participant, though. He would try to get away, and Mama would drag him back, crying. Kaliteyo used to enjoy telling about how Bob used the dish towel to wipe his tears and blow his nose.

In the winter, Bob and I had to gather kindling for Mama's wood-burning stove. Willie was always the first one up in the morning, and he would go in and get the fire started. Then we'd all run downstairs and stand around the stove while we got dressed.

We always had a cow when I was a child, and I took my turn milking her. It was unpleasant work, especially during winter. One of our cows was named Fidget, because she wouldn't stand still, and one day she knocked me up against the side of her stall. It made me so mad I got a board and hit her across the back with it. Mama scolded me for that. She said I shouldn't get mad at a dumb animal.

Tom had a deformity of his chest called pigeon breast, which Dr. Callaway said would make him susceptible to consumption. He was a finicky eater, and Mama just couldn't get him to gain weight, so Dr. Callaway advised her to get a goat and feed him goat's milk to build him up. The plan worked well. Tom actually liked goat's milk, and because I had the smallest hands, it became my job to milk the goat. I remember when the goat's udder was full, I could only use two fingers. As I got some milk out, I could use three fingers, and finally four.

We had a barn in the lot next to our house, where the goat and the cow stayed during the night and where Bob and I used to see the descendants of Snip's white rats. We played out there a lot. We'd climb up in the hayloft and jump off. It was five or six feet down to the ground. One day Bob and I decided that we could use Mama's nice monogrammed parasol like a parachute. We ruined it and earned ourselves another whipping.

There was also a little house out in back for a servants' quarters. Odessa, our maid, stayed there sometimes when she wasn't getting along with her husband, but when it was vacant, Bob and I played in there. It was our "office." We didn't play "house" like other children. We played "business." Bob was Bill, and I was Jenson. We dressed up in some old clothes of Papa's and pretended to chew tobacco, smoke cigars, and make big deals.

Sometimes Mama would let us walk home with Odessa. She lived in West Town, the colored section of town, which was about a block from our house. Odessa was pretty, and she lived in a little house with a big mulberry tree out in front. She also had a phonograph. She would play records for us and serve us mulberries with sugar and cream.

Bob and I looked forward to the ice man coming by on his rounds. We had an ice box, and Mama would put up a sign in the window if she wanted ice. There was one sign for a twenty-five-cent block and another for a fifty-cent block. The ice man would strap a big piece of leather across his back, swing a block of ice across his shoulder with a pair of metal tongs, and carry the ice up to the house. We always ran out to his truck when he came by to pick up ice chips to suck on.

Farmers drove their trucks down the street from time to time, selling fruit and other produce. Mama would buy fruit, wrap it in newspaper, and store it in the hall closet to keep it from spoiling. Lots of vendors came to the door in those days. They sold buttons and thread, ribbons, jewelry, tonics, and books. There was also a man who came around to sharpen scissors.

Some evenings Willie would bring home ice to make ice cream. Back then, every housewife had her own ice cream recipe. Mama's was like a custard. She would cook up her batter, and Willie would put it into our ice cream maker. Then we would compete for the privilege of sitting on the lid to hold it down while Willie turned the crank.

Sometimes we would venture down the street to play with the neighbor kids. There was an older girl who liked to play with us, but she was slow-witted, and we would play tricks on her. Mama told us not to do that, because it was cruel to take advantage of her. We asked Mama why the girl was slow-witted, and she said it was because her parents were cousins.

Sometimes Bob and I got into trouble with the neighbors. There was a man who lived down the street from us named Joe Raines. He had a big orchard of fruit trees, and we would climb over his fence to steal fruit. When he caught us, he would run us off. I don't think he really minded that much, though. When I got married, Joe made a serving tray from different kinds of wood and gave it to me as a wedding gift.

Every spring, as soon as it got warm outside, Bob and I would start working on Mama to give us permission to go barefoot. She'd put us off as long as she could because she was afraid we would step on a nail and get lockjaw. Sure enough, after she gave in, one of us would step on a nail. Mama's treatment was to make us soak our foot in coal oil. We never got an infection, either.

What Bob and I enjoyed most was going out to the farm. When we were little, Mama wouldn't let us go by ourselves, but Willie would take us with him when he went. We would climb the big elm trees that grew along the road and eat the possum grapes that grew on the vines up in their branches. They were mostly seed, but they tasted good.

A grove of persimmon trees grew next to the old house at the farm, and that's where Bob and I played "Tarzan." We would pull the branches down and then hold on as they flipped us up into the air. One day while we were playing Tarzan, a big snake chased us. We ran as hard as we could to where Willie was working in his garden. He followed us with his hoe to where we had seen the snake, but when he got there, it was gone.

Rush Creek went right through Willie's farm. We waded in it and caught crawdads and little fish in jars. Willie tied a rope to a limb so we could swing out over the water. Usually there was more mud than water. After a rain, when the water was up, Bob would get out in Rush Creek and try to swim. He used a big jar as a float at first, and eventually he was able to swim without it. I was too chicken to try. Since my narrow escape during the flood of 1922, I was scared of the water.

In about 1925 the county came up with the idea of digging a new channel for Rush Creek to bypass Pauls Valley and prevent our annual floods. We called it the ditch. The ditch didn't work very well for the flooding, but it did give us an unexpected bonus. It caused Rush Creek to dry up for a while, and Bob and I pulled twenty catfish out of the mud. We brought them home to Mama, and she fried them up for us.

There was an area of sandy ground close to Rush Creek where Willie grew watermelons. We used to find arrowheads there, buried in the sand. We would imagine stalking deer in the forest with bows and arrows like our ancestors.

Bob and I used to climb the big trees along Rush Creek. We'd sit up there and talk about our hopes and dreams. I'd tell Bob about how when I grew up, I was going to live in a tree house. I'd live all by myself, and when I got hungry, I'd just eat fish out of the creek. Bob had different dreams. He was going to be a cowboy, riding horses and roping steers. He also spent a lot of time telling me about the boys he knew. They were divided into two groups: those he could "whup" and those he couldn't.

Up on our perch in the trees, we could also look out across the countryside. They raised sheep on a neighboring farm, and we would watch as the sheep slowly meandered around the field, grazing. We watched as the lambs frolicked, and the rams challenged each other. There was a road on the other side of the creek, and occasionally we would see a car. We saw one particular car several times. It would drive off the road and park. The car belonged to a prominent businessman in town who was having an affair with his secretary. His daughter was in my class in school. We couldn't see inside the car, but we knew that what they were doing in there was nasty.

Snip and Haskell helped Willie at the farm. Sometimes chickens would fly into the well, and someone would have to get them out before they fouled the water. One time Haskell went down into the well to rescue a chicken and lost his grip on the rope. He was strong and agile, though, and somehow managed to brace his legs against the walls to keep himself from falling. The well was eighty-five feet deep, so the fall could have killed him. Willie was there and pulled him out.

I also had a close call in that well. One day when we were all out at the farm, Snip noticed a chicken had fallen into it. He wasn't as energetic as Haskell, and he asked Bob and me if one of us would go down to retrieve the chicken. I volunteered. I was feeling brave that day. Snip tied the well rope to a singletree and had me straddle it while he lowered me down into the well. Down and down I went. It was cold and dark down there, and I got scared. I gripped the rope so tight, I pulled myself up off the singletree, and it started to slide out from under me. I screamed for Snip to raise me up.

Snip got me up as fast as he could, and as he lifted me off the singletree I noticed he was as white as a sheet. He was just as scared as I was. He looked worse after Mama got through with him, though. She gave him a tongue-lashing. I remember her saying, "You'd better not ever endanger the life of one of my children again."

Sometimes Mama would let Bob and me go out to the farm by ourselves. We'd walk down past West Town, follow the ditch to Rush Creek, and walk along the creek out to the farm. We loved to ride the horses, Mack and Maggie. They were big workhorses. It was hard to get a bridle on them because they would raise up their heads so we couldn't reach them. I usually rode Mack. He was gentler. Maggie had some mustang blood in her and was more spirited. We rode bareback. I always had to find something to stand on to get up on Mack, but Bob was like a squirrel. He'd just climb up Maggie's leg.

Another thing Bob and I did for entertainment was go to religious services. The Baptists used the vacant lot across the street from us for revivals, and sometimes Mama would let us go. We enjoyed the singing, and we enjoyed watching the people. The preacher would give his sermon, and then everyone would sing "Bringing in the Sheaves," while those who wanted to be saved would come down to the front to receive the Holy Spirit.

We had a cousin who drank like Papa, and one time we noticed him with his wife at one of the camp meetings. I'll call them Frank and Nellie. Nellie had brought Frank there hoping that he would get saved and stop drinking. After the sermon, we watched them as the congregation began to sing "Bringing in the Sheaves." Nellie looked up at Frank, but he didn't budge. Near the end of the song, the preacher called out, "Won't you please come while we sing the last stanza?" Still Frank didn't move. When the singing stopped, the preacher said, "Will those of you who are still sinners please face the back?" Nellie watched in horror as Frank turned around. His face turned red, and he looked like he wished he could sink down into the ground. As Bob and I watched, Nellie pulled on Frank's sleeve. She finally got him to turn back around, but he never went down to receive the Holy Spirit. I just know that as soon as they got home Frank started drinking again.

Bob and I also went to brush arbor meetings down in West Town. We got invited by Shorty, a black man who worked for Willie and sharecropped. He lived in a little house out on the farm. Shorty's mother was a devout

Pentecostal, and the brush arbors were built up against her house. A brush arbor consisted of a wooden framework which was built out from the side of a house, and it was laced with brush to make it shed water. It wasn't big enough for the whole congregation, but the preacher and the choir could get under it. Mama let us go, but she gave us strict instructions to behave ourselves and to be respectful.

We enjoyed the brush arbor meetings even more than the Baptist revivals. The people who attended the services were Holy Rollers. They sang, they spoke in tongues, and sometimes they "rolled" out of their chairs in rapture. We learned some of the songs, and we would sing along with them. Bob had a pretty voice. Watching the preacher was worth the trip. He would get to the climax of his sermon and jump right straight up in the air for emphasis. He must have jumped four feet high. It was amazing.

One evening while Bob and I were sitting among the congregation at a brush arbor meeting, we noticed a woman holding a baby in her lap. After a while she started to rock back and forth and hold her hands up in the air, so we could tell she was feeling the Holy Spirit. Bob and I kept our eyes on her baby. We began to discuss, as quietly as we could, whether the baby was going to fall off her lap.

As the mother continued to sway, her baby tilted more and more dangerously toward the edge of her lap. Finally, just as she rolled off her chair in rapture, the lady next to her grabbed her baby.

CHAPTER 14
- More Adventures -

The year 1923-24 was Snip's third as a senior in high school, and Mama was determined he would graduate. Every morning she'd make sure he went to school, and every evening she'd nag him to do his homework. Haskell, three years younger than Snip, was a junior. He had almost caught up with him.

My older brothers were spoiled. Mama was partial to the boys. It was because of the way she was raised. Back in her day, men were deferred to. She didn't make our older brothers responsible for us—she spent all her time being a mother—but she did give them permission to boss us around. In the summer, when it was hot, I would try to get as cool as possible. I can still hear Snip or Haskell yelling: "Mama, make Jim put on a slip."

Snip and Haskell both had tempers, but Snip would flare up and then be over it, while Haskell would sulk. Snip had a sentimental side, too, unlike Haskell, and he was superstitious. One night he rode in from the farm, all upset. He rushed into the kitchen where Mama was and told her that the "headless horseman" had followed him on the road. He was serious, too. Mama teased him about it, but she was just like him. It was her French blood.

Willie was totally different from Snip and Haskell. He wasn't ambitious like them. He never thought about going to college or of striking out on his own—except for the time he and Preston Burch set out to seek their fortunes, but that was long before my time. For as long as I can remember, Willie worked hard to make a living from his allotment and to help Mama and Papa pay the bills. He even operated a little hamburger stand in town to make extra money.

Willie always had time for us, too. I remember him taking Bob and me over to Wild Horse one day to see a sorghum mill. Mama had sent him out there to buy some molasses. She loved sorghum molasses. She'd put it on biscuits or pancakes. It was too strong for me.

Wild Horse was a Negro community south of Pauls Valley on Wild Horse Creek. It had originally been home to a group of freed slaves, and later it was a refuge for outlaws. Old Dr. Branum told us that once he was taken out to Wild Horse at gunpoint to treat a man who had been shot. It was a much tamer place when we went there with Willie.

The sorghum mill was fascinating. There was a mule hitched to a long pole walking in a circle, turning two heavy metal rollers which squeezed the long strips of sugar cane. A green, sugary liquid trickled out into a vat below, where it was boiled down to make molasses.

Willie had a girlfriend about that time. She was self-centered and vain, though, and she and Willie didn't go together very long. Willie quit asking her out after Snip told him he had seen her with another guy.

In 1923, Bob was in the third grade and I was in the fourth, still in class with the little kids because of my trouble with long division. Oteka had just started to school and was in the primer, leaving Tom the only child still at home with Mama. Kaliteyo matriculated to junior high that year. She thought she was so big.

Kaliteyo still treated me like a pest, even though Mama kept trying to cultivate a relationship between us. We had been sleeping together for about a year, but that certainly didn't endear us to one another. Kaliteyo was fanatical about me staying on my side of the bed. Even in the wintertime, when it was cold and I'd try and snuggle up to her, she'd tell me to stay away. I can still feel her elbow in my ribs.

One summer, our neighbors, the Jerden girls, had a niece who came to stay with them. She was Kaliteyo's age, so they invited her over for a visit. I wanted to go, too, so Mama made Kaliteyo take me. Mama cleaned us up, combed our hair, and altered some of her clothes for us to wear so we'd look nice. I was real excited and proud of the way we looked, and when the Jerden girls complimented us on our dresses, I blurted out that Mama had altered her own dresses for us to wear. Well, Kaliteyo was mortified. You would have thought I had told them Mama was a bank robber.

The Jerden girls, Tilia, Julia, and Jeanette, were three old-maid sisters who lived across the street from us. Their name was actually Jordan, but everyone pronounced it "Jerden." Julia and Jeanette worked down at the courthouse, and Tilia stayed home and kept house. There was a banker named Harry Gage who was smitten with Tilia. He would drive up in his car every Sunday afternoon and take her and her sisters driving. Tilia would sit in the front seat with Harry, while Julia and Jeanette sat in the back. Tilia and Harry courted for years, but they never got married. The Jerden girls were good neighbors to Mama. After we were all grown and living away from home, Tilia used to come over to check on Mama, and she would bring her food when she was sick.

Mama made Kaliteyo take me along with her another time when she went swimming with some of her friends. We were at a lake, and we were the only ones there. I got out in the water too far and had to call for help. Kaliteyo was embarrassed, but she saved me, and then made me suffer for it later. She told me she only saved me because she knew if she didn't Mama would get mad at her.

Kaliteyo and I both had trouble with prejudice from the other children at school. I remember her coming home one day crying because the teacher referred to Indians as savages. Mama told her not to feel bad about being an Indian. "The amount of Indian blood in you wouldn't be enough to fill my thimble," she said.

I didn't feel like I belonged to my class in school because I was older than they were, but I also felt isolated because of the color of my skin. I was a lot darker than any of my brothers and sisters, except Willie. He was dark like me. Anyway, one day we had a little party at school, and we were each assigned someone else in the class to give a gift to. My gift was a bottle of bleach. I didn't cry like Kaliteyo, though. It just made me mad. I decided then and there that I could get along just fine without friends from school.

Our family was pretty independent. We had our farm, and there were plenty of things for us to do at home. We all liked to read, and Mama had plenty of books. When I was in school, I never had to go to the library to prepare a report. I could always find what I needed at home. We had fun together, too. Mama would tell us stories. We loved to hear her tell about her childhood in Arkansas and about territory days. One of Teker's friends once said about us, "You all don't need anybody else, you entertain yourselves." And it was true.

90

Kaliteyo had a bad toothache that winter that bothered her for weeks. It had festered and caused her jaw to swell on one side. One day she was riding one of the horses across the yard, and a tree limb caught her right under her chin, knocking her off the horse. It caused the festered place to break open and pus to flow out of it. Mama took her down to see the dentist, Dr. Laird.

Dr. Laird's office was in a railroad car that had been pulled off on a side track behind the Royal Theater. He owned the car, and he and his family lived in it. He would work in one town for a while, and then move on to another. When Mama took Kaliteyo down to see him, I got to go along, too. He pulled Kaliteyo's tooth, and she had to go back to see him several times afterward. The railroad car was really fancy inside. There were thick velvet curtains over the windows, and the pull cords had tassels on them. Dr. Laird had a daughter named Mignon, who was an accomplished harpist. We heard her play. She was also a dancer. They say she later moved to New York City and danced professionally.[1]

Mama had cause to celebrate that spring. Snip finally graduated from high school. She said she felt like going out on the porch and shouting, "Hallelujah!" We all got dressed up and went down to the school to watch him walk across the stage. It was the only time I ever saw Willie dressed in a suit.

Now that Snip had satisfied Mama by graduating, he went out to find a job, and it wasn't easy. He was turned down several times, and then Walter Hart got him a job in Claremore, working for the Oklahoma Farm Mortgage Company.

Snip had always been close to the Harts, who lived across the alley from us when he was younger. There were two brothers, Dean, who was Snip's age, and Jack, who was mine. Their father, Walter Hart, got a job with the state when I was little, and the family moved away from Pauls Valley. Walter later became secretary for the School Land Commission, running the largest department in state government.[2]

After Haskell finished his junior year, he asked Papa if he would send him to college. Papa said, "Son, I can't help you. I just don't have the money." So Haskell went to work in the broomcorn. Cutting broomcorn was hard work, and dangerous, too. Broomcorn was cut by hand in those days, with long knives. Haskell would come in every night dog tired, but he kept it up, and put his money aside. By the end of the summer, he had almost enough to pay for college tuition. Papa was still dealing in real estate at that time, but he wasn't making much money. He'd still give it away, though. He was an easy mark for a farmer who couldn't make a payment on his mortgage. Mama used to fuss at him about it.

When Papa wasn't around, Mama complained about our poverty and about Papa's drinking. She shouldn't have done that, but she didn't have Dr. Spock to advise her. She berated Papa to his face, too, and I remember one time when she played a dirty trick on him.

Bob and I were in the kitchen with Mama one morning when Papa came downstairs to the bathroom to get cleaned up—the bathroom was right behind the kitchen. All of a sudden we heard him cussing and spitting. We looked over at Mama and she was giggling. Papa had hidden a bottle of whiskey behind the toilet, and when she found it, she emptied it out and filled it with soap suds.

That spring, after Snip's graduation, Papa took us swimming, this time at Wynnewood, where there was a big pool. We all rented suits. Papa got a suit, too, and he went in swimming with us. He floated on his back while we splashed around. I was terrified of the water after my experience in Rush Creek, so I stayed back in the shallow end of the pool with the little kids. It was Teker who rode on Papa's belly, this time. She was five years old and a little pistol. She disappeared for a while, and then out of nowhere she came hurtling through the air into the deep end of the pool. Everyone watched in horror, waiting to see whether she would come back up or not. Pretty soon, there she was, sputtering and paddling, just like she had been swimming all her life. That's the way Teker was—fearless.

Oteka got sick after our trip to Wynnewood. She must have swallowed too much water from the pool. First her stomach was upset, and then she got a fever. Dr. Callaway had retired by this time, and his son, John, had taken over his practice. Dr. John had been a military doctor, and his bedside manner wasn't up to his father's standards. What especially irritated Mama was that he would cover his face with a handkerchief when he examined the children. Dr. John knew his business, though. At first he said Teker just had the stomach flu, and she'd get right over it, but she didn't. She got worse. Her fever stayed up and she couldn't eat. Finally Dr. John made the diagnosis. Oteka had typhoid fever. He put the red quarantine sign on our door.

Mama banned everybody from Teker's room except herself, and she washed all of her dishes and clothes separately. Teker was sick for a long time. Mama fed her custard and gave her purgatives. She was afraid she was going to lose another child. She relied on prayer to pull Teker through. The Episcopal priest visited, and the congregation offered up prayers for her.

It was several weeks before Teker's fever came down, and the doctor said she had passed the crisis. Mama always said it was the prayers that saved Teker's life. She remained a loyal Episcopalian for the rest of her life, and so have I.

When Mama started letting us visit Teker, we saw how much weight she lost. She was skinny already, but now she looked like a little skeleton. She was pale; her cheeks were sunken in, and she had lost her hair! That's what upset her the most. We told her not to worry, that her hair would come back in, and when it did it would be brown and curly. She never liked her straight black hair.

Bob and I got stir crazy while we were quarantined. We didn't miss playing with the neighborhood kids so much. We had each other and a big yard, but we really missed going out to the farm. When Dr. John finally took the quarantine sign down off the door, the first thing Bob and I did was to beg Mama to let us go out to the farm. She said we could go, but as we left, she made us promise not to run the horses. We had fun at the farm, climbing the trees and riding the horses, and when the sun started going down, we decided to ride home instead of walking. Bob rode Maggie and I rode Mack. We went along the Rush Creek road and then along the ditch.

When we got to the road into town, Bob said, "Let's race." We kicked the horses in the flanks, and away we went. Maggie was faster, so Bob got out ahead, right away. I bounced along, hanging on for dear life, while Bob stuck to Maggie's back like a flea. As we were going through West Town, Mack, who wasn't as sure-footed as Maggie, tripped in a chughole. I flew over his head and landed right in front of him. Mack jumped over me, but one of his back hooves scraped me on the forehead and opened a big gash. I was fine, actually, except for all the blood streaming down my face. Bob was hysterical. He bent over me, crying "Jim, I didn't aim to do it. I didn't aim to do it," as if it was his fault. A black lady rushed out of her house to see about me. She wiped away the blood with a wet washcloth, and when she saw I could walk, she told me to go straight home.

Mama was furious. While she doctored my cut, she said, "I told you not to run the horses, and then what did you do? You ran them, anyway. That's what you get when you disobey!" I don't know what she did to Bob, but she had a special punishment for me. She had been having trouble getting Teker to take her medicine, so she made me stand at the foot of Teker's bed and take it for her. Teker got tickled, watching me cry as I choked down the awful-tasting stuff. Then she laughed and agreed to take the medicine herself.

We had one more adventure that fall before school started. Willie took Bob and me hunting with him. There was snow on the ground, and we didn't have any boots, so Mama wrapped our feet and legs in tow sacks to keep us warm. Willie shot twenty rabbits that day. When we got home, we helped him skin them, and Mama cleaned them and left them out on the back porch, where they froze. We ate rabbits all winter long.

CHAPTER 15
- Growing Up Poor -

For us the Depression started eight years early, in 1921, when we moved back home from Arkansas. Papa's real estate business was no longer profitable, and Willie's farm barely brought in enough money for him to make payments on his mortgage. Also, Papa's health was failing. He had arthritis, and the years of drinking had damaged his liver and caused him to have dropsy. His legs would swell, and sometimes he couldn't walk downtown to his office.

Thanks to Willie's farm, we always had something to eat, but there were no extras. We didn't celebrate birthdays. Santa Claus didn't come to our house, and neither did the tooth fairy. No one in our family got new clothes at Easter time, like the other kids in town. Mama did color some eggs and hide them in the yard on Easter morning, and we would get some fruit and sometimes a silver dollar in our stockings on Christmas, but that was about it.

Mama saved everything. She would save pieces of cloth and try to decorate our outfits to make them look different, and she would alter her old clothes for us to wear, like when Kaliteyo and I went over to meet the Jerden girls' niece.

Mama worked like a dog. She cooked on a big, wood-burning stove. It was about seven feet long, with a big stovepipe extending through the ceiling and the roof. The burners sat on the left, above a big compartment where the wood burned. On the right was an oven, and on the other side of that was a copper basin for heating water. The stove was nice in the wintertime, when we could all go in the kitchen to get warm, but it really made the kitchen hot in the summer.

Mama was a good cook. I remember her using an old cookbook her mother had brought from Georgia. She baked pastries—biscuits, cornbread, cobblers, pies, and little sweet rolls she would make by spreading sugar and cinnamon on dough, rolling it up, and slicing it. She carefully rotated the pans in the oven so that the pastries would bake evenly. We couldn't afford to buy light bread, so on days when we didn't come home from school for lunch, Mama would make us biscuit sandwiches. They tasted good, but I was embarrassed because we couldn't afford light bread sandwiches like the other kids ate.

Gas was installed in 1926, when I was thirteen. Bob and I were ecstatic because we didn't have to bring in kindling wood anymore, but Mama complained. She said the gas heat didn't cook as well as her old wood-burning stove.

Mama made everything from scratch. She had a big kettle in the backyard that she used to make hominy from corn and lye. We had hominy grits for breakfast, and we also ate it like popcorn. She made butter by skimming the cream off slightly fermented milk and then churning it until it was thick. Mama loved to drink the buttermilk that was left over, and she used it for pancakes and baking. She made her own cottage cheese by letting the skim milk clabber and then straining it through cheesecloth. She'd tie up the ends of the cheesecloth and hang it up on the clothesline to drain. The cottage cheese tasted really good with fruit.

Mama had a cellar dug out in the backyard behind the porch, and she used it to store the fruits and vegetables she canned and her homemade jelly. Willie grew vegetables, melons, and strawberries in his garden at the farm, and we had a big pear tree out by the garage that bore plenty of fruit.

We ate lots of chicken. Mama would wring their necks and scald them to loosen up their feathers. Mama was strong. She could catch a chicken and wring its neck in a minute. Also, Snip would go out and shoot quail, ducks, and doves and bring them home. On Christmas, Willie would buy us a goose. Mama wouldn't cook a turkey. She said the meat was too dry.

Bob and I had to do the dirty work. If there were potatoes to peel or chickens to pluck, we were recruited. What I hated most was plucking the chickens. There was something about scalding them that caused a terrible odor. It ruined chicken for me forever. I still hate the smell of chicken.

Plucking a goose is even harder than plucking a chicken, and scalding them doesn't help much. It just makes the feathers greasy. The other thing about a goose is the down. It's thick and hard to get hold of. Mama always had to help us because we couldn't get it all.

We didn't have much money, but we always had indoor plumbing. There was even a bathroom upstairs. The water in Pauls Valley was really hard, though. It left a residue on cooking pots, and you could hardly get the soap to lather. People used to call it "jit water." We used rainwater from the cistern to wash our hair.

Mama was our entertainment, especially in the wintertime. We would gather around her in the kitchen and she'd tell us stories while she cooked. Then after she finished in there, we'd follow her into the dining room or the bedroom, wherever she decided to go next. When it was cold, we would stay in the kitchen where it was warm, even after Mama finished cooking. One winter, Joe McClure, one of our cousins, stayed with us. He had some health problems that year and needed to be close to the doctor. Joe could dance a jig, and he used to do the jig for us while we gathered around the stove.

Mama was always teaching us. She told stories from her life and stories from history, and she quoted proverbs. She had one for every situation. Someone with poor judgment was "a fool for the want of sense." "Willful waste makes woeful want," taught the value of thrift. Advice to women: "A giggling girl and a cackling hen never can come to a good end," or "Pretty is as pretty does," or "If you don't act like a lady, people won't treat you like one." Mama illustrated patience with the saying, "A watched pot never boils." She described a quiet but wise person with, "Still waters run deep." Mama taught the importance of friendship with the saying, "A friend in need is a friend indeed," and family loyalty with, "A house divided against itself cannot stand," or "Blood is thicker than water." Some of Mama's sayings were just for fun, like her toast, "Up to my mouth and down to my toes, where many quarts and gallons go," or when we were eating she'd say, "I've noticed that every time you bend your elbow, your mouth opens."

Through all the hardships Mama endured, she never whined, and she wouldn't let us whine. She'd say, "I'll give you something to whine about." That's one of her phrases engraved in my memory. We weren't allowed to tattle, either. Me and Bob would tattle on each other, and then we'd both get a whipping. One thing I am grateful for: we always had plenty of space. We had a big house, and since we owned most of the block, we had plenty of room to run and play. We had trees to climb, the barn, the garage, the servants' quarters, and the cellar to explore, and if we got tired of each other, we could always find a quiet place to be alone. After I was married, I always felt claustrophobic living in small houses with small rooms. It wasn't until we had raised our son and could afford to buy a larger house that I was comfortable again.

We lived on the corner of Grant and Pine, and paved sidewalks ran along both sides of the house, even though neither street was paved. We could sit out on the porch in the shade of our big pecan tree and face either street. In the evenings we'd sit out there with Mama, listen to her stories, and greet people as they walked by.

Our porch had a railing that connected the big pillars supporting the roof, and one of the boards on the railing was brown and smooth where Bob Dog liked to scratch himself. He was called Bob Dog to distinguish him from my brother Bob. Willie originally bought two bull terriers, Bob and Queen, but Queen was mean, and one day while Willie was standing out in the yard talking to a friend, Queen charged the man. Bob Dog got there first, though. He ran into Queen and knocked her to one side, saving the man from being bitten. Willie got rid of Queen after that, but he kept Bob Dog.

Bob Dog had to put up with a lot from Oteka and Tom. They rode him, dressed him up, tied tin cans to his tail, and made him pull their wagon, but he loved them, just the same. I was in charge of Bob Dog's baths. I could usually catch him if he didn't know what I was up to, but if he heard Mama say, "Bob Dog needs a bath," he would run off and be gone for two or three days. When Bob Dog disappeared, he went to West Town. He had a girlfriend over there.

The only thing that scared Bob Dog was thunder and lightning. One evening, we went to a movie and left him in the dining room with the doors closed. Our dining room had big oak doors separating it from the living room and heavy green velvet curtains that hung in front of them. The curtains had a red leather border decorated by a fleur-de-lis pattern. They were beautiful.

While we were gone, there was a thunderstorm. Usually during a storm, Bob Dog would hide under Mama's bed, but this time he couldn't get in there since the doors were closed. When we got back, he had torn those big green curtains to shreds.

Paul house, 1917

We all loved Bob Dog. He was with us through all our crises. He even seemed to have a sixth sense about where we were. When I was living in Oklahoma City, and would ride the bus home for a visit, he used to meet me two blocks from home. Teker said he met her, too.

One day, long after we children left home, Bob Dog came home to Mama covered with blood. Someone had stabbed him. He was seventeen years old when he died.

Our house was spacious, with large rooms, ten-foot ceilings, and big windows that let in plenty of light. Wallpaper with bright designs covered the walls, and the baseboards were made of heavy oak. A portrait of my grandfather, Sam Paul, hung by the front door, and a large charcoal drawing of a lion—Mama's masterpiece—was displayed above the fireplace. Lace curtains covered the windows, and a genuine Tiffany lamp sat on a writing table. There was a large pendulum clock sitting on one of the bookcases. It had been given to Mama and Papa for a wedding present in 1898. The water buffalo horns from our family's vacation to Galveston in 1913 were mounted above the door into the hall.

Two big bookcases covered one wall of our living room, full of books we read for pleasure and used for reference. There was a set of encyclopedias and a big unabridged dictionary. Mama never told us the meaning of a word. She always made us look it up. We had a set of books about European history—Mama especially loved French history—several volumes of English literature, and a series of children's books called *The Children's Hour,* which I especially loved. There were individual classics by Dickens, Hawthorne, Longfellow, Shakespeare, Edgar Allen Poe, Edgar Rice Burroughs, James Fennimore Cooper, and many others. Mama bought books everywhere she went. Once she even found an old copy of the Dawes Commission Rolls.

Mama's old rocking chair sat in the corner, and in the center of the room was a magnificent set of furniture that matched Mama's charcoal lion—a couch, and two chairs with wooden backs topped by lions' heads and legs carved into the shape of lions' paws.

The dining room adjoined the living room, and the big, rolling doors between them were usually open, making the two rooms one. Our dining room table was six feet across, plenty of room for all of us. Mama usually put a lace tablecloth on it, with a vase of flowers sitting in the middle. When he was grown and should have known better, my little brother Tom used to run through the house with Mama's dog, Spot, chasing after him. Spot would try to jump over the table to keep up with Tom and land on the tablecloth, sending the vase and flowers flying. Then Mama would chase them both out of the room with her broom. Tom never grew up.

There were two china cabinets in the dining room, displaying, in addition to china, Mama's collection of milk glass bowls, figurines, and knickknacks. And about head high was a plate rack displaying ornamental plates from Mama's and Papa's travels. Mama stored her table linens in a large sideboard, and on top of it sat her punch bowl, where Grandpa used to toss his hat.

Several of Mama's paintings graced the dining room walls. There were two still lifes. One was a teapot, a cup, and a lemon. The teapot looked as though it had just been washed and polished. The other was a glass and sugar bowl sitting next to two lemons and a lemon squeezer, simple but elegant. Mama's largest painting hung high above the sideboard. It showed a vast plain covered with snow, and in the center was an Indian brave standing outside his teepee, wrapped in a blanket. You could almost feel the chill. She worked on that painting for years trying to get everything just right.

We had some good times in that dining room. I especially remember Christmastime. We didn't have presents, but we ate well: goose, stuffing, sweet potatoes, okra, biscuits, and especially ambrosia. We loved it. Mama would buy a coconut and cut a hole in the end to drain out the milk and give us each a taste. Then she'd shred the coconut meat and mix it with fruit to make the ambrosia. My little brother Tom worked in the Philippines after World War II and drank so much coconut milk he made himself sick.

Mama's parlor had big, rolling doors like those into the living room, and its own entrance from the porch so it could be closed off for entertaining. She had a table and chairs in there for guests and an easy chair for reading or sewing. More of her artwork hung on the walls—a portrait she had painted of Snip and a charcoal drawing of a cherub next to a vase filled with brushes. Mama also cut pictures out of magazines and pinned them to the walls.

A hall led past the living room to the back porch. Mama's bedroom was on the left and the stairway up to our bedrooms was on the right. In the summers, it was especially hard to sleep at night because of the heat, so we'd all stay downstairs where it was cooler. Mama would open the front and back doors so a breeze could blow through the house. The coolest place to sleep was in the doorway between the living room and the hall. That was my spot.

There was an old crank telephone in the hall. Back then, all calls went through an operator, and "party lines" served several homes at a time. Each phone had its own special ring, but if you were nosey, you could listen in on other people's conversations. This made people careful about what they said on the phone. It was handy, though, because you could leave messages with the operator when you couldn't get someone on the phone right away.

In the hall under the stairs was a large closet. Mama stored a variety of things in there: linens, coats, shoes, and tools. There was also a barrel filled with fruit. The hall closet was also a good hiding place if you were in trouble.

There were no closets in the bedrooms. We kept our clothes in dressers or hung them on our bedroom doors. Mama had an armoire in her bedroom for her nice things.

At the top of the stairs hung a big picture of prancing horses, one of France's national pictures. It was rolled up and ruined when we moved to San Antonio like the portrait of Aunt Sippie. We had six bedrooms upstairs. Kaliteyo and I slept in the one at the head of the stairs. Willie's room was to the left, over the parlor. There were two rooms on either side of the stairs where Bob and Papa slept, and later Teker and Tom, and in the back of the house over the porch were Haskell's and Snip's rooms. Snip's room was over the kitchen, and Bob and I used it to climb out on the roof. Haskell's room was over Mama's bedroom, and one of his windows opened out over the sidewalk that encircled the house.

That was where I performed an experiment with a cat. In our family, we generally didn't like cats. I guess we got that from Mama. She didn't like them because they scared the birds away. Anyway, that's my excuse for mistreating the cat. Someone had told me that cats always land on their feet, so one day I decided to test out the theory. I caught a stray cat in our yard, took it up to Haskell's window, and tossed it out. Sure enough, it landed on its feet. Just to be sure, I caught it and tossed it out again, this time giving it an extra little push. It landed on its feet the second time, too. I couldn't catch it after that.

I was Mama's errand girl. Pauls Valley was a small town, so I went just about everywhere. Our house was only three blocks from downtown. Grant Street, which bordered our house on the east, was the main road coming into town from Whitebead, where Aunt Sippie lived. It was a dirt road back then—well, all the streets were, except for the ones downtown, which had been bricked over to control the mud and the dust.

Pauls Valley had boardwalks originally so people could walk without stepping in the mud. When I was little, the boardwalks were being replaced by concrete sidewalks. The old boardwalks that remained were run down, and you had to be careful where you stepped on them. Bob and I learned where all the loose boards were. There was one in front of Mr. Rennie's law office.

The bricks and the sidewalks didn't help during our annual floods, when the water would get so deep downtown that "reckless fools," as Mama called them, would row boats down Main Street, which was later renamed Paul Avenue. Our house was on higher ground than the downtown area, and the water never made it up to the top of our front steps, but during floods ,Mama would send Willie out every few hours to measure the depth of the water. The ditch diverted some water away from town, but years later they were still paddling boats down Paul Avenue. Once, after a flood, Haskell claimed he pulled a catfish out of one of his desk drawers.

I didn't pay much attention to the names of the streets when I was running my errands—they weren't even marked back then, except for the ones downtown—but those running north and south read like a history of the area. Grant Street was named after Calvin Grant, a partner in the first general merchandise store in Pauls Valley and co-founder of the first bank. The next street over was Paul Avenue, named for our family, with its many famous and infamous members. After that was McClure Street, named for our great-uncle Tecumseh McClure, who had once served as Chickasaw governor. Then there was Garvin Street, named after Sam Garvin, the enterprising freighter who married a Choctaw woman and became the wealthiest man in the county. Garvin County was also named after him. There was also a street named for William Guy, governor of the Chickasaw Nation during the turbulent times of our grandfather, Sam Paul; Arbuckle Street, named for the fort that protected the valley against marauding plains Indian tribes before the Civil War; and Rennie Avenue, named for Albert Rennie, the attorney who brought his family all the way from Canada to seek his fortune in Indian Territory.[1]

The main street running east and west was Chickasaw Street, named in recognition of the original owners of the valley. It crossed Paul Avenue downtown, and ran parallel to the railroad tracks. The other cross streets were named for trees: Pine, Pecan, Ash, Willow, Walnut, Cedar, Oak, and Elm. That was appropriate, since most of our streets were covered like an arbor by one kind of tree or another.

Most of my errands were for groceries and medicine. Shumate's Grocery was downtown on Chickasaw Street. Back then they didn't have grocery carts. You just told the grocer what you wanted and he filled your order. I'd give Mama's list to Mr. Shumate, and he'd send me home with a sack of groceries.

Crabtree's Drugstore was where I went to pick up medicine. It was also on Chickasaw. Mr. Tethers was the pharmacist there. All I had to say was that Mama wanted some stomach medicine, and he knew just what to give me. Stomachache was our most frequent complaint. Mama's stomach medicine was clear with a white sediment that settled to the bottom of the bottle. She shook it up before she gave it to us. The medicine was peppermint-flavored. It tasted good, and it relieved a stomachache right away, too. Crabtree's had a soda fountain, so it was a popular hangout for teenagers, and we got our schoolbooks there.

Bragg's Meat Market was one of my favorite places. I loved the smells of the sausage links, and the cuts of beef, lamb, pork, and catfish. Mama usually sent me there for a soup bone and some cheese. She would fix soup for us, and crackers with cheese melted on top. Sometimes Mama would let me buy a pickle out of the big vat of vinegar sitting next to the counter. I would eat it on the way home. Mr. Bragg's daughter married Papa's nephew Ikard, so the Braggs were practically kinfolk.

The icehouse and the produce house were down by the railroad tracks. Ice was delivered, but Willie would sometimes bring a watermelon in from the farm and take it down to the icehouse to cool before bringing it home. The icehouse also stored meat—you could rent a locker—and milk or cream.

The produce house was next to the icehouse, and Mama would send me down there to buy flour and corn meal. They also had other grains, as well as peanuts, pecans, sorghum molasses, fruits, and vegetables. Mr. Pyle owned the produce house. Bob and I used to gather pecans out of the yard and sell them to him for a nickel a sack. That was enough to pay for a ticket to a movie.

The Royal Theater was on Paul Avenue, about a block from the railroad tracks. Kaliteyo preferred romantic movies starring Lillian Gish, Mary Pickford, or Rudolph Valentino, but Bob and I liked cowboy movies with Tom Mix or Al Jennings. Tom Mix had worked as a cowboy in Oklahoma before his movie career. He won the National Rodeo Championship in 1909. Al Jennings had been the leader of an outlaw gang—really—and served time in jail for bank robbery. After writing a successful book about his adventures and starring in a movie about his exploits, he actually ran for governor of Oklahoma—a good background for a politician, don't you think? We also enjoyed comedies with Buster Keaton or Charlie Chaplin.

Movies were silent until after 1927. The only dialogue was printed on "intertitles" shown between scenes, and the plot was illustrated mainly by the actors' exaggerated movements and melodramatic facial expressions. Action scenes were speeded up to make them more exciting, and there was always an organist at the front of the theater playing music to match the mood of the scene.

One time there was a movie playing that I especially wanted to see. The pecans hadn't fallen yet, so I had nothing to exchange at the produce house. I took some of Mama's cream down to the icehouse and sold it to get the money to buy a ticket. Mama must have known, but she never said anything.

There were also live performances at the Royal Theater. We had plays and musical performances. Vaudeville didn't make it to Pauls Valley, but we did have variety shows called Chautauquas. They were sponsored by the Chautauqua movement, which was started by philanthropists in order to spread culture, religion, and education to rural communities. Teams went all over the country. They would come to town and stay for a week or so, presenting plays, musical performances, lectures, and religious services. Some noted intellectuals of the time, including William Jennings Bryan, traveled on the Chautauqua circuit. I didn't go to any lectures, but I do remember the plays. The girls all fell in love with the leading men.

Across Paul Avenue from the Royal Theater was the Alvis Hotel, owned by Alma Alvis, a good friend of Mama's. Mrs. Alvis' daughter Imy was Tom's age, and they were friends all through school. Probably the most imposing building on Paul Avenue was the First National Bank. Classic Roman columns flanked its doors, quite a leap from the bank's origin as a small office in the back of Calvin Grant's dry goods store. Dr. Callaway's office was up a stairway in the back of the bank, so we went there a lot. St. Mary's Episcopal Church was also on Paul Avenue, as was the Masonic Lodge, which Papa had built during better times.

Papa was a 32nd-degree Mason. He said that the only way you could go higher than that was to travel to England. He was in charge of teaching the Masonic ritual to the younger members, but he had trouble with his eyes—"granulated eyelids," they called it—and when his eyes were bad, Mama would read the rituals to him to refresh his memory. Papa had to go into Oklahoma City to have his eyes treated. Kaliteyo described the procedure to me in great detail. She said the eye doctor would pull Papa's eyeballs out on his cheek and then scrape them to get the granules off. I believed that story for a long time.

Papa also built the First Baptist Church and a two-story building on McClure that had his name, "W. H. Paul," embossed on the cornice across its top. It housed a J. C. Penney store for a long time.

Mama had my hair cut in a Buster Brown style, and she sent me to the barbershop, just like the boys. My favorite barber was Big Frank. He used to tell me my hair was so tough he had to resharpen his scissors every time he cut it.

Downtown, next to Shumate's grocery, was an electrical shop that sold lighting fixtures and the latest advance in technology of the time, the radio. Not many people owned radios, but the electrical shop always had one playing near its entrance, and there were usually a few people standing around the door listening. I always made a detour by there myself when I went downtown. During the Jack Dempsey-Gene Tunney fight in 1926, practically the whole male population of Pauls Valley was clustered around the electrical shop's radio.

One of the main stores downtown was Wacker's, one of the nation's first five- and ten-cent stores. The idea was so successful that Wacker's became a national chain. The store's founder, G. F. Wacker, continued to live in Pauls Valley and was one of the town's most enthusiastic supporters, serving both as mayor and as president of the Chamber of Commerce.

Walnut Street was a couple of blocks north of our house. A block east on Walnut, in front of the water tower, was the fire station. Ivy Baldwin was our fire chief, and he also had a bicycle shop. He'd fix bicycles for the boys and carve dolls for the girls. We all loved him. He also made a large model locomotive that he used to ride in parades.

One day Mama sent Bob downtown on some kind of errand. It was winter, and he was running with his head down and his hands in his pockets to keep warm. He ran right into the side of the fire station and knocked himself out. Mr. Baldwin picked Bob up and took him inside until he was warm and alert. Then he brought him home to Mama.

City hall was in the same building as the fire station, and there was a room in the back that housed a small library. I'd go down there every Saturday to see if they had any new books. I read the adventures of the Bobbsey Twins, and my brothers read the Hardy Boys mysteries, and the adventures of Tom Swift. I remember how excited I was when the library got a copy of *The Wonderful Wizard of Oz.*

Mama instilled a love for reading in all of us. Willie ruined his eyes reading in poor light. He used to read Zane Grey novels about the Wild West, and he subscribed to the magazine *Grit and Steel,* which had stories in it, but was mainly devoted to game fowl, Willie's passion. Snip and Haskell appreciated great literature and especially poetry, like Mama. Kaliteyo read a lot, too. She used to tease Mama about creating a jungle of plants in her yard, calling her the *Girl of the Limberlost,* after a book by that name about a young girl who lived with her mother in an isolated cabin in the woods.

Walnut Street extended east across Rush Creek, and passed by the Old Cemetery where my oldest brother, Little Samuel, was buried. Mount Olivet, the newer cemetery, where my oldest sister, Victoria, was buried, was further out from town, on the road to Wynnewood. Mama often visited both cemeteries to tend their graves. She planted flowers around them and cut the grass. She pulled up the fence around the front part of our yard and put it out at the Old Cemetery to protect the family plot there. Mama used to point out to us a mound of earth on Roy Burks' place, across from the Old Cemetery, where many of the Caddo that had died in the smallpox epidemic of the 1860s were buried.

The courthouse was on Willow, just a block north of Walnut Street. There were big trees on the courthouse lawn, and men would stand out there in the shade in the afternoons and talk. During political campaigns, a platform was set up there for the candidates to give their speeches. Mama's lawyer, Alvin Pyeatt, had his office on Willow. She used to go see him every year or two to ask him to get her a divorce from Papa, and he would always talk her out of it.

Our grade school, Lee School, was nine blocks from home. We walked there and back twice each day, since Mama had us come home for supper at noontime. Most of the children took sack lunches, but Mama believed you should eat your main meal in the middle of the day, so we came home. Sometimes it was pretty hard to get back to school in time for class. In the evening I liked to dawdle, especially in the springtime. I loved the smell of the catalpa trees that lined the fence around the Grant home. Sometimes I'd take one of the blossoms home to Mama.

Some of the most exciting events in our lives were the parades. The circus parade was my favorite. They unloaded their wagons from the train and then drove them through town, the performers marching alongside. There were wagons with lions and tigers inside, women in beautiful costumes riding horses and elephants, jugglers, clowns, and acrobats, all parading to the music of the calliope and the circus band. The parade would progress down Paul Avenue to Walnut, where they would turn and continue down to the park. There the circus crews would begin setting up their tents. Bob always went down to where they were working and tried to get a job, but they never hired him. They must have been used to little boys trying to join the circus.

We also had a parade on Armistice Day, which commemorated the end of World War I, with bands and soldiers marching and dignitaries making speeches.

The biggest parade of all, though, was at the start of the Garvin County Fair. Everett Baker always led off, riding atop his Conestoga wagon—anyways, a wagon he'd fixed up to look like one—pulled by a team of six horses. Mr. Baker was one of the old settlers, and he and his wife were my godparents. Ivy Baldwin would drive his model locomotive. There would be marching bands and floats and cars with representatives of different civic groups like the Masons, the Lions Club, the Elks Club, the Eastern Star, and the Rebekah Lodge. There would also be some lucky people riding horses. I wanted so much to ride a horse in the county fair parade!

It was in the fall of 1925 that I got my chance. I had an entry in the fair that year, a picture of a flower that I had turned in for a school art project. I hadn't wanted to do it myself, so Kaliteyo drew it for me, and Mama painted it. It was so good that my teacher decided to enter it. I didn't really care about the flower, though. I just wanted to ride in the parade.

Mama knew how much I wanted to be in the parade, so she talked to Hazel Hart, who was in charge of the celebrations, and got me on the list of riders. I was so excited. Mama bought me some riding pants, and Willie managed to buy riding boots cheap from a neighbor of ours who had outgrown them. On the day of the parade, I shined up my boots and put on a nice shirt and a cowboy hat. Willie helped me saddle up Maggie, and I got in line with the other riders.

As we started down Main Street, I was riding just in front of Jack Grimmett, a boy in Bob's class in school. All of a sudden, Jack's horse decided he didn't like the look of Maggie's rump, so he bit her. Maggie jumped and then took off running at full speed. She had a wild streak, and she didn't let anything get in her way. She ran past the other riders, and she ran past Ivy Baldwin's locomotive and Mr. Baker's Conestoga wagon and just kept on going. I pulled on the reins as hard as I could, but it had no effect. All I could do was just hang on. As I went flying past the crowd, I heard Mrs. Sprague, the wife of our optometrist, yell, "Ride 'er, Jim!" Maggie didn't slow down 'til she got to Rush Creek.

So my big moment was over pretty quick, and I was so embarrassed I could hardly hold my head up afterwards. There was only one consolation. My flower won a blue ribbon.

CHAPTER 16
- *Branching Out* -

I guess I was in the fifth grade when I gave up on kissing my elbow. That was when I started spending more time with girls, and my brother Bob started hanging around with other boys.

It was about that time that I started spending more time with Kathleen Williams. Kathleen's grandfather, Grant Kimberlin, was an old-timer who had come to Indian Territory in the late 1800s, married a Chickasaw girl, and then became a wealthy farmer like Smith Paul. His wife, Puss, had been Aunt Sippie's best friend, so our families had been close for years.

Kathleen lived on a farm near Whitebead, and sometimes Mama would let me go out and stay with her. Her mother, Susie, was a really good cook. They had a peach orchard, and Susie made her ice cream with peaches. Also, Kathleen's father, Harve Williams, raised bees, and Susie used honey a lot in her cooking. Kathleen and I liked to chew on the honeycombs after the honey had been drained out of them. I got interested in music about that time, too, and Kathleen could play the piano. She played for me while I sang. We couldn't afford a piano ourselves, but Mama bought me a little ukulele while we were living in San Antonio, and I learned a few chords on it, so I could accompany myself.

Kathleen would also come into Pauls Valley and stay with me at our house. We talked and sang and went to the show together. I tried hard to talk Susie into letting Kathleen come to Pauls Valley to school, but she wouldn't agree to it. We still got together, though, when we could. Kathleen and I remained friends for the rest of our lives.

Snip did well in his new job, selling insurance policies to farmers, and he also fell in love again, this time with a pretty girl who worked in a beauty shop downtown. He was serious, too, just like he had been in Arkansas. He even tried to talk Mama out of a diamond ring that Papa had given her, so he could give it to the girl. Everyone told Snip that the girl was shallow. Papa couldn't stand her. He called her "that damned killdee," because her high-pitched voice reminded him of the chirping of a killdeer bird. They finally broke up, to everyone's relief.

Mama lightened up after she got Snip out of high school, and she really tried to enjoy her two youngest children, Oteka and Tom. She knew they would be her last. She helped them with their homework. She let them get involved in activities. Mama used to set up her quilting frame in Willie's room overlooking the front yard so she could watch them play while she worked on a quilt. Often Kaliteyo would sit with her and help her thread needles.

Kaliteyo used to entertain us with stories about Teker and Tom. One of their games was to act out movies that they had seen. Tom would play the part of the hero, and Teker would be the heroine. When they got to the part in the movie where they were supposed to kiss, they would hug and kiss a tree instead of each other.

During the summer of 1925, I got a chance to make some money. Mrs. Stewart was supplying cream to a boarding house on the other side of the railroad tracks, and she paid me fifty cents a week to deliver it for her. The boarding house was in the old McClure Hotel, which had been built by Papa's uncle Tecumseh in the old days. Every morning I would go over to Mrs. Stewart's house, pick up her cream, and carry it downtown.

That summer Bob also cooked up a scheme to make money. The Baptist preacher's daughter was in Bob's class in school, and he used to go over to her house to play. One day he asked the preacher if he would pay him to sweep out the church after the services were over. The preacher told Bob that he would hire him, but that he would have to join the church. Bob said that was just fine with him.

Things went along well until one afternoon, two or three Baptists knocked on our front door. When Mama answered, they asked her if "Brother Robert" was ready for his baptism. Mama indignantly informed them that "Brother Robert" had already been baptized once, and there was no need for him to be baptized again. As soon as Mama's unexpected visitors left, she hunted Bob down and gave him a lecture on baptism. Unfortunately, he had to give up on his new job.

Actually, we weren't going to any church then, because the Episcopal bishop of Oklahoma, Thomas Casady, had decided to sell St. Mary's, our little church. I always resented him doing that. I suppose he figured it wasn't worth the cost of sending a priest out to such a small parish, but the church had meant a lot to Mama through the years. Our congregation may have been small, but we were loyal. There was an Episcopal church down in Sulphur, but we didn't have a car to get there, so we stopped going to church, for the most part. Every once in a while, the Stewarts would invite us to ride down there with them, but Mama didn't like to accept favors she couldn't pay back. We did occasionally go with them, though.

We had another change in our lives in 1925. Aunt Sippie moved to California. She had a son, William, out there who had tuberculosis. There was no treatment then for tuberculosis, and William had become an invalid, so Aunt Sippie went out there to take care of him. Eventually all of her children followed her to California, except for Tamsey, who was married and had a family of her own in Pauls Valley. Mama and Papa helped Aunt Sippie move.

There was a widow lady, Mrs. McCrimmon, who lived down the street from us. Her brother, Mr. Doolin, owned a ranch near Byars, and now and then he would come down to visit his sister. He and Papa were old friends from Papa's ranching days, so he'd come by to visit while he was in town. My brother Bob was always full of questions when Mr. Doolin came by, asking about cattle, about horses, and about ranching in general. Mr. Doolin took a liking to Bob, and in the fall, he told him he had a little bull calf that had just been weaned. He asked if Bob would like to raise him. "Of course," Bob said, and he could hardly wait to see his new calf. Sure enough, about a week later, Mr. Doolin showed up with a little Black Angus calf. Bob was tickled to death.

Bob and I took care of that little bull all winter long. We played with him like he was a dog. We'd chase him and he would chase us. He was really tame, and when he got a little bit bigger he would let us ride him. After a while Bob got tired of feeding him, though, so I ended up taking care of him most of the time.

In the spring of 1925, Haskell graduated from high school. He was president of his class like Snip, but unlike Snip, he had made good grades and was eager to go on to the University of Oklahoma to study law. Mama was corresponding with some of the Pauls back in North Carolina at the time, and they wrote to her inviting Haskell to come out there to school so he could get a "decent education." I remember Mama being offended at the idea that Haskell couldn't get a good education in Oklahoma.

Haskell may have gotten an education at OU, but it certainly wasn't easy. Slaving away in the broomcorn during the summers was only the start of it. He made enough money to pay for his books and tuition that way, but it wasn't enough for room and board, so he got a job waiting tables in downtown Norman, about a mile away from the campus. His schedule was tight. He had a class from ten until eleven in the morning, and he had to be at work at eleven, so he would sit next to the door so he could be the first one out when the class was over. Then he'd run downtown. Haskell was hardy to begin with, but after running that mile to work every day for a semester, he was really in good shape.

One day when Haskell was sitting in the student union, he heard a boy on the track team boasting about his accomplishments. Haskell could never stand pretense, and he never lacked self-confidence, either, so he went over and challenged the boy to a race. I can just hear him. "Well, you think you're so fast, let's just see how fast you are." The track star accepted the challenge, of course, expecting to teach Haskell a lesson for his arrogance, and the two made arrangements for the contest. Haskell suggested they start at the campus and run to town, just the course he was used to.

On the day of the race, Haskell met the track star at the administration building. Word of the race had spread, and a little crowd gathered, both on campus and in town at the finish line. Haskell's customers at the restaurant were all eager to see how their waiter would fare. When the track man saw Haskell dressed in street clothes—the only ones he had—and regular shoes, he offered him a chance to back out. There was obviously no way he could compete with a trained athlete, especially without proper shoes, but Haskell said he had agreed to race, and he was determined to go through with it, so off they went.

The track man ran easily for the first block or two, but when Haskell didn't slow down, he began to realize that he might have a race on his hands. After half a mile, they were still neck-and-neck, but after eight or ten blocks, Haskell started to pull away. Haskell won the race, and it was the track star who learned a lesson—a lesson in humility.

Haskell hadn't been at the university long when he realized that members of fraternities and sororities considered themselves better than other students. Some of his high school classmates who had joined fraternities and sororities wouldn't even speak to him when they passed him on the sidewalk. Haskell never forgot those slights, and many of those men and women lived to regret snubbing Haskell Paul.

Haskell was always proud, and it embarrassed him that he couldn't afford to buy decent clothes. His shoes had holes in them and so did his pants. He wore an overcoat for two years to cover the holes in his pants, no matter what the weather. After that he never wore an overcoat again.

By the time Haskell finished his first semester at OU, he was really homesick, but he couldn't afford a train ticket to go home for a visit, so in desperation, he decided to hop a freight train. Back then, the train companies hired guards to go from car to car looking for hobos. Those they found were thrown off the train as it went full speed down the track. Haskell hid behind a bale of hay in the corner of one of the freight cars, trembling with fear, while the guards went from one car to another, banging on the doors, and then shining their lights inside. Luckily they didn't see Haskell, and he made it home all right, but he didn't try that again.

Haskell made good grades that first year at OU, and he returned home in the spring to spend another summer working in the broomcorn.

In the meantime, Snip had done so well with the Oklahoma Farm Mortgage Company that he bought himself a car, a sleek brown Packard. He also got himself a new girlfriend, Helen Lafferty, a secretary at the mortgage company. Helen was even prettier than the beauty operator in Pauls Valley. Mama used to tease Snip by saying that he had found Helen on a pinup calendar. Helen was different from the other girls he had dated, though. She was the daughter of a minister. She was smart and responsible. She had substance, and we all liked her.

Willie had done better during the year with his farm and his hamburger stand, too, so he also bought a car, an old Model T Ford. He needed it to drive himself back and forth to the farm and to haul supplies and produce. Snip sold him an insurance policy on it.

Now, I don't want to give the wrong impression of Snip. He may not have been as down-to-earth as Willie, but his heart was in the right place. He not only bought a car with his earnings that year, he also had gas installed in our house. Like I mentioned before, Mama missed her old wood-burning stove, but we had a hot water heater, there was a new furnace in the dining room that heated both the living and dining rooms, and Bob and I didn't have to gather kindling any longer.

That spring when Willie sold Bob's calf, he gave me half the money, because I was the one who really took care of it. Snip complained. He said that Willie should spend the money on the house, but Willie said that the calf belonged to Bob and me, and that we should have the money. I didn't spend my money on shows or even clothes. I gave it to Mama to keep for me. I wanted to save it for something special.

And sure enough, during the summer of 1926 there was a woman staying with Mrs. Stewart who had danced in the Ziegfeld Follies. She advertised that she was giving dancing lessons, and I asked Mama if I could use my money to take lessons from her. Mama said yes, so I spent the summer dancing.

The big event of the summer, though, came from Snip, naturally, and it took everybody by surprise, especially Mama and Papa. He decided to run for the state legislature! How he got the idea, I'll never know, but Snip never lacked self-confidence, and in those days, when jobs were scarce and there were no laws limiting political patronage, elected officials had tremendous power and influence. I think that Snip saw holding political office as a way to get ahead.

When Mama's friends found out about Snip's candidacy, they came to her and asked if he was old enough. "Why, he just got out of high school," they said. Mama had to reassure them that he really was twenty-one. Snip faced serious obstacles in his campaign. Not only was he young and inexperienced, he didn't have much money. His job selling insurance paid well, but not enough to pay for a serious political campaign. Not only that, he was running against a wealthy opponent, Jimmy Thompson. Thompson was a successful Pauls Valley businessman, and he wanted to win.

Using slanderous rumors in a political campaign is not a new tactic, and Snip felt the effects of it early on in his career. One of Mama's old friends, Becky Bell, sold Avon products, and she heard all the local gossip. One day she reported to Mama that Jimmy Thompson was calling Snip a cattle rustler. Mama laughed at that. She said that if Snip was stealing cattle, she didn't know where he was putting them.

Snip's campaign consisted mainly of traveling around the county, talking to anyone who would listen, and giving speeches at every opportunity. He was down at the courthouse every day, talking to the crowd that gathered there. He spoke to the Masons, the Kiwanis Club, and the city council, and he went door-to-door. Then there was Papa. Everyone knew Papa, and he worked hard to get Snip elected.

One day, early in his campaign, Snip casually mentioned to Mama that he was going to Whitebead that afternoon to give a speech. Mama pricked up her ears when she heard that. She knew that Snip didn't have much experience in public speaking, and she was worried that he had bitten off more than he could chew in running for office, anyway. She hadn't seen him working on his speech; he had just been lounging around all day. So that afternoon after supper, she asked him, "Don't you think you should make some notes for your speech?" No response. Then she started giving him advice. She told him to talk to the crowd like he was talking to an individual, to be natural, and to tell stories. "Wouldn't you like to practice your speech on me?" she asked. No response. Finally, frustrated with him, Mama told Snip that he had better give a good accounting of himself in Whitebead, because those old settlers were her friends, and she didn't want to be embarrassed. When the time came to go, off Snip went, leaving Mama to stew.

Snip didn't say much after he got home, and Mama was afraid to ask. She prepared for the worst. Several days later, Mama ran into one of her old friends from Whitebead. The lady just raved about the speech. "Oh, Homer was marvelous. He talked to the crowd like he was talking to each person individually. He was relaxed, and he told stories. He talked about the old settlers and the history of the community. He even quoted poetry." It turned out that Snip had a natural gift for oratory.

When the votes were counted, Snip came off the winner. It surprised everyone but him. In the end, I think it was Papa's influence that really tipped the balance. When Snip went to the state capitol the next January, he would be the youngest man ever elected to the Oklahoma State Legislature.

CHAPTER 17
- *Bloomfield* -

During the summer of 1926, while Snip was campaigning for the state legislature, Mama and Papa got a visit from a lady representing the Indian Field Service, a Mrs. Reeder. Mrs. Reeder had come to talk to them about sending one of us to the Bloomfield Academy, a Chickasaw boarding school for girls in Ardmore.[1]

Mrs. Reeder made a good impression on Mama and Papa. She told them that Bloomfield had high academic standards, and that in addition to academic subjects, they taught manners, etiquette, and "industrial arts," which included laundering, sewing, gardening, dairying, and housekeeping. Mrs. Reeder also emphasized that the school gave young Indian girls an opportunity to be with others who shared a common heritage. She and her husband were both Chickasaw, and they had two daughters who attended the school, Julia and Sophia.

After Mama and Papa talked with Mrs. Reeder for a while, they asked me to come into the room. They introduced me to Mrs. Reeder, and she asked me if I would be interested in going to a school for Indian girls. I was excited right away. I was tired of feeling different in a predominantly white school. The idea sounded almost too good to be true. In fact, I got so excited that Mama had to calm me down. I remember her telling me, "Jim, Indians are just like everybody else. They're just people." Papa was tickled at the way I reacted, but he didn't seem as impressed with the idea as Mama. I guess he remembered his own experiences attending Indian boarding schools, and they weren't all good. Mama and Papa didn't push me either way, though. They let me make my own decision. I told them I wanted to go.

There was another thing in the back of my mind when I decided to go to school at Bloomfield and that was the fact that it was located in Ardmore, where Grandpa was living at the old soldiers' home. I imagined that I would be able to visit him whenever I wanted.

When Kaliteyo found out about the plan, she begged Mama to let her go to St. Elizabeth's, a Chickasaw girls' school located in Purcell. Bloomfield only went to the eighth grade, but St. Elizabeth's went all the way through high school. Mildred McClure, Iman's daughter, attended St. Elizabeth's, and she had told Kaliteyo all about it. Kaliteyo told Mama that if I got to go away to Bloomfield she should be allowed to go to St. Elizabeth's. So it was settled. That fall we both went to boarding schools.

While Kaliteyo and I were waiting for school to start, we tried to get Papa to teach us some Chickasaw words. He spoke the language fluently— he used to speak it with Iman and Uncle Buck—but he refused to teach us. He just laughed and told us it wasn't important. Finally we did get him to teach us to count to ten: *chufa, tuklo, tuchina, oshta, tulhapi, hunali, ontuklo, ontukchina, chukali, pokoli.*

When the time came to leave home, Mama packed my trunk. I got to take my roller skates and my ukulele, and Mama made me two new dresses. One was a nice dress for special occasions. It had a sash that hung down the back and flowers that Mama embroidered on the front. My other dress had a checkered pattern and was nice, but was more of an everyday dress. The only problem was that Mama left me with orders to wear union suits under my pretty dresses. I liked to never got out of those union suits.

On the day we left for school, I hugged and kissed everybody goodbye, and Willie drove me down to Bloomfield. After the matron signed me in, Willie left. That's when I started to feel alone. I thought about getting to visit Grandpa, though, and that kept my spirits up. That evening after supper Mrs. Hill, the matron, took me back to the main residential building where I would be living and started telling me the school rules. One of them was that I wouldn't be allowed off campus except for an official school activity.

I asked her if that meant I couldn't go visit Grandpa, and she said that it did. Well, that did it for me. I told Mrs. Hill that if I couldn't go to see

Grandpa, I was going home. I cried and demanded that she call my mother. When she refused, I cried all the harder. She tried to get me to go upstairs to bed, but I refused to budge. I kept demanding that she call Mama. After much pleading on Mrs. Hill's part, and crying on mine, I finally agreed to spend the night, but only if I could talk to the superintendent in the morning.

Even after agreeing, though, I still didn't want to go up to my room. At that point Mrs. Hill began to insist. I still remember our trip up the stairs. I would take a step up, then turn around to go back, and Mrs. Hill would slap my bottom. Then another step, and another slap, all the way up the stairs.

The next morning, Mrs. Hill was true to her word, and she took me in to see the superintendent, Miss Allen. I remember meeting Miss Allen that first time. She seemed to tower above me. I met her years later, and she was actually a small woman, but when I was a child, she seemed like a giant. Miss Allen listened patiently as I demanded that she call my mother to come take me home. I explained to her that the only reason I had agreed to come to school there was so that I could visit Grandpa. Miss Allen was very kind. She told me that my mother had sent me there to go to school, and she would want me to stay. She asked me to make a bargain with her: if I would just try it out for a month, then, if I still wanted to go home, she would call my mother.

Miss Allen's strategy worked. I had settled down a little, anyway, since the night before, and although I was still upset, what she said made sense, so I agreed to stay for a month. I did get homesick, but I also enjoyed going to school and being with the other girls. Mama wrote me letters, and Willie sent me a little sewing basket filled with candy.

Every Friday was letter day, and we were all required to write a letter home. Some of the girls complained about writing letters and said that the teachers told them what to write, but I looked forward to letter day. I wrote a letter to Mama on Valentine's Day, 1927. It was sent to her along with my grades:

> Mother this [is] the report for January. I am getting along just fine. I couldn't write you last Sunday because I couldn't get a stamp. But I will write next Sunday if I can get a stamp.
> Your Loving Daughter, Wenonah Paul.

Bloomfield was a beautiful school. Everything was neat and clean, and the buildings were well maintained. There was a lake in front of the main building that had an island in the center, and there were pergolas built over the walkways that were covered by flowering vines. Concrete sidewalks connected the buildings, so I got a chance to use my roller skates. Ardmore seemed to have a milder climate than Pauls Valley, even though it was only forty miles to the south. It never got very cold or very hot, and it didn't snow all winter.

My room was in the main building where the hospital was located. The little girls and the girls who spoke only Chickasaw or Choctaw also stayed there. The school nurse, Mrs. Wright, was Choctaw, and since Chickasaw and Choctaw are almost the same, the girls who couldn't understand English could talk to her.

I really wanted to learn Chickasaw, but it was forbidden for the girls to speak their native language. The US government officials who ran the school thought that was the best way to teach them English. There was an old Indian man who did maintenance around the school who taught me a few Chickasaw words, and I learned some words from the other girls on laundry day. That was one of my jobs, to work in the laundry room. The mangle we used to press the sheets made a lot of noise, and the girls would hide behind it and speak Chickasaw. I still remember a few words they taught me, like *chukma*—"hello," and *minti*—"come here."

At Bloomfield, the girls performed most of the school maintenance. In addition to the laundry detail, there were girls assigned to sweeping, dish washing, gardening, feeding the chickens, and gathering eggs, and then there were the milkmaids. Only the older girls got to milk the cows. I so wanted to be a milkmaid.

Every month the school published a newsletter, and I still have one of them. It is dated March 27, 1927. It begins with an editorial by one of the teachers:

We are glad to welcome springtime again for with it comes the sweet perfumed flowers and the happy birds. Everywhere life bursts forth in all its beauty. Joy and happiness are everywhere. Yet it is not only earth's springtime but it is the springtime of life for our Bloomfield girls. It is the best and happiest time of their lives. They should try and realize this fact and cultivate in this springtime of youth those things which will enable them to grow into beautiful and useful women.
Jewell Crummey

There was an article about Bird Day:

On March 19th, we had a splendid Bird Day Program given under the direction of Miss Roberts and Mrs. Risser. The entire program was about birds and their help to man. The girls who took part in the play wore bird masks and costumes which made them look very real. There were robins, bluebirds, crows, and owls. Two toads in costume proclaimed themselves as great helpers of man also.

A report about the school garden:

Gardening has been progressing very well this month. Each eighth grade girl made a garden of her own in which she has planted twenty-five different kinds of vegetables. These plants are nearly all well above the ground. The other classes have also worked at planting so that Bloomfield has a garden it can be proud of.

And a project by the eighth grade girls to redecorate their rooms:

The eighth grade girls under the direction of Miss Owens, our Home Training Teacher, have completed redecorating their bedrooms. Their first step was to select the color scheme to be used in each room. The varnish was removed from the furniture and it was sandpapered before painting. They have given the walls and woodwork two coats. The floors have been covered with linoleum. The girls have made all the room furnishings including window curtain draperies, bedspreads, dresser scarfs and floor pillows. We expect an invitation to a "house warming" before long.

Ernestine Trout

There were also articles about world news, visitors, religious activities, illness—some of the girls had measles—news about the girls' families, and news from other Indian schools.

Finally, there were honor rolls for both academic and industrial classes. I was on both. I even made a good grade in arithmetic.

One girl from each dormitory was chosen as nurse to report any girls who were sick and to help out the school nurse, Mrs. Wright. I was chosen as nurse for my dormitory, and I was very proud of my position. Since Mrs. Wright's office was in my building, I got to help her more than the other student nurses did. One of my jobs was to help process new students when they first came to school.

Each new girl was required to take a shower and to put on clean, freshly laundered clothes. It was my job to take each girl to the shower room for her shower and to run a fine-toothed comb through her hair to check for lice. I felt very important performing this duty, especially since some of the girls were older and bigger than me. After I ran the comb through each new girl's hair, I would put it on a clean white towel, and take it back to Mrs. Wright. I remember being uneasy until I got rid of that towel.

Since I lived in the same building as the hospital, I saw all the girls who were sick. There was one little girl I remember who came to the school weak and emaciated. Mrs. Wright tried to make sure she ate good food, but her condition continued to deteriorate. Finally a doctor from Ardmore was called in to see her.

The doctor prescribed medicine, but the little girl's condition still didn't improve. Then one day an old man came walking up the road. He had walked all the way from his home. He was the little girl's grandfather, and he was also a tribal healer. The old man spoke with Mrs. Wright, and then he went in to see his granddaughter. He stayed with her for a long time. When he left, I watched him walk back up the road until he was out of sight. The little girl started improving after that, and she finally recovered.

Health was an important part of Bloomfield's curriculum, and the state of our health was reported monthly to our parents, along with our performance in class. The health report included our weight at the beginning and the end of each month, our hours of sleep, hygiene, exercise, and diet—we were supposed to drink one pint of milk and six glasses of water each day, along with eating a helping of fruit and a green leafy vegetable.

The cooking and sewing classes at Bloomfield were a challenge for me. I hadn't learned much from Mama about either, except for the little bit of crocheting she taught me when I was sick. My worst grade was in sewing. Our project in sewing class was to make a dress, and the teacher ended up doing most of the work for me. Then there was cooking class. I remember baking a cake. We were supposed to whip the egg whites and then "fold" them into the batter. The other girls all knew what to do, and I remember how horrified they were when I just dumped in my egg whites and started stirring. I didn't learn much in sewing class, but I did learn to fold in egg whites, and when I came home in the spring Mama let me bake a cake for the family. I still have the little cookbook I made at Bloomfield. In it are directions for making a "Standard Cake."

We also had a class in basket weaving. We learned to soak reeds in water to make them pliable and then to weave them into baskets. We planted flowers in our baskets and took them home at the end of the year. My flower was a narcissus.

My favorite class at Bloomfield was chorus, and that was when I got seriously interested in singing.

In the spring we all got to go to a park in Ardmore for an outing. The highlight of the trip was a big slide. Instead of going straight down, the slide had ripples. Some of the older girls came prepared with bread wrappers from the bakery for us to sit on so we would slide faster. It really worked. We got to going so fast that those ripples actually launched us into the air as we went over them. We had to hit the ground running.

It wasn't long after that last outing in the park that the school year was over. Snip came to get me, driving his big brown Packard, and I was so glad to see him. He sat with the parents and watched the school's final presentation for the year, a May Day Festival play. I was especially excited because I had been chosen to play the role of Queen of the May.

The play was performed on the island in front of the main building with the parents sitting around the edge of the lake. The girls were dressed in costumes representing the animals of the forest. They danced around the May Pole, holding colorful streamers, and then I was crowned. I wore the pretty dress that Mama had made for me and a crown of flowers. After the play, we gathered up my stuff: my roller skates, my ukulele, my sewing box, my basket with the narcissus planted inside, my cookbook, and my crown. Then Snip took me home. On the way home, Snip told me I had done a good job, and he was proud of me. That meant a lot.

It was so good to be home. Mama said she was proud of me, too. She was especially pleased with my manners, how I said "yes ma'am" and "no ma'am" when I talked to her. She even let me help her with the cooking. Bob and Kaliteyo teased me about being the Queen of the May, but I was glad to see them, anyway.

CHAPTER 18
- Oteka Falls into a Hay Mower -

The summer of 1927 started off well. I was so happy to be home with my family, especially with Mama. I helped her in the kitchen and in the garden, and I told her I didn't want to go back to Bloomfield. It's not that I didn't miss Mrs. Wright and all of the girls. I did, but the homesickness had just been too hard for me. Now, I'm sorry that I didn't go back to Bloomfield. While I was there, I really felt like I belonged.

It was different with Kaliteyo. She was anxious to go back to St. Elizabeth's again. She did well in school and she didn't get sick, which must have been a relief to Mama. Kaliteyo was always trying to assert her independence.

St. Elizabeth's was in Purcell, about twenty miles north of Pauls Valley. It was founded by an order of nuns who established a convent there before statehood. One of the sisters told the girls how she had stood on top of a hill and watched the first land run opening Indian land to white settlement in 1889. St. Elizabeth's got its financial support from Mother Katherine Drexel, a nun from a wealthy family in Philadelphia who used her fortune to support schools for black and Native American children.

Kaliteyo came back home that summer full of stories about her school year. The sisters there weren't strict with the girls, and they let them cut up a little. One of Kaliteyo's best friends at St. Elizabeth's was Tula May Graham, and Kaliteyo kept us in stitches telling us stories about their escapades together. She told us how she and Tula May would laugh and joke and entertain the other girls after the lights had been turned out for the night.

I always envied Kaliteyo because she got to take piano lessons at St. Elizabeth's, but of course, she didn't take music seriously like I did. She told about one time she was mimicking Mrs. Potter[1], the pianist who played background music for silent movies at the Royal Theater. Mrs. Potter was quite rotund, and during the action scenes, she'd get excited and bounce up and down on the piano bench, jiggling all her generous body parts. Kaliteyo's imitation of her was hilarious. Anyway, Kaliteyo was imitating Mrs. Potter for Tula May one day when a nun walked by and caught her in the act. I would like to have been a little mouse in the room to hear how Kaliteyo explained herself.

The funniest story Kaliteyo told was about her friend Tula May trying to smuggle apples into her room. There was an apple tree on the school grounds, and when the apples got ripe, Tula May came up with a plan. During their free period, she was going to pick some apples and stuff them into her bloomers to take back to their room.

For those who don't know, bloomers were blousy pantaloons that had drawstrings that tied at the ankles. The girls at St. Elizabeth's were all required to wear them under their skirts.

Well, during recess that day, the nuns didn't notice as Tula Mae picked apples and slipped them under her skirt. Everything went smoothly until the girls filed back into the building to return to class. That's when the drawstring on one leg of Tula Mae's bloomers broke. One by one, the apples fell, rolling out on the sidewalk behind her.

Kaliteyo said that one of the nuns was watching as Tula May walked by, and when she figured out what was going on she got tickled. It was funny the way Kaliteyo told it. The nun was overweight. She was trying to be stern, but the girls could tell she was laughing by the way her belly shook.

Haskell didn't come home that spring. He had gotten a job at the Meyers' Funeral home in Norman, driving the hearse and helping out with funerals. Mr. Meyers let Haskell live in a room in the back, so he stayed there and worked while he took courses during the summer.

Haskell also had another reason for not coming home. He had gotten married. He didn't tell Mama. She found out from Snip, who read it in the newspaper. Mama's first reaction was to try to have the marriage annulled, but Papa talked her out of it. Haskell would be twenty-one in February, and then he could do what he wanted, anyway.

Haskell's bride was Eve Thomas, one of his classmates in law school. Eve was working as a grade school teacher in the nearby community of Goldsby to put herself through school. By combining their incomes and living in Haskell's little room in the back of the funeral home, she and Haskell both lived a little better.

Haskell still didn't have enough money to buy clothes. The next year he earned himself a place on the law school's debate team, and when he competed, he had to borrow a suit from one of his classmates.

Snip spent his first year in the legislature learning the ropes and making connections. One of the friends he made was a veteran legislator from Purcell, Jim Nance. Nance was editor of the *Purcell Register* and an influential man in state politics. He took an instant liking to Snip.

From the start, Snip used his political position to help out the family. One of the first things he did after taking his seat in the House of Representatives was to get our brother Willie appointed game warden over Garvin County. This was a big help to the family. With Papa sick most of the time and five children still living at home, Willie's little income from his farm and hamburger stand was stretched to the limit.

Papa's dropsy was bothering him that summer. It caused his legs to swell, so most days he stayed home with his feet elevated. A neighbor from across the street, Mr. West, would come over to visit him from time to time. Mr. West was a retired pharmacist, and he would give Papa advice. I remember that one of the remedies he suggested was to drink tea made from dandelion leaves. He said it would clean the poisons out of his system as well as get rid of the fluid. Papa laughed at the idea of dandelion tea, but there may have been something to it. Dandelion tea is still recommended for fluid retention.

The other thing Mr. West did was to share with Papa his knowledge about dropsy. We all joked about the way Mr. West chose to cheer Papa up. He would say with his thick German accent, "The svelling affects first the legs, and then higher and higher it comes. Ven it hits your lungs, you're a goner."

Papa laughed about Mr. West's predictions, too, but I know he was worried. He suddenly became afraid of the dark and always made sure there was a light on when he went to sleep. I didn't understand why at the time, but since then I have learned that there was an old Chickasaw belief that when a person dies, his spirit needs a light to find its way to the spirit world. In the old days, the Chickasaws would keep a light burning near a person who was near death. I think Papa was just preparing himself.

Papa didn't die, though. He improved—it was probably because he was too sick to drink. Anyway, by the middle of the summer, he was getting up again every morning and walking to town.

Now that I was older, I started paying more attention to my little brother and sister, Tom and Oteka. Tom was six, and he had a little friend named Victor Swinney, who would come over and play with him. Vic's father, Claude, was Pauls Valley's sheriff for years and years, and the Swinneys had always been good friends of Mama and Papa. Vic was actually named for Mama. Vic and Tom would spend all morning digging in the dirt and wrestling, and by the time Mama would call them in for supper, they would be filthy. When Mama sent them into the bathroom to wash up, they would just go in and splash a little water on their faces. I'll never forget seeing them come in to eat, their dirty little faces streaked with water.

Oteka was nine now, and she was still the same spunky little girl who had called out to Papa from under the bed and who had leaped into the deep end of the swimming pool before she learned to swim. Teker was popular, and everywhere she went she had a gang of little girls following her.

Teker and Tom loved to go out to the farm with Willie, just like Bob and I did. When it was time to make the first cutting of hay, they begged to go, so Willie took them along. He hitched up Mack and Maggie, and let Teker and Tom ride them as they pulled the mower, its six-foot-long cutting blade slashing back and forth—I don't know what he was thinking. Willie steered the horses up and down the field as the children laughed and pretended to be cowboys. At the corner of the field, there was a big pecan tree that had a limb hanging out over the field. The limb was lower than Willie thought, and before he knew it Maggie had ducked under the limb and it had struck Teker, knocking her off the horse right into the path of the mower.

Teker screamed and Willie's heart stopped. He reined in the horses, jumped down from the mower, and looked in horror as his little sister lay there on the ground, blood gushing from an eight-inch gash in her leg. He picked her up, grabbed Tom, and ran for the car. He wrapped up Teker's leg as best he could to staunch the bleeding and then raced into town. Teker was as brave as a lion. As they rode into town, she calmly picked a piece of bone out of her leg and threw it out the window of the car. Willie took her straight to the hospital, where she was seen by a doctor. I'll call him Dr.

Cutter. Soon Mama and Papa were there too. Dr. Cutter took one look at Teker's leg and said it had to come off. He told them he would operate the next morning.

That evening Mama, Papa, and Willie met with Snip, who had driven down from Oklahoma City as soon as he heard the news. They all stood out on the front porch and talked about what to do. I remember Mama saying, "They're not cutting my daughter's leg off. I won't give my permission." Snip got on the phone and called the most influential man he knew, Lieutenant Governor Bill Holloway. He told Holloway about his little sister being hurt and that he wanted to find the best surgeon in Oklahoma City. Holloway didn't disappoint him. He called a doctor he knew at the medical school who recommended a young orthopedic surgeon named Donald O'Donahue, who was becoming nationally known for his skill and innovative surgery. Snip called him that night, and Dr. O'Donahue told him, "Bring your sister to Oklahoma City, and I'll see her in the morning." Oteka was taken by ambulance to Oklahoma City that night.

The next morning, Dr. O'Donahue saw Oteka. "Yes," he said, "there's a chance I can save her leg." He took her into surgery that morning and did what he could to put her leg back together. Tense hours of waiting followed the surgery. That afternoon, when Dr. O'Donahue made his rounds, Oteka's toes were still pink. He told Mama, "It looks like her circulation is still good. If infection doesn't develop, I think we'll be in the clear." The nurses set up a cot in Teker's room for Mama, and she slept next to her. Each day that passed without complications raised Mama's hopes further. Finally, after a week, Dr. O'Donahue told Mama he thought it was safe for her to go home. Mama said, "I'll leave when my daughter leaves." So, she stayed. It was a long wait. There was the slow process of healing, and then came the rehabilitation with the pain of stretching out the torn muscles and scar tissue.

Teker got regular visits from Homer, Willie, and Papa. I didn't get to go to the hospital, but Kaliteyo did. She gave Teker a little black doll baby when she went to visit her, and Teker kept it for the rest of her life. After two months of healing, Mama and Teker left the hospital together. Teker had a wicked scar, but she still had both of her legs. Mama never forgave Dr. Cutter. She always referred to him as "the Butcher."

CHAPTER 19
- Back to School in Pauls Valley -

Teker started the fourth grade in the fall. She was so strong. She limped, and there was a hideous scar on her left calf, but come September she was able to walk the eight blocks to Lee School with our little brother Tom, who was just starting the first grade.

I was in the eighth grade that year, back in Pauls Valley. I missed the girls at Bloomfield, but it was good to be home with Mama. She must have missed me, too. Every morning she'd tell me to come right home from school to help her in the garden.

Bob was in the seventh grade that year, so we started walking to school together. Pauls Valley Junior High was only five blocks away, on the other side of the courthouse. My year at Bloomfield had put me ahead of my class, and that made me proud of myself and proud of having gone to Bloomfield. I did well in school that year.

My cooking class at Bloomfield hadn't completely made up for my years as a tomboy, though. I had to take a domestic science class in the eighth grade, and one day our assignment was to bake a date loaf. I brought my ingredients from home, including cream from our cow. We had to boil the cream down to a caramel consistency and then add dates and pecans. As I boiled my cream, it gave off a funny smell. Pretty soon the teacher noticed it and came over to where I was working. She asked me where I got my cream, and I told her it was from our cow. She said, "Has the cow recently had a calf?" Well, as a matter of fact, she had. The teacher informed me that you shouldn't use milk from a cow with a new calf.

I was embarrassed because all the other girls seemed to know this important rule of cooking, but I finished baking my date loaf anyway, and I ate it. It tasted good, too. I figured that if the milk was meant for the calf, then it had to be okay.

Since I had enjoyed singing at Bloomfield, I signed up for the glee club at Pauls Valley, and I did well. Miss Shi, our choir director, complimented my singing, and after the first semester, she chose me to be a member of the girl's quartet. The only problem was that I had to have a blue skirt to dress like the other girls. I finally screwed up my courage and asked Papa if he would buy one for me—I remember he was talking to Crocket Scrivner at the time. Somehow Papa came up with the money and bought me a skirt. Once I got acquainted with the other girls, we had a good time together. The quartet performed at school functions, and in the spring, we got to compete at the district meet in Ada. When I went, Papa gave me ten cents to spend, and I bought a little bracelet made out of wooden beads.

We had a good Christmas that year. Mama invited Haskell and his new wife, Eve, to come down from Norman, and Snip brought his girlfriend, Helen Lafferty—they were serious now. Papa was there, of course, and Kaliteyo came back from St. Elizabeth's for the holidays. Bob and I plucked a goose and Mama cooked it, along with all the trimmings, complaining all the while about how she missed her wood stove.

Mama, now over the shock of Haskell's secret marriage, was trying to make Eve feel welcome. This was the first chance I had to be around Eve. She was kind of stiff, and she seemed anxious to show us how smart she was. I didn't much care for her. Snip's girlfriend Helen, on the other hand, fit right in. She pitched in and helped Mama in the kitchen, and she seemed to enjoy being with our family.

Helen took a special liking to me. I told her about my schoolwork and about singing in the glee club. Helen dressed stylishly, and I was starting to get interested in clothes.

Snip's term in the House of Representatives was only for two years, so in 1928 he was up for re-election. In the spring, he got a lesson in political dirty tricks. His opponent accused our brother Willie of mismanagement of funds and got him fired from his job as game warden. Our family suddenly lost the security we had felt with Willie's state job.

Willie was philosophical about losing the job, though. He told Mama not to worry, that he still had his farm and his hamburger stand, and now he would have more time to spend on his passion, cockfighting. Willie bred his own gamecocks, and he rented his best fighters out to breed. He also operated his own "runs" for breeding and conditioning the roosters, and he organized tournaments, which could be lucrative. Cockfighting was popular back then, and there was betting involved, which wasn't exactly legal.

In the spring, school was out. It had been a good year. I had enjoyed singing in the glee club and in the girls' quartet, and I had made good grades, especially in English and Latin. I made some good friends, too.

I recently ran across my junior high memory book. We couldn't afford yearbooks, so it's all I have to remember my junior and senior high school friends. Kaliteyo wrote my name in the front and made page headings for me using her beautiful calligraphy—she was always artistic like Mama—and then she wrote this sarcastic note:

> *Dearest el' - ol' - bitsy - baby - Jim:*
> *Well! "Nuter -Jender" how are u progressing by now? All I have to say for n with my "sisterly love" is just "stay rite in there and fight 'em"—cause I'm bettin' on u.*
> *Kaliteyo*

And there's a note from Helen Lafferty, Snip's fiancée, who later became the big sister I never had:

> *Dearest Jim:*
> *Adjectives curl up and die when trying to describe you, so I'll only say that you are very very sweet—and I'll always remember you—no foolin!*
> *Your ever devoted "sister"*
> *Helen Lafferty*

The book is full of notes. Some, of course, are silly or from people I hardly knew, but not many. Most are from good friends, teachers, or family members, and they mean a lot to me, even now. In light of the tragedy that would soon darken our lives, it strikes me how happy and optimistic we were.

Here's a note from one of my teachers, Oma Patton:

Dear Wenonah,

The chapter of your junior high work is just about written isn't it? I hope it will all sound as good as your record in here. You are one I am sending into high school and expect to make good. I have enjoyed having you in my class. Am wondering who will take the place of the little black-eyed girl who always sat near my desk. She will have to be a good one to really take your place.

Always with love,
Oma Patton.

And from our neighbor, Vera:

Dearest Twin Sister

I guess it is useless to say I love you because you know that. We have always lived so close together you seem more like a twin sister than just a friend. May you always remember the girl who loves you. I shall always and forever remember you.

Love,
Vera Ashurst.

And my sweet little sister, Oteka:

Dear Jim:

You are passing into high school aren't you? I am passing into the 5th grade and passing out of Miss Marie Monro room which I am very glad of because she is cross.

Your loving sister,
Oteka Paul

When school was out, Willie taught Bob and me to drive his Model T Ford. Bob was thirteen and I was fourteen. Bob was really proud when Willie let him drive. One day he took off in Willie's car to run an errand for Mama, and as he headed out onto Grant Street, he steered the car around the corner with his right arm, resting his left arm on the window like he had seen someone else do. When Willie saw him steering with one arm, he yelled for him to stop. Bob just kept on driving—he couldn't hear for the engine noise—so Willie ran the car down on foot, made Bob stop, and then yanked him out of the driver's seat. I'll tell you, that got old Bob's attention. After that he remembered to keep both hands on the steering wheel.

Soon after we learned to drive, Willie let Bob and I take his car out to the farm. We enjoyed ourselves, as usual, and when time came to drive back home, I bent down to crank the engine—it was my turn to drive. The old Model T's weren't like modern cars. The gears and the brake were pedals on the floor, and there were levers by the steering wheel called the throttle and the spark. The throttle regulated the amount of fuel going to the engine, acting like a modern accelerator, and the spark regulated the amount of electricity going to the cylinders. You had to crank the engine to start it. There was a crank down under the front bumper, but before turning the crank, you had to pull back on the spark. If you didn't, the car could backfire, causing the crank handle to jerk back violently. It could break your wrist.

Anyway, I forgot to pull back on the spark before I cranked the engine, and the engine backfired. The handle jerked so hard, it raised me clear up off the ground. My wrist swelled up as big as an apple, and Bob had to drive us home. The next day I went in to see Dr. Callaway, and he gave me a splint to wear. He didn't have an x-ray machine, so I never knew if my wrist was broken or not. It didn't heal right, though, and it still gives me trouble sometimes.

CHAPTER 20
- The Tragedy That Changed Our Lives Forever -

At the beginning of the summer, it finally seemed like things were getting better. Willie's stint as game warden had given us a temporary boost in our income. Snip and Helen were now engaged, and Snip was running for a second term in the state legislature. Haskell was in his last year of law school, and he and Eve were about to have a baby.

The rest of us were out of school for the summer. I was looking forward to getting time to visit with my friend Kathleen, and Bob was spending most of his spare time with Toodles Jackson, whose father owned a garage and filling station. Oteka seemed almost back to normal after her injury. She was running around with her little friends again, just as if nothing had happened, and Tom had gone back to spending his days outside, wrestling with Victor Sweeney. Kaliteyo had enjoyed her second year at St. Elizabeth's, and after spending a couple of weeks at home, she had gone back to Purcell to visit Tula May Graham.

Mama and Papa were still at odds. Mama had made another trip down to see her lawyer, Alvin Pyeatt, about a divorce, and Mr. Pyeatt had told her that if she divorced Papa, she would lose custody of her children, just like Mrs. Paul had lost custody of Papa and Uncle Buck after her divorce from Sam Paul. I don't know if there was any truth to what he said, but it stopped Mama from going forward with the divorce.

I'm sure that Papa heard about Mama's visit to the lawyer. There aren't many secrets in a small town, and it must have caused him to feel even more alienated and isolated from the family. He had finally given up on his real estate business and had taken a job with the police department. He worked the night shift. I think Uncle Buck got him the job. It was a big comedown from making real estate deals involving thousands of dollars, but times were tough, and it did bring in a little money. Mama wasn't happy about it, though. She didn't like the idea of Papa carrying a gun.

Willie was Mama's rock. He helped her with all her decisions, and of course, he was supporting us with the income from the farm, his hamburger stand, and what little he made off his gamecocks. Every evening, Mama would pour out her troubles to him. She would list all of Papa's failings—how he had lost his business, his health, and his standing in the community, all because of that damned alcohol. Now they were ruined financially, and she could no longer hold her head up among her friends. Willie would calmly take it all in and then tell Mama not to worry, that things were getting better.

We all relied on Willie. Even the older boys deferred to him. He always looked at things in a positive light. Willie was actually more of a father to us than Papa was. He'd take us to the show and bring us treats from the farm. He was always there to listen to our troubles and to smile at our accomplishments.

Willie had aged. He was only twenty-eight, but he seemed older. He wore glasses. He had ruined his eyes by reading in the dark, but he still spent most of his free time reading. He had started to put on a little weight, like Papa, so every evening he would run down Pine Street to the Traherns' house and back for exercise. It was about twenty blocks, round trip.

That spring there were two big events in Haskell's life, both on June 20. In the morning, he found out that he had passed the Oklahoma State Bar exam. He still had another year of law school to complete, but when that was over, he would be able to practice law. On the evening of that same day, his wife Eve delivered a baby boy in their little room in the back of the Meyers' Funeral home in Norman. They named their son Thomas, Eve's maiden name. We immediately gave him the nickname of "Little Tom" because our little brother was also named Tom.

Everyone was anxious to see the new baby, but Eve wanted to give herself a while to recover before she made the trip down to Pauls Valley. Finally, on July 28—a Sunday—she agreed to come. Haskell was studying, so Willie drove up to Norman to get her and the baby. Oteka and Tom went along with him for the ride, and Bob and I stayed home with Mama. Kaliteyo was still in Purcell, visiting with Tula May.

When Willie got home, we all "oohed" and "aahed" over the baby, and then I took him upstairs for Papa to see. Papa was just getting up to go to work. He took a look at Little Tom, smiled at me, and then went back to getting dressed. I took the baby back downstairs and rejoined the family. Later, we heard Papa in the bathroom getting cleaned up, and then we heard him come downstairs. He didn't come into the dining room to say hello. He just walked straight through the living room and out onto the porch, slamming the front screen behind him. He was mad about being excluded.

When Bob heard the front door close, he ran after Papa to say goodbye. A moment later, he came running back into the house and said, "Mama, are you gonna let Papa shoot that dog?" Apparently, a stray dog had wandered into the yard, and Papa had told Bob he was going to kill it.

Willie told Mama to keep her seat; he would go out and talk to Papa. Then he got up and walked out onto the porch. Mama followed him, anyway, and Bob and I followed her. Bob went out and stood by Mama while I looked out through the screen. What I saw next is burned into my memory. I can still see it like it was yesterday.

Papa was standing over the dog with his pistol drawn, and Willie was trying to reason with him. He argued that the dog hadn't caused any harm, and he was probably somebody's pet, but Papa wouldn't listen. Finally, Willie just bent over to pick up the dog, and as he did, Papa fired and the bullet struck Willie!

I watched in horror as Willie dropped the dog. He staggered back toward the door. Mama opened it and said, "Honey, come lie down in my room"—she always got that right, the proper use of "lie" and "lay." I stepped back as Willie opened the door to come inside. He took one step into the living room, and then he fell, right in front of me.

Mama was right behind him. She looked up at me and said, "Jim, run and get Dr. Johnson!"

I ran out onto the porch and down the steps; Dr. Johnson lived right across the street from us. As I ran, I saw Papa standing in the street, backing away from the house. He still had the pistol in his hand. It was as if he thought the devil himself, or maybe Mama, was coming after him. I didn't stop. I ran straight across the street and into the Johnsons' living room. The doctor was sitting in a chair, reading. Somehow I managed to blurt out that Papa had shot Willie, and he was hurt bad. Dr. Johnson grabbed his bag and followed me back across the street, but there was nothing he could do. The bullet had gone straight through Willie's heart. He was dead by the time we got back to the house.

When I saw Willie lying still on the floor, I fainted, and then I fainted again and again, every time I looked at him. Finally, someone carried me next door to the Ashursts. Mrs. Ashurst laid me on her porch swing and gave me water and juice until I could stand up again. Then I walked back home.

The police had already been there and had talked with Mama. She told them that Papa had murdered Willie, and she wanted him to hang. Then the undertaker came and carried Willie away. When they had all gone, Mama was still frantic. She cried, and she railed at Papa; she blamed Bob for bringing the news about the dog. When she saw me, she told me to go call and tell Uncle Buck. Uncle Buck said he'd send Kenneth over. Uncle Buck's son Kenneth was about my age.

Late that evening, Snip, Haskell, and Kaliteyo arrived. Snip sat with Mama until the early hours of the morning. Kaliteyo and I slept together that night, and we cried together. She kept saying that Papa never would have shot Willie if she had been there, and she was probably right. Kaliteyo always had a way with Papa. Haskell probably felt the same way about himself, but he didn't say it.

The next day was Monday. Willie's casket was placed in our living room, and Mama sat next to it and cried. All day, people filed by Willie's body and tried to console Mama. Papa's family—Uncle Buck, the Waites, the McClures—were all there. Friends came from Whitebead, Elmore City, and Wynnewood. Everyone brought food. Ministers from the Baptist, Methodist, and Presbyterian churches all came by to say prayers.

The funeral was held on Tuesday at the Methodist Church. I don't know how we all got there. Mama couldn't help us. She couldn't even take care of herself. The church was filled with flowers and with people. There was standing room only. An excerpt from Reverend Douglass' eulogy was printed in the newspaper:

> *No pastor ever feels more helpless than when he stands before an open casket, surrounded by a broken-hearted family who look to him for words of comfort. Were it not for the faith we have in a blessed immortality, life would scarcely be worth the effort. All roads are rough, sin and tragedy often meet us, sickness and sorrow are*

everyday occurrences. Faith and faith alone bids us to look up to a star of hope where angels wait and loved ones linger, and where God sits on His throne, high and lifted up. This little mother and her grief-stricken children may remember that God loves them, and that in an eternal heaven, loved ones wait their coming.

Willie Paul, born November 28, 1900, was never a child. From an early age he cared for his mother and her other children. Denying himself every luxury, and even many of the necessities of life, he gave himself unreservedly to the comfort and happiness of the family.

He loved books and children, birds and flowers. All the neighbor children knew him and loved him. Squirrels playing in the front yard seemed to recognize in him a friend.

Young Mr. Paul could be best described as quiet, self-sacrificing, stoical, tender-hearted, and trustworthy. No effort was too great which would bring comfort or assistance to his mother and her children.

The mother told the preacher that she could truthfully say to the world that her son went before his God with clean hands. That while he belonged to no church, yet he believed in God and trusted in prayer. He lived and died believing in a God who loves us and who hears us when we call.

There is no oratory but which falls helpless in a time when tragic sorrow tears the heart of a family, bathing their faces in tears, and blinding their weeping eyes. The several visiting pastors in the church today can bear witness before this great audience that any true Christian would bind up every broken heart and brush away every falling tear, only we have not the power and authority. But the Heavenly Father has promised to be with us in our sorrows, and his words never fail.

This wonderful floral offering and this large congregation of sympathizing friends will ever stand before the memory of the sorrowing family as a picture of hope and a gleam of consolation. Faith of Jesus Christ and the fellowship of those who love will ever linger as a balm of healing to this family weighed down by sorrow and overcome by grief.

There is no better prayer which could be offered on this occasion, than that some day this little mother might be able to walk by faith through the gates of glory, and there meet the boy whom she loved so ardently. May the peace of God rest the soul of the dutiful son, and may his mercies and blessings guard the entire family through the darkness of this sad hour, and into the portals of a happier day. When the storms and sorrows of this life shall have passed, may the sunset be serene. May the tears of this sad company, like the raindrops on the living branches, be changed by the setting sun into gems of precious memory, so that we may be able to say with God's prophet, "At eventide it shall be light."[1]

Mama would have just as soon followed Willie through "the gates of glory," sooner rather than later. After the funeral, all our friends and neighbors came over to the house, but Mama couldn't stop crying. Finally, Hazel Hart, a good friend of Mama's, said to her, "You just have to get over it." Mama just stared at her. Hazel loved Willie, too. She just didn't know what to say, but Mama would never get over it. None of us would.

CHAPTER 21
- Aftermath -

The Sunday after Willie's funeral, Mama decided that we should go to church. So Kaliteyo, Bob, Teker, Tom, Mama, and I all piled into Willie's Model T Ford and started off for the First Baptist Church. Snip wasn't with us, so I drove. Just as I turned left onto Ash Street in front of the church, I saw a big truck barreling down on us, but it was too late. The truck hit us broadside and turned Willie's little car over on its side.

Bob and I helped Mama and the little kids climb out of the car, and then we realized that Kaliteyo was pinned underneath the canopy, so we climbed up on the car and somehow managed to lift it off so she could get out, but her collarbone was broken. Fortunately, hers was the only injury. Mama's dress was burned by battery acid, but she wasn't hurt. She attributed our survival to Providence. She said, "If we hadn't been in front of a church, we'd have probably all been killed."

After my wreck, Snip did himself proud. He stayed home with us for a while, and during that time he spent a lot of time with Mama. It was good for her. She needed someone to confide in, even if it wasn't Willie. Snip promised her that he would try to take Willie's place. He took the money from the insurance he had sold Willie on his car and used it to fix up our house. He had it repainted, a new roof put on, and the old electrical wiring replaced. He even managed to get Willie's car running again. That convinced Mama that she could count on Snip, so she started letting him make decisions for her, and she gave him permission to boss us around, which he enjoyed greatly. Needless to say that didn't go over well with me. I didn't cross Snip, though. I agreed to whatever he told me, and then I did what I wanted.

Mrs. Paul died two weeks after Willie was killed. It must have been too much for her to see the suffering Papa had caused. Hers was the second death in our family that summer, and it caused me to believe we were under some sort of curse.

I don't remember much about that time in our lives. Everything was so confused. Snip was there, but I don't remember seeing him that much. I guess he was busy with his re-election campaign. Kaliteyo was gone. Snip had sent her to Purcell, to stay with the Townleys, Mrs. Paul's people. Haskell wasn't at home, either. He and Eve were living in Norman while he finished up his last year at OU. Mama spent most of her time in bed. She could hardly walk. She had to have her head propped up just to breathe. Young Dr. Callaway checked her and said her heart was failing. He prescribed medicine, put her on a special diet, and told her to stay in bed.

Mama had a lot of visitors, and they would bring food, so we had enough to eat, for a while, at least. Her most regular visitor was Mr. West, the old pharmacist from across the street who used to visit Papa when he was laid up with the dropsy. He came over every day, and every day Mama would relive the shooting. I had to leave the house when he was there, because I couldn't stand to listen to her talk about it.

I saw Willie everywhere—in the hall, in the kitchen, out on the porch. When I looked outside, I could see him walking up the street. When I slept, I saw him in my dreams. It scared me. I cried. I tried to talk to him. I promised him I would do my best to take care of Mama, Teker, and Tom.

It wasn't long before the food gifts stopped coming, and with Mama sick in bed and Kaliteyo gone, it was up to me to do the cooking. I could scarcely function, but I had to. Mama would give me a list, and I'd go buy the groceries. She had to have special bread, baked without salt. I picked that up at Worley's Bakery. I had no idea how to cook. All I had ever done was cook a cake and some date bread for school. Now I was cooking for the whole family. I remember running back and forth to Mama's bedroom to get instructions on how to bake cornbread. She would show me on her fingers: "this much meal, this much buttermilk, this much salt, and this much lard."

Bob helped me with the errands. One day he took Teker out with him to get something and ran the car off the road. Luckily, neither of them was hurt. We had no money to buy clothes. Bob wore the same clothes all summer, a khaki shirt and pants, with one white sock and one brown sock. Oh, how they stunk!

There was really no one around to help Teker and Tom deal with our tragedy. Bob and I were too upset ourselves to pay much attention to them. One day, I found little Oteka standing in the middle of the kitchen with a butcher knife in her hand saying, "I'm going to kill myself." I ran over and took the knife away from her. There was nothing I could think of to say, so I just hugged her. I don't know how Tom handled Willie's death. I guess he just went off by himself.

School started in the fall, and the nightmare continued. Kaliteyo came home to spend her last year of high school at Pauls Valley. Mama was still weak. Sometimes I cooked, and sometimes Kaliteyo cooked. Most of the time, everybody just fended for themselves.

I went through the motions of going to school, but I had no interest in my classes. Everyone in town knew us and knew about our tragedy. My classmates couldn't think of anything to say, so they just stared at me. It was unbearable.

Papa had been arrested right after the shooting and was in jail awaiting his trial. His cell was on the top floor of the county courthouse, and it overlooked the sidewalk. I had to walk by there every day on my way to school. When he saw me, he would call out, "Jim, Jim, Jim, Jim..." When I heard him, I would start running and keep running until I was out of his sight.

In September, Grandpa died. Like I said before, Mama took me to see him before he died, and I also went to his funeral. He was confused at the end, so I don't know whether he knew about Willie's death or not. I hope not. Grandpa had been close to Willie, too. So that made three deaths: Willie, Mrs. Paul, and Grandpa. After that, I had a phobia that deaths would come in threes. Whenever there was a death in the family, I always had a fear that another one was coming, and then another.

After watching us flounder all summer, Snip's fiancée, Helen, moved in with us. She took over the cooking and cleaning, and she got us back into a routine. At night, she slept upstairs with us girls. Helen was compassionate and good-natured, and boy, was she a good cook. Even my finicky brother Tom liked her cooking. That year she cooked Thanksgiving dinner. Tom walked into the kitchen while she was cooking a lemon chiffon pie, and she told him that he could eat as much as he wanted. He tried to eat the whole pie. We all loved Helen.

Helen knew I was embarrassed by not having nice clothes, so she told me she would help me make myself a dress. We went downtown and picked out some material, and then we worked on the dress together. One day while we were sewing I told Helen I was scared about what would happen to us now that Willie was gone, and she told me a story. Helen's father was a minister, and he had passed away several years earlier. She said that once when she was scared, her father had told her that she should never worry, because no matter what happened, God would be there to protect her. So every night I prayed for God to take care of us.

When Bob and I found out Helen didn't know how to drive, we took her out to an old country road to teach her. We got the car started, and then let her drive. She was doing pretty well, until we came to a gate. I got out, opened the gate, and as I was standing there waiting for her to drive the car through, she swerved and almost ran over me! I guess she got mixed up on which way to turn the steering wheel. Anyway, that day I initiated her into the family. She found out that Papa wasn't the only one of us with a temper.

Everyone dealt with our tragedy in their own way. Kaliteyo adopted a little stray kitten and named it Vera Dell, after the mailman's wife, who she thought was pretty. One day we all went out to the farm together, and Kaliteyo took Vera Dell. Snip and Helen were with us. When we were ready to leave, Kaliteyo couldn't find Vera Dell. She called for her, and we looked everywhere we could think of, but the kitten was nowhere to be seen. Finally, Snip said we couldn't wait around any longer, and he told us to get in the car. As the car pulled away, we felt a bump. It was Vera Dell. She was crushed under a wheel. Kaliteyo screamed, and then she cried and cried. It was as if someone in the family had died.

Snip was reelected in November, and afterward he started making trips to Oklahoma City to get ready for the next session of the legislature. In the meantime, Mama had recovered enough to be up and about and to help with the cooking.

In December, Papa went on trial for murder. All of us were named as witnesses, but Bob and I were the only ones called on to testify. They paid us three dollars each. The prosecuting attorney was Mac Q. Williamson, the senator from Garvin County. After I got up on the stand and swore to tell the truth, he asked me the day of the week and the month. I could hardly talk, but I answered him. Then he asked, "Do you want your father to die in the electric chair?" I couldn't speak. I just started to cry. The judge reprimanded him, but it was too late. The damage was done. I couldn't stop crying, so the judge dismissed me. The jury probably thought my tears were for Papa, but they weren't. I had no feelings for Papa after he killed Willie, none whatsoever.

They wouldn't let Mama testify, so my brother Bob was the prosecution's star witness. Apparently, he didn't have any trouble telling his story like I did. The jury found Papa guilty, and he was sentenced to five years in the state penitentiary. The local newspaper covered his trial:

W. H. Paul Guilty of Manslaughter
Jury Gives Him Five Years After Short Deliberation.

About eleven-thirty Tuesday night, the jury returned a verdict of guilty against W. H. Paul, charged with the killing of his son, W. G. Paul, of manslaughter in the first degree and assessed his punishment at five years in the state penitentiary.

This brought to a close one of the most spectacular trials ever staged in Garvin County. The jury received the case after argument about eleven o'clock, and reached a verdict in less than thirty minutes.

The case went to trial Monday, but the jury was not elected until Tuesday morning. The evidence of the state and the defense both closed by four o'clock, the first argument was had before supper and the concluding arguments after the supper hour.

Several citizens of the town testified in the case to the effect that after the shooting, Paul refused to return home and ascertain the condition of his son. It developed that there were two eyewitnesses, Robert Paul and Mrs. Victoria Paul. The son, Robert, was the only eyewitness allowed to testify. This thirteen-year-old son of the defendant made a splendid witness for the state. The state then offered the testimony of Mrs. Paul, but the defense objected for statutory grounds and the court refused to allow her to testify. Paul took the stand and gave his version of the shooting. His testimony was not clear as to the actual shooting. Claud Seymour and Calvin Phelps testified that they saw Paul backing off the porch with his pistol pointed back toward the house. Several other circumstances were offered in evidence.

A great deal of emotion was displayed on the witness stand, by the defendant himself, and the children who testified. The case carried more tragedy throughout than any case tried for considerable time in the county.

Able and eloquent pleas were made to the jury by attorneys on both sides. Carroll Moody, Homer Hurt and Mac Q. Williamson handled the prosecution, and S. J. Goodwin and J. H. Mathers of Oklahoma City appeared for the defendant.[1]

Just before Christmas, Bob and I went downtown together to spend the six dollars we had been paid for testifying at Papa's trial. Bob bought a toy gasoline pump for our little brother Tom, and I bought a ceramic teapot for Mama.

CHAPTER 22
- A Wedding, Politics, and Family Conflict -

In January, Snip and Helen were married. Their wedding was held in the home of Jim Nance, then Speaker of the Oklahoma House of Representatives. Nance was Snip's best man. No one in the family attended the wedding. I don't know if Mama was even invited, but I doubt it. We were a political liability.

Here's the article that appeared in the *Pauls Valley Democrat* after the wedding:

Homer Paul Becomes a Benedict.
Garvin County Solon Weds Claremore Girl In Oklahoma City.

Homer Paul, representative to the state legislature from Garvin County, and Miss Helen Lafferty of Claremore were married at the home of Mr. and Mrs. James C. Nance at 530 West Twenty-third street in Oklahoma City, Sunday night, according to announcement in the daily papers, Monday.

The wedding ceremony was performed by Rev. J. R. Cartwright, a House member from Johnston County and father of Congressman Wilburn Cartwright of the Third District, and the wedding, said to be informal, was attended principally by members of the legislature and a few other close friends.

The guests included J. P. Burch and wife of Pauls Valley; Miss May Carter of Pauls Valley; Sen. Paul Stewart of Haworth, wife and daughter, Martha Genia; H. Tom Knight of Claremore, Rogers county representative, and wife; C. C. Hester of Blanchard, McClain county representative, and wife; Tom Collins of Oklahoma City; H. L. Hunter of Purcell and wife; and Mr. and Mrs. Nance and two daughters, Rosamond and Betty; Sen. Dave Boyer of Walters and Mrs. Boyer.

James Nance, who is one of the "anti" leaders, was master of ceremonies for the wedding, the report says, getting the marriage license and arranging all the details. He and Mrs. Nance moved to their city home for the session a bit early so that the wedding could be held there instead of at a local hotel, where, he explained, politicians are too thick for cupid's comfort.

Mr. Paul, who was reared in Pauls Valley, is a great-grandson of Smith Paul, founder of this city, and one of the earlier settlers of this section of Indian Territory and Oklahoma. He was graduated from the Pauls Valley high school, later attending the Oklahoma University at Norman.

Mr. Paul is serving his second term as a member of the state legislature and is expected to be one of the leaders of the twelfth session of this lawmaking body.

The bride is the daughter of Mrs. James Lafferty of Claremore, one of the prominent families of that city, and a leader in social circles.

After the close of the legislative session the happy couple will make their home in Pauls Valley.

The many friends of the contracting parties, both in Pauls Valley and Claremore, will join in wishing them a long, happy and prosperous wedded life.[1]

After the wedding, Snip and Helen moved to Oklahoma City for the 1929 session of the legislature. At the time we were oblivious to what went on there, but Snip was in the thick of things, and it wasn't long before his name was in the headlines. The House was investigating the state highway commission on bribery charges.

During the discussion, J. T. Daniel was speaking against a motion made by Snip to stop the flow of federal money during the investigation, and

Snip raised a point of order, saying that Daniel had already spoken. He was obviously trying to cut Daniel off.

Daniel replied, "You were just asleep."

This raised Snip's hackles, and he replied, "Suppose you put me to sleep."

"I will," said Daniel, as he pulled off his glasses and started toward Snip.

Snip said, "Let him come," and he stood up to meet Daniel.

The sergeant-at-arms, along with other legislators, restrained the two, and they sat back down, but the conflict wasn't over. After exchanging threatening glances, Snip and his antagonist stood again, ready to go at each other. This time the Speaker, Jim Nance, called out, "Put those gentlemen in their seats." Again the two sat down.

Amused by the fracas, Rep. J. Woody Dixon, said, "I move the inkwells be removed." The motion carried.[2]

Snip was getting a reputation for being a young firebrand, but also a force to contend with. This session he had bigger fish to fry than the state highway commission. He was planning to impeach the governor.

Governor Henry S. Johnston was a shy, pious man who spent hours meditating and studying Rosicrucianism. He alienated his own party, not because of his eccentric ways, but because he ignored the legislature and its treasured patronage system in making appointments. Instead of conferring with them, he consulted a medium.

There were a lot of Republicans elected to the House in 1928 on a tide of Republican support for Herbert Hoover. Johnston, a loyal Democrat, had made enemies in both parties by supporting Al Smith, Hoover's opponent. A group of nine Democrats, including Snip and Jim Nance, known as the "Irreconcilables," joined the Republicans in the House in drawing up impeachment charges against the governor. This is the reason that Jim Nance was referred to as an "anti" leader in the newspaper article about Snip and Helen's wedding.

Snip said it was a sad sight to see the governor grilled by the senators. Johnston was on the stand for a week. He was actually guilty of nothing more than misplaced trust. He defended his principles before the senators and was genuinely surprised to hear about some of the things done in his name. Johnston earned everyone's sympathy and respect for his honesty and sincerity. The trial was hard on Snip, especially since he was one of the ones responsible. Afterward he told us, "I never want to be a part of anything like that again." The governor was finally convicted of "incompetence" and forced out of office. In March of 1929, he was replaced by Snip's friend,

Lieutenant Governor Bill Holloway.[3]

In spite of Snip's distaste for the impeachment process, he came out of it with more political power than he had before. After only two terms in the state legislature, he had become one of the most powerful men in the state. From the start of his career, Snip had a knack for picking the winning side.

When the legislature adjourned, he and Helen moved back in with us. Kaliteyo and I were both graduating that spring, she from high school and I from junior high. Snip and Helen came to our graduation ceremonies, and I asked Helen to write another note in my memory book. She wrote:

> *Dearest Jim:*
>
> *Remember you used to say you would be glad when I could write "sister" without the parenthesis, so since last writing in your memory book a ceremony has been consummated that has made this possible and truly that is what I want to be—a sister to you. May you never feel any hesitancy in asking me anything, and I'll always live in hopes and with the thought of being a real sister to you. Perhaps these are not the exact words of what I'm going to write but at least the sentiment is there.*
>
> *"As onward thru this life you go, five things you should remember: Of whom you speak, to whom you speak, and how, and when, and where."*
>
> *Space will only allow me to say one more thing and that is—when many, many years have passed may you and I always have the most pleasant memories of each other.*
>
> *Your Sister,*
>
> *Helen*

By this time, things were different at home. Mama had recovered her health, and she had taken charge of the family again. When Snip and Helen moved back, tension began to build between her and Helen. Helen was a strong woman, and she was used to taking charge, so I suppose it was inevitable. Things came to a head one day at suppertime. Mama snapped at Helen about something, and they started arguing. It wouldn't have been so bad if Snip hadn't been there. He lost his temper and shouted at Mama. She stood her ground, and finally Snip got so mad he picked up Mama's silver cream pitcher and threw it up against the wall.

The next morning, Mama packed us up and moved us out to the farm. She said she wasn't going to live in the same house with "that woman." Soon afterward, Snip and Helen got themselves a garage apartment a few blocks away on Chickasaw Street, and we moved back in. Snip knew he couldn't change Mama's mind. He didn't abandon us though. He continued to visit, and she continued to tattle to him.

Her main concern was Bob. She told Snip she was worried he would get into trouble and asked Snip to send him away to military school. I never understood it. Bob wasn't rebellious, and he hadn't got into any trouble, but Mama probably remembered the trouble she had with Snip at that age, or maybe she still blamed Bob for Willie's death.

Snip, always the negotiator, said yes, but only on one condition. He wanted Willie's farm. Snip already had an allotment of his own—it was over by Blanchard—but he had always been jealous of Willie's allotment, which was on Smith Paul's original homestead. Snip called us all together— Mama, Haskell, Kaliteyo, me, Bob, Teker, and Tom. We all got a say, and we all agreed to let Snip have the farm. For my part, I told Snip I didn't mind him taking it. I just wanted it to stay in the family.

So Snip sent Bob to the Oklahoma Military Academy (OMA) in Claremore. Maybe Mama did what was best. We were poor, and boys think of things to do when they are poor and bored, but I missed my brother. He was my best friend.

I had made a plan for myself, anyway. The next year I would be in high school, and I figured that if I took extra courses I could graduate a year early. I could graduate with my original class and then go to work to help Mama, Oteka, and Tom. My childhood was over, anyway.

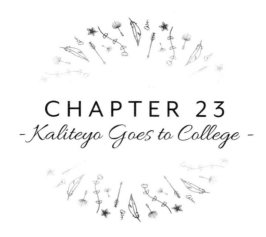

CHAPTER 23
- Kaliteyo Goes to College -

Snip once said he could get more done by manipulating other people than he could by doing things himself, and I can testify to that, because he practiced on us. Bob used to call him "the Manager." Usually I appreciated Snip's wheeling and dealing, even though he took our farm, because most of his deals were for our benefit. I don't know how we would have made it through the Depression without him.

In the spring of 1929, when Haskell graduated from the OU law school, Snip went to our old neighbor, Walter Hart, who had gotten him his first job with the Oklahoma Farm Mortgage Company, and asked him to give Haskell a job. At the time, Mr. Hart was secretary of the Oklahoma School Land Commission, and he hired Haskell as an attorney for the department. The School Land Commission was created by the Oklahoma State Constitution to manage a trust consisting of lands set aside for the benefit of schools. The School Land Department, run by the secretary of the commission, then Mr. Hart, leased land and made loans on property. It carried on a lot of legal work in dealing with the loan contracts, assessment of property values, and collections, so Haskell was busy. He traveled constantly and became acquainted with lawyers and judges all over the state. He was suddenly an important man.[1]

In his new job, Haskell made two hundred dollars a month, which was good money back in those days. His salary would look even better in a year or so as the country sank into the Great Depression. Haskell and Eve could afford to move out of the funeral home. They rented a house in Norman, and Eve continued taking classes in law school. That was a bone of contention between them. He thought she should be content to stay home and be a housewife, but Eve was resolute. She had helped support him during his schooling, so now she felt it was her turn to finish her education. The way things turned out, it's a good thing she did.

Snip made another arrangement that summer. He convinced Haskell to send Kaliteyo to college. It didn't make much sense to me at the time. Snip hadn't even been to college himself. Mama didn't care. In her day, women didn't go to college. She just wanted us to be fed and clothed. I don't know. Maybe Helen had something to do with it.

I can picture Snip approaching Haskell with the idea. He would have told him, "Now that I've gotten you a good-paying job, you can help the family out by putting your sisters through college. You live right there in Norman, so you can give them a place to stay while they go to school, and they can help Eve with the baby." Little Tom was barely weaned.

At the time, it didn't occur to me that I would also become part of Snip's plan. Kaliteyo had just graduated from high school, and college was the furthest thing from her mind. After our family's tragedy, she had decided to dedicate her life to God and become a nun. She wanted to go back to St. Elizabeth's, where she had been so happy as a schoolgirl. Haskell was tactful. He argued that although she might be happy at first, the life of a nun would eventually be too confining for her. He said, "Why don't you just try college for a year? See if you like it." He and Kaliteyo had always been close, so she listened to him, and finally she agreed to go.

Well, when Kaliteyo started to school, she went from sublime to ridiculous. She transformed herself from a nun into a party girl. Soon she had pledged a sorority and was spending her evenings having a good time. Meanwhile, Eve was expecting her to help out with the baby. Haskell wasn't paying much attention to all of this until one night he came home to discover that Eve was missing a late class because Kaliteyo had gone to a party and had left her at home to take care of Little Tom.

Haskell was furious. He stormed out of the house, walked down to Kaliteyo's sorority house, and burst in on the party. When he found her, he loudly announced that she was needed at home and then proceeded to drag her out. Kaliteyo was humiliated. On the way, Haskell informed her that she was there to get an education, not to have fun. He went on to say that as a member of his household she had duties; he and Eve were doing her

Kaliteyo Mahota Paul

a favor in letting her stay with them, and in return she had an obligation to help out with Little Tom. How did she think they were going to pay sorority dues, anyway? He had a job, but that didn't mean he was made out of money. Haskell could make you feel about two feet tall when he wanted to, and he disliked fraternity and sororities, anyway, because of the way he had been snubbed by them when he was a student. So that was the end of sorority life for Kaliteyo.

She was well acquainted with Haskell, so she soon got over the shock of his outburst, and when she thought about it, she realized they couldn't afford for her to belong to a sorority, so she started taking her turn watching Little Tom. She didn't really mind babysitting; she loved babies. Soon, their lives settled into a routine. Both Kaliteyo and Eve went to their classes, and Kaliteyo watched Little Tom when she was asked.

Kaliteyo majored in fine arts at OU. She was a good artist, and she won a place in a special program for Native American art students headed by Oscar Jacobson, dean of the Art School. Jacobson's program would launch the careers of several Native American artists, including the famous Potawatomi artist, Woody Crumbo.[2] Kaliteyo started applying herself, and she did well, at least for a while.

One day, when she came home to babysit, she found Little Tom lethargic and weak, his diaper wet from diarrhea. She got Eve, and they rushed him to the doctor. Tom was badly dehydrated, and he had to be admitted to the hospital for intravenous fluids. The doctor told them Tom must have been sick for several days.

The experience scared Kaliteyo. She decided Eve couldn't be trusted to take care of her own baby, and that as long as she was there, she was going to see after him herself, even if it meant giving up her study time. For all intents and purposes, that was the end of Kaliteyo's college career.

Meanwhile, back in Pauls Valley, the Depression had started, but it didn't make much difference to us. Like Mama said, "You don't know what a depression is unless you've had prosperity."[3] Actually, thanks to Snip, we did better than most. In addition to providing for his family and sending Bob to OMA, he supported Mama and the rest of us still living at home. It must have been hard on him, especially after Mama had kicked him and Helen out of our house. He was always in a bad mood, and we didn't dare ask him for money. His stock answer was, "I don't have a nickel."

During Kaliteyo's first year at OU, I started high school, and I continued singing in the glee club and the girl's quartet. Mama still wasn't speaking to Helen, but I visited her anyway. She was expecting now, and she had gotten involved in Pauls Valley society, even though she was a newcomer in town. She invited me to sing for the Pauls Valley Music Club, but Mama wouldn't let me.

Mama immersed herself in her gardening and in her younger children, Teker and Tom. They used to talk about the whippings Mama gave them, but actually, they got off easier than we did. Mama knew she couldn't have any more children, so she was lenient. They'd run all over the house with their little friends, yelling and slamming doors. We could never have gotten away with that.

Tom was Mama's baby, and she especially spoiled him. If it was cloudy outside, he would say, "Mama, do I have to go to school today?" and she would let him stay home. I'd say, "Mama, Tom needs to go to school," but it didn't make any difference. She enjoyed having Tom at home. Of course, he got behind in his studies, and then Mama had to tutor him. She wasn't easy on him—I'll give her that. She'd drill him until he got it right.[4]

In the spring, Bob came home from OMA. His natural skill at riding horses had earned him a place on the polo team, and he even made good grades. He used the little bit of money he saved from the allowance Snip had given him to buy a trombone. He tooted on that thing all summer long, trying to get good enough to try out for the OMA band.

He spent the rest of his spare time that summer matching fights for our little brother Tom. He had decided Tom needed to be educated in the manly arts. Mama didn't find out about it until he got Tom into a fight with somebody who was a little too big for him. Tom got mad and took out after Bob with our BB gun. Bob wasn't afraid of getting shot, but he ran away from Tom just for fun and climbed up into the pear tree next to our garage. That little BB gun was so puny you could barely feel the BBs when they hit you—I used to play with it myself—but when Tom shot him, Bob fell out of the tree, laughing all the time. It was about then that Mama caught them. She took the gun away, broke it in two, and threw it into the fireplace. After what had happened to Willie, Mama had a phobia about guns.

After destroying our little BB gun, Mama took up the issue of Bob arranging fights for Tom. I remember Bob's response: "But Mama, don't you want Tom to learn how to fight?" To him, it was just a necessary part of Tom's education.

CHAPTER 24
- Papa Passes Out of Our Lives -

Papa got out of prison in the summer of 1929. His lawyer had filed an appeal, and he was released on bail. He got a room down at the Royal Theater, upstairs next to the neon sign that announced what movie was playing. We knew where he was, but we didn't talk about it. I'm sure Papa had plenty of visitors, though. He still had a lot of friends—John Garvin, Ed Low, Iman McClure, Ikard Paul, and of course, Uncle Buck. I found out later that Haskell went down to see him too, and also Helen. She took him food and washed his clothes. It was just like her to be loyal and caring.

Papa started drinking again—he must have been trying to kill himself—and his dropsy came back. His legs swelled, and his belly filled up with fluid. He spent several months in Oklahoma City at the University Hospital. I learned about all of this later. He was released from the hospital in April of 1930, and he came back to his room at the Royal Theater. After that, he went back to Oklahoma City from time to time to get his fluid drained off.

Being in the hospital must have been a relief for Papa. There he was treated like an ordinary patient, not having to endure the looks of his neighbors who knew that he had killed his own son. Years later, I met a nurse who had taken care of Papa at the hospital. She knew nothing of our tragedy. She was Chickasaw, and evidently Papa had taken a liking to her during his hospital stay. She said he never complained, but teased and joked with her in Chickasaw and called her his "little Indian Princess."

156

Finally, after one of his visits to the hospital, Papa fell on the stairs going up to his room and busted open the place where they had drained his fluid. After that, he developed a fever, and the doctor diagnosed him with peritonitis. Papa told the doctor he didn't want to go back to the hospital. Helen came to Mama and told her Papa was dying, so Mama took us all up to his room to see him one last time. I remember standing there, not knowing what to do or what to say. Papa was real sick, but he seemed glad we came. Finally as we were leaving, Mama leaned over and kissed him on the forehead.

Papa had always been a Presbyterian, I suppose because of the Presbyterian missionaries back in Indian Territory, so his funeral was at the Presbyterian Church. We all sat down in front with Mama. All I can remember about the service was Ed Low speaking. Papa had staked Mr. Low when he first came to Pauls Valley, and Ed was always loyal to him. The newspaper summarized his comments:

Funeral Services Held for William H. Paul
Native Citizen Died Monday Night, Following Long Illness

Funeral services for W. H. Paul, 54 years old and native citizen, were held from the Stufflebean-Meyer funeral home Tuesday afternoon, September 23 at 4 o'clock, conducted by Rev. P. D. Tucker, pastor of the Presbyterian church. Interment was made in Mt Olivet cemetery.

E. W. Low, an old friend of the Pauls, paid a beautiful tribute to the achievements of the deceased during the constructive periods of this community, pointing out some of the joys and successes and the trials and disappointments that characterized the life of W. H. Paul.

The deceased was born March 5, 1876, a mile and a half southwest of Pauls Valley, and died Monday night, September 22, his exact age being 54 years, 6 months and 17 days. Diabetes was the cause of his death.

Paul became dangerously ill in September 1929 and was carried to Oklahoma City, where he was in the hospital under medical care until April of this year when he returned home. His condition was such, however, that but little hopes were entertained for his recovery. He was confined to his room and in bed most of the time, until the end came.

157

He was a son of Mr. and Mrs. Sam Paul and a grandson of Smith Paul in whose honor Pauls Valley was named. His mother, before her marriage, was Sarah Lambert. She died a few years ago in Chickasha.

W. H. Paul was a man of unusual ability and at one time wielded a great influence in this community, according to old timers who knew him best. Many brick buildings in Pauls Valley, including the Masonic temple, stand as a monument to the untiring energy of this man, who so often was sorely tried and tempted, and who probably yielded to his temptations more often than he resisted them.

The deceased is survived by his wife and seven children and one brother, all of whom were present at the funeral services. The children are: Homer Paul member of the state legislature, Haskell, Tom, Robert, Kaliteo, Wynona, and Oteka. The brother is Sam W. (Buck) Paul of this city.

In the passing of W. H. Paul another old landmark has been removed from this community. To the surviving wife, brother and children, whose minds have been disturbed and whose hearts have been bleeding, goes out the sincere sympathy of the people of this entire community.[1]

I've spent most of my life hating Papa for what he did to Willie. One time I took all the pictures I had of him and Mama together and cut his image off. Another time I came upon a picture of him looking confident and smug, and I got the scissors out and cut it to pieces. I shouldn't have done it. Later I tried to repair the picture, but there was a lot of damage. I wish I had those pictures back now, but I hated Papa so much at the time.

My brothers and sisters didn't all feel the same way about him. Haskell and Kaliteyo thought that Mama drove him to drink by her nagging, but they grew up during happier times and knew a different side of him. Bob agreed with me, and I think Snip did, too. Snip admired Willie and looked up to him. Teker and Tom loved Willie, too, but I don't think they hated Papa like I did.

I can also see now that Mama was partly to blame for Papa's troubles. She should never have shut him out after little Victoria died, and she should have stopped having babies after Kaliteyo. The responsibility was too much for Papa. There were just too many of us.

Still, I could never have any feelings for Papa after what he did, although I can't deny he was a remarkable man. He was proud and ambitious, cheerful and popular, and he became wealthy during a time in history when men succeeded or failed by their native intelligence and by the strength of their personalities. He rejected the violence, the promiscuity, the irresponsibility, and the hard-heartedness of his father, Sam Paul, but he did things his family never forgave him for. I don't think he ever forgave himself, either.

When Papa was found dead in his room, there was a book of poetry lying next to him opened to this poem. He must have wanted us to read it.

The House by the Side of the Road by Sam Walter Foss

There are hermit souls that live withdrawn
In their place of their self-content;
There are souls like stars, that dwell apart,
In a fellowless firmament;
There are pioneer souls that blaze the paths
Where highways never ran-
But let me live by the side of the road
And be a friend to man.

Let me live in a house by the side of the road,
Where the race of men go by-
The men who are good and the men who are bad,
As good and as bad as I.
I would not sit in the scorner's seat,
Or hurl the cynic's ban-
Let me live in a house by the side of the road
And be a friend to man.

I see from my house by the side of the road
By the side of the highway of life,
The men who press with the ardor of hope,
The men who are faint with the strife,
But I turn not away from their smiles and tears,

Both parts of an infinite plan-
Let me live in a house by the side of the road
And be a friend to man.

I know there are brook-gladdened meadows ahead,
And mountains of wearisome height;
That the road passes on through the long afternoon
And stretches away to the night.
And still I rejoice when the travelers rejoice
And weep with the strangers that moan,
Nor live in my house by the side of the road
Like a man who dwells alone.

Let me live in my house by the side of the road,
Where the race of men go by-
They are good, they are bad, they are weak, they are strong,
Wise, foolish – so am I.
Then why should I sit in the scorner's seat,
Or hurl the cynic's ban?
Let me live in my house by the side of the road
And be a friend to man.[2]

The poem didn't make sense to me when I first read it, because it's about a generous man who asks for no reward. Papa certainly was generous, but it still didn't seem to fit him. But then, as I read the poem again and again, it began to dawn on me that Papa wasn't identifying with the man in the house by the side of the road. Instead, he must have thought of himself as one of the poor, miserable failures who sought comfort in spite of their failings.

He was asking for forgiveness.

Papa was buried in our family plot out at Mount Olivet Cemetery, and thirty years later, when Mama died, she was laid to rest next to him.

CHAPTER 25
- I Graduate from High School -

Kaliteyo was a "butt-insky," always butting into my life where she didn't belong. In 1930, Pauls Valley High School announced plans to restore the girls basketball program, a proud tradition during the early days. The "Bloomer Girls," as they were called, had won the state championship in 1911, and OU's renowned coach, Bennie Owen, said they were "the best team that ever played on the University of Oklahoma gymnasium floor."[1] I wanted to play on the team so bad I could taste it. It didn't matter to me that I was only five feet tall. I just knew I could play better than those bigger girls.

But butt-insky Kaliteyo said, "No," as she reminded Mama of my fall from the swing in the third grade. "Jim shouldn't play. Her side is weak from her fall, and she might reinjure herself." So Mama didn't let me try out. She should have asked Bob how weak I was. I could certainly stand up to him.

Anyway, I didn't play basketball that year, but I did keep singing, and I also represented our school in Latin at the district meet. My plan to graduate a year early was still intact. I made sure all my courses counted toward graduation, and I took Spanish in summer school. I also made a new friend, Carrie O'Harro, who lived down the street from us. She and I would walk home from school together. We went to the show sometimes too, when Carrie's father would give her the money. He had plenty. He was just stingy.

In the fall of 1930, Snip was re-elected to the state legislature, and "Alfalfa" Bill Murray was elected governor. Murray was an attorney who had moved to Indian Territory from Texas in 1898. He settled in Tishomingo, where he met and later married Mary Alice Hearrell, the niece of Douglas Johnston, the Chickasaw governor. Murray represented the Chickasaw Nation at the Sequoyah Convention, and the next year he was elected chairman of the Oklahoma Constitutional Convention.

Murray had been out of politics for fifteen years when he ran for governor, but the Depression was right up his alley. He claimed to represent the "common man" and he certainly acted the part. He borrowed forty dollars from the Bank of Tishomingo and went on the campaign trail, subsisting on crackers and cheese.

Murray's opponent, a wealthy oil man named Frank Buttram, treated Murray's candidacy with contempt, but the farmers and workers of the state saw in Murray a kindred spirit, and they voted him into office.

Snip had the political sense to support Murray's candidacy, so his star became brighter after the election. His name began to be mentioned as a prospect for Speaker of the House.[2] He must have swallowed hard, though, when Alfalfa Bill released two thousand felons from the state prison as a cost-cutting measure.[3]

On November 25, just three days before Willie's birthday, Helen delivered a baby boy. She and Snip named him William George Paul, after his uncle, and we immediately dubbed him "Little Willie." Willie was a chubby little baby, with jet-black hair. Every day after school I would go over to Helen and Snip's apartment to see him. I'd hold him and sing to him. He'd just coo.

The birth of Little Willie softened Mama's resentment against Helen, and we had a real family Christmas that year. Snip and Helen were there with Little Willie, Bob was home from OMA, and Haskell and Eve came down from Norman with Little Tom and Kaliteyo.

During the Christmas break, Bob looked up his old friend, Toodles Jackson. Toodles' father had bought him a motorcycle for Christmas, and it had a sidecar, so after spending Christmas with their families, Toodles and Bob went over to the ditch, and drove the motorcycle up and down the side of the levee, with Bob in the sidecar. On their third or fourth pass,

Toodles crested the levee going all out, and the motorcycle flipped over, dumping Bob out. As Bob fell, his head hit a rock and he was knocked out cold. Toodles brought him home and carried him up the steps. He was as limp as a rag. Mama had Toodles lay him down on her bed.

Mama called young Dr. Callaway, who came right over. After he had examined Bob, he told Mama he didn't think Bob was paralyzed, but since he was still unconscious, he couldn't be sure he was okay. He said there was nothing he could do. We would just have to wait and see what happened. He said if Bob woke up before morning, he would probably be all right. We all sat in Mama's bedroom and watched. Toodles was scared to death. He'd pace back and forth for a while and then go out and get firewood. He kept the fire in Mama's bedroom going all night long. Finally, early the next morning, Bob woke up. We all breathed a sigh of relief.

After the Christmas holidays, the legislature convened. They rejected Murray's proposals to increase taxes on corporations, but they did create a tax commission, and through it Murray was able to improve collection of corporate taxes and reduce property assessments on farm land to give the farmers a break.[4] The School Land Department, which handled leases and loans to farmers, was critical to the plan. Soon after the election, Murray called Haskell into his office and told him to go easy on loan foreclosures.

One day, early in April, Mama got a call from Haskell. Kaliteyo hadn't come home the night before. He wanted to know if she had come back to Pauls Valley. No, Mama said, she hadn't seen her. Haskell called Snip, and both of them drove down to Pauls Valley. Still, no one had heard from her. I was scared to death. I knew Kaliteyo hadn't been happy at school, and I was afraid something bad had happened to her. I asked all of her friends if they had seen her, and then I searched everywhere—the house, the garage, the barn, and the cellar.

Finally, after Snip and Haskell left, Kaliteyo appeared out of nowhere. Mama didn't seem surprised. She must have known where Kaliteyo was all the time. She told us she refused to go back to school. She said she had been unhappy living with Haskell for over a year, now, and she just couldn't take it any longer. Mama told Kaliteyo she didn't have to go back to school if she didn't want to. Later that night, Mama called Snip and Haskell and told them she was all right.

It was years later that Kaliteyo told me where she was hiding. She was right there in the hall closet, the only place I didn't think to look.

She moped around the house for the next week or so. She didn't look for a job. She didn't visit any of her friends. I couldn't figure it out. It was out of character for her, at least the part about not visiting her friends. Then finally the truth came out. Kaliteyo admitted she was married, and pregnant, but not necessarily in that order. Mama was embarrassed and hurt.

Kaliteyo's new husband was a country boy named Richard Willingham, from Paoli, a small town just north of Pauls Valley. Kaliteyo had met him in high school, when he and his buddies would come down to Pauls Valley to have a good time. Why Kaliteyo was attracted to Richard, I couldn't fathom. He was real tall, wore his hair slicked back with grease, and thought he was God's gift to women. He also had a big stomach. I used to call him a "tub on two sticks." It wasn't that Kaliteyo didn't have a choice. There was an engineering student down at OU named Cooksey who was just crazy about her, but Kaliteyo was never sensible about anything.

Mama decided to try and make the best of the situation. She invited Richard over to meet us, and she threw a shower for Kaliteyo. Helen helped out, and I sang "A Gypsy Love Song"—appropriate for Kaliteyo, I thought—accompanying myself on my ukulele. Kaliteyo must have laid it on thick when she gave the story to the Pauls Valley newspaper. They reported she was a member of the Kappa Upsilon sorority, the one Haskell had dragged her out of, and she and Richard would be living in Kilgore, Texas, where "Mr. Willingham will engage in the real estate business."

What "the real estate business" actually amounted to was Richard's father renting a farm for the rest of the year. The whole Willingham family was moving down to Kilgore to try and bring in one good crop and make some money. It was the beginning of a hard year for Kaliteyo. She knew nothing about being a farmer's wife.[5]

While Kaliteyo was ruining her life, I was trying to carry out my plan to graduate from high school with my original classmates and then go to work to help the family.

I figured I had enough credits, after carefully choosing my courses and going to summer school. In my mind, the only problem left was to prove that I was old enough to be in the senior class. The school records showed my birthday as November 16, 1913, which made me a year older than most of my fellow juniors, but I still wouldn't have been quite five when I started school in 1918. I asked Mama, and all she would say was, "you were all born three years apart." Well, Kaliteyo was born in 1909, and Bob 1915, so maybe my birthdate was actually 1912, which would definitely make me old enough to be in the senior class, so I went down to the courthouse to look at my birth certificate. The date looked like 1913, but it was smudged, so I went back to Mama.

I asked Mama if she could remember anything that happened about the time I was born—anything I could look up—and finally, she said: "I do remember that Mrs. Bradley lost a baby boy just before you were born. He died of pneumonia. She thought she'd never be able to have another child. You might be able to find his grave out at the cemetery." So the next Saturday, I walked out to Mount Olivet Cemetery.

It was a long walk, probably a couple of miles, and on the way the sky started to cloud up. I found the Bradley plot, and as I started looking at the headstones, it started raining. Soon, I was sloshing through the mud from one grave to the next. I found two or three headstones that may have been for babies, but they were weathered so badly I couldn't make out the dates. I was drenched to the bone when I got home.

What I did next I've never admitted to anyone, but I was desperate. It just meant everything to me to be able to walk across the stage with my original classmates.

I changed the date on my birth certificate to 1912.

Armed with "proof" that I deserved to be in the senior class, I went to Mr. Morrison, the principal. I explained to him that since our family had moved around so much when I was little, I had fallen behind the other children in my class at Pauls Valley, so they had put me back a grade. I went on to say I had taken extra courses to catch up with my class, and I had proof (my forged birth certificate) that I was old enough to be a senior.

Mr. Morrison listened patiently while I presented my case. Then he looked at my record. He said the date on my birth certificate didn't matter. I still hadn't satisfied all the requirements to graduate. I needed one more course, American literature. That was a total surprise to me. I thought I had it all figured out. "Please, Mr. Morrison," I begged. "I can take American literature in summer school. Just let me walk across the stage with my classmates." But he was firm. I wouldn't be allowed to graduate with my class.

I performed with the girls' quartet at the graduation ceremony, but afterward I had to sit there and watch while Carrie and all the rest of my classmates filed by to pick up their diplomas without me.

That summer I took American literature, and I got my diploma in the fall, so technically I was included in the class of 1931, but it wasn't the same as walking across the stage with them. The only bright spot was Snip—old, grumpy, "I don't have a nickel" Snip. He bought me a class ring, and he told me once again that he was proud of me.

CHAPTER 26
- Haskell Tricks Me into Enrolling at OU -

Snip and Helen moved out to the farm that summer with Little Willie. They had built their house over the foundation of Sam Paul's old house, where Papa was born. It didn't have modern conveniences like gas and electricity, and Helen cooked on a wood-burning stove, like Mama used to do.

Snip did have a water tank built at the farm, and he had a windmill put in to pump water up from the well, so there was running water in the kitchen, even though they still used an outhouse for a while. Helen planted a garden, and Snip bought some chickens, hogs, and cattle. They also cleaned out the old dairy barn that had been built by a family who rented our farm while we were in San Antonio, and they started selling milk. It was an off year for the legislature—they only met every other year—so Snip had time to spend on the project.

In spite of the hardships, Snip and Helen were soon relatively comfortable. Mama and Helen were still getting along, so we visited back and forth, especially Snip. He was a nervous father, and it seemed like every time Little Willie got the sniffles, Snip would come into town to ask Mama what she thought they should do. It tickled me to see my brother's softer side.

Since jobs were scarce, and since Snip was in the state legislature, people often came to him looking for work. One day during that summer, a job hunter came knocking on his door, and Snip recognized him as one of the men who had turned him down when he was looking for a job after his high school graduation. He told the man, "I'll give you the same consideration you gave me when I needed a job. Get off my porch before I throw you off!"

I tried to get a job in Pauls Valley that summer, since my American literature course didn't take up that much of my time, but to no avail. The only jobs to be had during the Depression were at the courthouse, Wacker's,[1] or the laundry, and those were all taken, so my plans to go to work to help Mama, Teker, and Tom were frustrated.

It was about that time that Snip and Haskell started working on me to go to college. You would have thought they'd give up, after failing so miserably with Kaliteyo, but they kept after me all summer. I said no, that I was planning to get a job, but as the summer dragged on and I still didn't have one, my resistance started to break down. One weekend, Haskell invited me to come home with him for a visit. "Eve would like to see you, and you haven't seen Little Tom for a while. He's growing like a weed," he said. Haskell could be very charming. So I agreed to go home with him for a couple of days. As we drove toward Norman, he said, "Say, Jim, the OU entrance exam is tomorrow. Why don't you take it? Just for fun. See if you can pass it." So I took the college entrance exam. I suppose Haskell's challenge awakened my competitive nature. The test wasn't really that hard. I remember that for my English composition I wrote my stock theme, "My Narrow Escape," about almost drowning in Rush Creek.

The next day I had a nice visit with Haskell and Eve, and I played with Little Tom, who was three, and just old enough to get into things. On Sunday Haskell took me home, and I settled back into my routine. Three weeks later, to my surprise, I got an acceptance letter from OU. I had almost forgotten about taking the test.

Once the letter came, it was hard to say no. Snip and Haskell were more excited than I was, but I wasn't doing anything, anyway, so I started planning to go to college. I talked with Miss Shi, the choir director at Pauls Valley High School, and she encouraged me to go to the Fine Arts School and major in voice. She said I had real talent, so I started dreaming about becoming a choir director like her, or even an opera singer. Miss Shi had graduated from OU herself, and she gave me a nice letter of introduction to her sorority.

It was just about this time that Richard and Kaliteyo came back through town from Kilgore, Texas, where they had been farming. They were driving a big car. I forget what kind it was, but Richard had bought it with his share of the fall harvest money. They seemed happy, but Kaliteyo was pale and thin. She was working herself to death out there on the farm. She wasn't used to hard work, and she was pregnant, to boot. It upset us to see her that way.

As soon as they left, Mama called Snip and asked him to try and get Richard a job in town so Kaliteyo wouldn't have to live on the farm. Once again Snip pulled strings, and soon he had found Richard a good job with the highway department in Cement, a little town near Paoli, where the Willinghams lived.

After Richard had gotten settled in his new job, Kaliteyo invited me to come up to Paoli to spend a week with her. She drove down to get me in their fancy new car. Kaliteyo was bubbly and full of sisterly love, not at all like her. She spent a couple of nights at home with us in Pauls Valley, and while she was there, Mrs. Garvin came by.[2] Mrs. Garvin would walk over to see Mama from time to time, and when she was ready to go, one of us would walk her home. While she visited with Mama, Kaliteyo and I went into Mama's bedroom and pierced my ears. I wanted to be able to wear earrings at OU, and Kaliteyo had seen the other girls pierce each other's ears at St. Elizabeth's, so she experimented on me. She pinched my ear lobes until they were numb, stuck a sewing needle through each one, and then pulled the needle through, leaving a ring of thread through the holes. When we finished, we were proud of our work, but when Mama found out, she was furious. "I can't turn my back on you girls without you getting into trouble!" she fumed. Mama was sure my ears would get infected. Mrs. Garvin just smiled.

The next day Kaliteyo and I left for Paoli, with detailed instructions from Mama about how to take care of my ears. Kaliteyo was excited about me going to OU, and she filled me with stories about how much fun I was going to have there. It was all a lot of hooey, of course, but I believed her at the time.

It was during this visit with Kaliteyo that I found out what kind of man she had married. Like I said before, I never liked Richard from the start, so I avoided him, but it was a little hard in a one-bedroom house. One day, while Kaliteyo was hanging out the laundry, Richard cornered me in the hall, put his big arms around me, and tried to kiss me! I slapped his greasy face, pushed him away as hard as I could, and then ran outside. I didn't dare scream for fear Kaliteyo would find out what had happened. That would have been the end of our newfound sisterly love. During the remaining two days of my visit I was terrified he would try something again, but he didn't. I was never so glad to get away from anyplace in my life. I never told Kaliteyo what happened.

A couple of weeks later, Haskell took me to Norman, and I started school. I didn't get to come home for a while, but I carried on a lively correspondence with Teker, and she kept me up on all the gossip. According to what she heard, Richard and his brothers still came to Pauls Valley on weekends and caroused with the local girls. The old man would even come down with them. Teker tattled to Kaliteyo, too—she was fearless—but Kaliteyo stayed with Richard, at least for the time being.

My first couple of weeks at OU were exciting. I enrolled as a fine arts major, and in addition to the usual freshman courses, I took voice, chorus, and Italian. Voice majors all had to take Italian and German in order to sing operas.

I took Miss Shi's letter over to her sorority, and the girls seemed really excited to meet me. They weren't even put off by my dark skin. They started calling me their "Indian Princess," and they invited me to a party they were giving for pledges. At the time, I didn't know about Kaliteyo's experience with Haskell.

On the first day of class, I found out that I would have to audition to get into the OU chorus. One of the voice coaches took me aside and had me sing a little to get an idea of what my natural range was. She told me I was a mezzo-soprano, and then she gave me a part to learn for the audition. I had a week to get ready.

That stymied me at first, because I couldn't read music. Miss Shi taught me all my parts, and I always just sang by ear. So there I was with a piece of music to learn, and I didn't even know what it was supposed to sound like. Luckily for me, I met another girl that day who had signed up for the chorus, and she could play the piano. I confessed to her that I couldn't read notes, and I begged her to teach me my part. She said she would not only teach me my notes, she would also play an accompaniment for me on the piano. I was tickled pink.

We had about a week to practice our parts, my friend and I—I can't remember her name now—and we worked hard together. On the day of the audition, we went in and performed. I was really nervous, but I thought we did pretty well, considering we only had a week to practice. The auditions went on for several days, and we were told to return at the end of the week when the results would be posted. That Friday afternoon, my friend and

I returned and found out we had both been accepted. I rushed home to share the good news with Haskell and Eve.

Haskell came home early that evening, and he was sitting at the kitchen table, looking at some papers, when I came in. When I blurted out that I had passed the audition and had been accepted into the chorus, he turned around slowly, gave me this withering look, and said, "What do you think you're doin'? Do you think you're gonna be an opera star?" I was crushed.

Haskell explained he had just gotten a bill from the university for my fees, and the fee for the chorus was fifty dollars. Hell, I didn't know that, or I wouldn't have enrolled in the first place. Then he proceeded to lecture me on how he couldn't afford to subsidize foolishness.

His put-down ended my dreams, but maybe he was right. We didn't have the money for the chorus fee, and I had no background in music. I just loved to sing. His words cut me to the quick, though. I went out the next day, dropped the chorus and my other music classes, and then transferred from the fine arts school to domestic science. I figured I would just learn to cook and sew. I also went over to the sorority house and told them I wouldn't be back. I suddenly understood why Kaliteyo had quit school.

I did stay in my Italian class. I liked languages. Chemistry was required for domestic science, too, so I enrolled in that, and also in dress design. I couldn't afford books, so I just went to the classes and tried to take good notes. The chemistry lectures didn't make any sense to me, so I dropped that course after a couple of weeks. The only class I really liked was Italian. My teacher, Dr. Scatori, was from Florence, in northern Italy, where the people were dark like me. He even thought I was Italian, at first, and started calling me "Signorina Paul." I just loved him. It fascinated me to watch him talk. His teeth fit together perfectly, and he never opened his mouth when he spoke. He was a tiny, little man, and his wife was a huge German woman.

Meanwhile, back home with Haskell and Eve, I was miserable. It wasn't just Haskell and his nasty temper. He was my brother, and I was kind of used to that. It was Eve. She went out of her way to make sure I knew I wasn't welcome. Every night when Haskell came home, they would argue. They argued about money, they argued about her continuing in school, they argued about having to support me. The walls were thin, so I heard everything. I would have rather picked cotton or mopped floors than sit there and listen to that, but I felt an obedience, an obligation, or something that kept me from quitting. In other words, I was chicken. So the year dragged on. I did fairly well in English and Italian, but I barely passed the rest. All I wanted to do was to go back home, get a job, and help Mama.

Kaliteyo's daughter was born November 5, 1931, just before the Thanksgiving break. She named her Lahoma Oteka, after our little sister. Teker was beside herself. She wrote me a letter as soon as she got the news, and she put the most important piece of information on the outside of the envelope, so I would see it first:

> *I got a letter this morning and Kaliteyo has a baby girl & named it after me & will be home Xmas.*

The letter inside was written with Teker's usual bubbly enthusiasm:

> *Dear Jim:*
>
> *I have just finished writing to Kaliteyo but will take time to scribble a few lines to you before going to bed. May Lollar and Lib Pyeate are the sophomore canadats for Football Queen and Nellie Gross and Elizabeth Plaster are the Seniors and Juanita Harmon and another girl are for Freshman and I can't think of the Junior Canadates but we won a game Fri with Ada the score was 13 to 0.*
>
> *I will expect you Wednesday or Thurs. Tell Eve I have had her letter written 3 days but just have not had time to mail it and I had plans for this week end and was dissapointed (as usual) so will have to write another. I have two risens on my face. One as large as a nickle and One as large as a dime but they will be well before you come for they are healing fast. I had a risen on my leg as large as a 50 [cent] piece but it is well now. I have 3 in-growing toenails. One is almost well now though because I pulled the nail off of it nite before last. Will you be here for Thanksgiving dinner? How long is your vacation? We have been having quite a bit of cold weather. Bob has killed one duck and about 5 squirrels.*
>
> *Wonder what little Oteka looks like? I bet she is pretty because she has black hair and black eyes and her hair is curly when it rains.*
>
> *Wenona Hibdon's mother has a new baby girl and named it Jerry Anne. This is a very interesting letter isn't it? I sure will be glad when Christmas comes won't you? Santa Claus is coming and so is Kaliteyo and little Oteka.*
>
> *Jim what are you doing for shoes? Was the rain coat and socks*

ok? Haskell paid for the raincoat. I must go help Mama—this is next morning. I have something very important to tell you when you come.

Love,

Oteka.

Teker was so cute. I can't remember what the "important" item was that she wanted to tell me when I got home for Thanksgiving. All I remember is being glad to be home for a while with Mama and the rest of the family.

Once I was back at OU, I faced another obstacle. One of my assignments for dress design class was to design and make an outfit. I drew the patterns, and I did the other work for the class, but I simply couldn't afford to buy material for the dress. I only owned one skirt, and I tried to make my two blouses look different by wearing them with different colored scarves. My shoes had holes in them, so I put cardboard inside to keep my bare feet off the ground. Finally, Eve gave me a pair of her old shoes to wear. After seeing Haskell's reaction to my chorus fee, there was no way I was going to ask him for money to buy cloth to make a dress.

Our dress design teacher had scheduled a style show near the end of the semester for us to model our creations. I had already resigned myself to the fact that I would probably flunk the class, but I didn't want to embarrass myself by having to stand up and admit I was too poor to buy material for a dress. My plan was to skip class that day, and then just hand in my drawings and patterns later, but I got the date wrong. I walked in on the day of the style show and noticed too late that the other girls were dressed up. I was sitting too close to the front to slip out. My only hope was that the teacher would take pity on me and not make me stand up. No such luck. She called on me and I had to stand in front of the class and admit that I hadn't done the assignment. If looks could kill, she would have fallen down dead, right then and there.

That was it. After the class was over I went straight to the administration building and dropped all my classes. I was done humiliating myself.

It would have been hard to admit to Haskell what I had done, so I didn't. I just kept getting up every morning and leaving like I was going to class, and then I sat in the student union building until time to go home. I figured if I could just make it till Christmas break, it would be too late to re-enroll, but my plan didn't work. Haskell got the blue slips in the mail after about a week. He called Snip and then all hell broke loose. Snip drove up from Pauls Valley, and he and Haskell proceeded to lecture me about the importance of a college education, how persistence would build my character, blah, blah, blah. I ignored most of it, but Haskell did say one thing that has stayed with me. He said a college degree is an accomplishment nobody can ever take from you, and that's true. Of course, he had to repeat it a few more times before I graduated.

Anyway, I gave in and re-enrolled in my classes. I went to the office of the dress design teacher and told her I couldn't afford the material for the dress. She let me know that the look I gave her had made an impression. She told me no one had ever looked at her that way before. I figured she had just never been around any Pauls. I made it through the semester, though, and we had another family Christmas. It was so good to be home again. Everyone was so excited about Kaliteyo's baby, Bob was full of stories from his semester at OMA, Snip and Helen were there with Little Willie, and of course, Teker and Tom were as cute as ever. Even Haskell was in a good mood. When it came time to go back to Norman, things didn't seem so bad.

CHAPTER 27
- Getting Back My Self-Respect -

After the holidays, I went back to OU, but it wasn't long before I was miserable again. Haskell was still grumpy, and Eve still resented my living with them. In spite of his occasional pep talk, Haskell frustrated every attempt I made to make my life more bearable. He put a stop to my music, my social life—even something practical, like my dress design course. He robbed me of my self-esteem. So I gave up. I didn't have a major. I didn't have a plan. I took just what courses I needed to get by and waited for Snip and Haskell to give up on me so I could go home and do what I could to help Mama, Teker, and Tom.

I enrolled in courses with no fees, and I continued to get along without textbooks. I did enroll in one course I thought I might actually enjoy, a journalism class, working on the school yearbook. The teacher of the class was Savoie Lottinville, who later became head of the OU Press. He took a personal interest in the yearbook, and I learned a lot by working with him. He had me put together stories about some of the professors, interviewing them and learning about their backgrounds. Some of them were very interesting people, like Dr. Scatori, my Italian teacher.

Haskell was gone a lot, so Eve and I were thrown together much of the time, which was an ordeal, to say the least. She was cordial enough, but I knew she didn't want me there. I guess she had resigned herself to the situation the same as I had. She was taking law courses and getting ready to take the bar exam, so she spent a lot of time studying. I took care of Little Tom, like Kaliteyo before me. He was a sweet little boy and smart as a whip. Eve was trying to teach him to use proper grammar. Even at the age of three, she would correct him so much that it was hard for him to get out a sentence without being interrupted.

Little Tom was terrified of his father. I guess it was partly because he hardly ever saw him, but Haskell wasn't the gentlest soul, either, and he wasn't above spanking Tom. One day, Little Tom got invited to a birthday party. It was for the son of the director of OU's Extension Division, who lived across the street from us. Eve and I took Tom to a toy store and bought a toy golf club for him to give to the little boy for a present, and then we sent him off to the party dressed in his best clothes. Later that afternoon, Haskell and I were standing out in the front yard talking, and it started getting dark, so Haskell called out for Little Tom to come home. He didn't come until Haskell had called him several times. When he finally did, Haskell was angry.

Little Tom ran across the street to us, carrying that toy golf club. I guess he figured it was too good a toy to give away. When he saw the expression on his father's face, he could tell that he was in trouble. Haskell greeted him by growling, "Why didn't you come the first time I called you?" Poor Little Tom, trembling with fear and forgetting all his proper grammar, blurted out, "D-D-Daddy, I would have a c-c-comed if I'd a h-h-heered ya."

The whole situation, Little Tom taking his present back and then stuttering and forgetting his grammar—he usually spoke so properly— struck me as funny, so I started laughing. Finally Haskell laughed, too, and Tom didn't get a whipping.

There was one other time that semester I provided Haskell with some amusement. It was when I got appendicitis. My stomach had been acting up ever since I had been at OU. Living on toast and Cokes from Veazey's Drug Store made me constipated, and after a while, I was taking laxatives on a regular basis. One day, my stomach cramps were especially bad, and I developed a fever. Haskell took me in to the infirmary, and they diagnosed me with appendicitis. The doctor performed the surgery right there in the clinic, and Haskell watched, or at least, he claimed he did.

Afterwards he "entertained" me and whoever else would listen by describing my surgery in great detail. He would tell how the doctor pulled all my "innards" out on the table while he searched for my appendix and how he had then crammed them all back in when he was finished. Needless to say, I didn't enjoy his description. The only good thing about my appendicitis was that afterward I got to go home and stay with Mama for a couple of weeks.

There was a lot of catching up to do when I got back to school. I worked especially hard in Italian because I didn't want to disappoint Dr. Scatori. I had to drop my journalism class because it was just too much extra work. Life with Haskell and Eve soon returned to normal. Eve continued to complain, and Haskell went back to being in a bad mood.

Mama visited us once. We had been home for the weekend, and Haskell had insisted on Mama coming back with us Sunday evening. He said she could spend Monday visiting with Eve and Little Tom, and he promised to drive her back to Pauls Valley on Monday evening. Haskell was in a good mood, and it was hard to turn him down once he turned on the charm.

We visited for a while after we got back to Norman, and then we went to bed. The next morning, Mama got dressed and went into the kitchen. Pretty soon Eve came in, and there was an uncomfortable silence as Mama waited for Eve to make breakfast. Finally, Eve offered to open a can of pork and beans for her. Mama said, "That's okay, honey, I'll just have some coffee." After that, Mama worried about me getting enough to eat. When I came home for a visit, she would fill me full of good food, and when I left she would load me down with snacks.

That spring, Eve passed the state bar exam, and I got to come home for the summer. Bob was home, too, from OMA, and he spent most of his summer playing tennis with his friends and tantalizing our little brother Tom, who idolized him. Since there were still no jobs, I spent most of my time helping Mama in the kitchen and in the garden, with plenty of time left over to visit with my friends from high school and my little sister Oteka, who confided in me about all her teenage insecurities.

They say that absence makes the heart grow fonder, and it seemed to work that way for Kaliteyo and me. She actually composed a little poem for me and wrote it out in her pretty calligraphy:

> I'm thinking of you often
> Recalling, day by day,
> Some happy little way u often say
> A smile, a laugh, a friendly act
> That's "Just like You," somehow
> I'm thinking of you Often

Just the way I am, right now.
Kaliteyo

In retrospect, I think Kaliteyo must have been reaching out to us for emotional support. She wasn't willing to complain, but with a new baby and a philandering husband, she must have suffered. For our part, Mama, Oteka, and I looked forward to our visits from Kaliteyo and Lahoma, and between times we kept up a lively correspondence. Most of our letters were about clothes:

Fri. morn-

Dear lil' Jimmie,

Do you have your dress yet? Haskell hadn't come by when I left but he probably has by now. You will have to take a tuck on the sides some of those little tucks in the back and maybe the front. I hope you will like it—you can pull out the basting after you press it—that is the reason I left them in.

I am sending three dollars for you to get me a pair of shoes (sandles) like yours black patent leather high heels … go to that cheap place where you said you could get them for 2 something.

I am at Willingham's so send them here.

Mr. Willingham is waiting for me to write this so he can take it to town as he goes.

I got a letter from Oteka the other day and she said she had things all cleaned up for me to come back home. But I ought to stay up here where Richard can help make a living for me—because Mama can hardly get by financially with Tom, Bob, and Oteka much less me.

Can you hear the baby crying? Oh! yes—do you have any use for the material that is left of the white? If you don't I think I can get Lahoma one out of it and embroidery it in a pretty sky blue and if you want to get her some little shoes you can get little blue slippers or little pink ones either—you look around and see if you can find some blue ones and the price and I will rake up a few pennies some where to get them.

So long,
Kaliteyo

178

It was Kaliteyo who convinced Teker and I to let our hair grow long. When we were little, Mama had the barber cut our hair in a Buster Brown style, but about the time I graduated from high school, Kaliteyo decided that we should let our Indian heritage show. Maybe it was the beginning of the Indian Exposition in Anadarko in 1931 that gave her the inspiration. We all went that year and saw the Indians who came from all over the country representing their tribes. The women all wore their hair long and dressed in beautiful beaded costumes. It brought back memories of Bloomfield. So we let our hair grow. Kaliteyo and Teker had thick, coarse hair that they braided and coiled around their heads. My hair was always thin, so I just pinned it up in a bun.

That summer, Snip was in the thick of another political campaign. This time, he had decided to run for the state Senate instead of the House of Representatives. As a senator he would have more prestige, and since the term was four years instead of two, he wouldn't have to run for re-election as often. Since Snip had supported Bill Murray's policies, he had Murray's endorsement,[1] and since the Republicans had been blamed for the Depression, the Democrats were all shoo-ins. Snip won the election easily and became the youngest man up to that time to be elected senator, just as he had been the youngest man to be elected representative back in 1926.[2]

Soon after the election, Snip and Helen had another son, named Homer after his father. Little Homer was towheaded like his mother, and his hair was curly—both firsts in our family.

In the fall, I went back to school, but my attitude hadn't changed. I was still biding my time by taking general courses until Snip and Haskell would let me go back home. The first semester, I enrolled in a swimming class to try and overcome my fear of the water.

Haskell was busier than ever. After the state Senate went into session in January, they started investigating the School Land Commission. Governor Murray had accused some of the members of the commission of getting loans for their friends. Snip was heading the investigation, and Haskell worked for the commission. Their names were in the paper practically every day, especially Snip's.

I got acquainted with Little Homer that winter. Snip and Helen had come down to Norman to see an OU football game, and they left Little Homer with me. He was about six months old. I was excited at first, remembering how Little Willie used to coo when I'd sing to him, but as soon as Helen walked out the door, he started crying, and he didn't stop until she got back. I walked with him, I sang to him, I changed him, I fed him, I did everything but stand on my head, but he wanted nothing to do with me. I told Helen that if I ever kept him again, I would have to get myself a blond wig so I'd look like her.

Mama and I made the newspapers that next spring, thanks to Snip. The headlines read, "Paul Relatives on List of Deals Nance Urged," and "Farmers Wait While Few Get Favors."[3] It seems that Snip had taken out two loans, one in my name and one in Mama's, probably to fix up the farm.[4] I was so embarrassed. I tried to slip in and out of my classes without being noticed. The newspapers may have thought the scandal would ruin Snip's career, but he didn't miss a beat. He said the loans were on the up and up, and the payments were current, so the matter was dropped. He continued to head the committee investigating the School Land Commission. He was chosen to write the bill to reform it,[5] and Haskell was promoted to head attorney.[6]

Haskell's promotion didn't come until the end of the year, and in the meantime, he and Eve were having financial trouble. He never had any sense about money, anyway. Whatever he had in his pocket in the morning, whether it was one dollar or fifty, would be gone when he got home that evening. All of Haskell's traveling and eating in restaurants must have also put a strain on their budget. He loved to stop and have a cup of coffee and a piece of pie with his friends. He was starting to develop a paunch.

During the last part of my sophomore year, Haskell and Eve decided to rent out half of my room to make a little extra money, so I got a roommate. The girl was also a student at the university. She was pleasant and quiet, and she didn't have any boyfriends, so she and I got along fine. The unusual thing about her was that she was a Christian Scientist, so she didn't believe in taking medicine. I was naturally curious, because I had never met a Christian Scientist before. We didn't actually talk about religion, but one time she got really sick. I wondered if she would break down and go to the doctor, but she didn't. She just went to bed and read her book—she had a little red book of prayers—and pretty soon she got better.

It was about that time I decided I had to figure out some way to make a living. I figured I had wasted my time in school long enough. We had a neighbor named Viola Mead, who used to come over to visit with Eve and me. We'd discuss our problems over lunch, and Viola and Eve would smoke. Pretty soon I started smoking, too. Mama didn't approve. Later she blamed me when Teker and Tom started smoking, although I had nothing to do with it. Smoking was considered stylish at the time, and no one suspected it could be harmful to your health.

180

Viola would complain to us about being stuck with a philandering husband, and I would complain about wasting my time in school. One day, Eve came up with a suggestion for me. Why didn't I learn to type and get a job as a stenographer? Her idea sounded reasonable, so I decided to try it. I bought an old, banged-up typewriter from one of Eve's law student friends, and started teaching myself how to type.

Fortunately, Eve and Viola weren't my only sources of information. After fumbling with that old typewriter for a while, I found out from some of my classmates that the state would probably need to hire social workers to administer President Roosevelt's welfare program, so I went over to the School of Sociology and asked about it. Professor Ryan, the head of the department, was very enthusiastic about the program, and was impressed by my Native American roots. He said the new programs would especially benefit Native Americans, and there would be a great need for social workers in Indian country. When I left his office, I was all fired up about becoming a social worker. Right away I went over and changed my major to sociology.

Finally, I had a goal! If I got a degree in social work, I could get a good-paying job, and help Mama, Teker, and Tom. I sat down and wrote a letter to Mama telling her that I was finally going to make something out of myself.

My advisor helped me figure out which courses I would need to graduate. He calculated that if I took a heavy schedule and went to summer school, I would be able to graduate in two more years.

Math was my first stumbling block. I knew I wouldn't be able to understand math, and I confessed as much to my advisor. He thought about it for a minute or so, and then came up with an alternative—ancient Greek. I jumped at the chance. I knew I was good at languages.

Zoology was another requirement for the sociology school, but I dropped it after about a week. I couldn't stand the smell of formaldehyde. So I went back to my advisor and asked him if there was anything I could substitute for zoology. He told me that I could take botany, instead, so I enrolled in that. Like ancient Greek, botany didn't really have much to do with sociology, but I didn't look a gift horse in the mouth.

After my schedule was settled, I got down to work, and sure enough, my grades improved. Ancient Greek was a breeze. There was a student in my Greek class named Jimmy Demopolis who actually spoke Greek, and I did better than him. I guess he was overconfident. I also enjoyed botany. It made me appreciate Mama's fascination with plants.

One of my sociology courses was called "Town Ecology," on the sociology of towns, and our main assignment for the class was to make a study of a small town. I wrote my paper about Pauls Valley. It was easy to write, and I made an A on the paper without even half trying.

Having a goal and a little success gave me back some of my self-confidence. Late one afternoon, I overheard Haskell bragging to a neighbor about how he was putting his little sister through college. He was laying it on thick. He told him about how he had encouraged me, and how he was sacrificing to satisfy my every need. I waited until he came back into the house, and then I let him have it. I told him I had never asked to go to college. I had been pressured into going and into staying with him. He had never given me any encouragement, but had instead criticized and bemeaned me, making me feel like I was a burden on him and on his family. I let out all the anger and frustration that had been building up over the past two years, and I said it loud enough for the neighbor to hear, too.

Haskell waited until I was finished, and then in his most condescending tone, replied, "Well, if that's the way you feel about it, why don't you quit?"

I told him, "No, I've come this far. I'm going to get my degree."

CHAPTER 28
- I Get Free of Haskell -

The next summer, I went home on pretty good terms with Haskell. I think he was proud of me for deciding to stick it out and get my degree. It was good to be home, though. Mama was getting by somehow, with her garden, her cow, her chickens, and some financial help from Snip. She made regular trips to Mount Olivet, where Willie and Little Victoria were buried, and also to the Old Cemetery, to visit Little Samuel's grave. She planted flowers and kept the grass mowed. No one maintained the Old Cemetery now, so she took down the front section of our fence at home and put it up around the Paul plot there.

At home, she still gave most of her attention to Teker and Tom. Oteka was in the tenth grade, and Tom had just matriculated into the seventh. He was proud as punch to be out of grade school. He was learning to play tennis and could almost hold his own against Bob.

Bob was now a senior at OMA, and he was full of himself. Hazing was still practiced there, and he was looking forward to the next year when he would be at the top of the pecking order. He was still doing well at OMA. He played in the band, he was on the tennis team and the polo team, and he had made good grades, too.

Bob was also becoming a ladies' man. Somehow he had managed to get acquainted with some girls, even though he went to an all-boys school, and he carried on a correspondence with his girlfriends during the summer.

Teker helped him with his love letters. He would sit on the couch with his feet propped up on an ottoman and dictate letters to her like she was his secretary. She also advised him on his wooing strategy.

Here is a draft of one of his letters that I found among Mama's things:

> *Dearest Jean:*
>
> *I hope you will forgive me for not writing sooner, but I have been actually studying as when we returned we had our six weeks tests, and this is the first time I have had to breathe. Jean don't think I have forgotten you because I certainly haven't. And also if you don't think my intentions were absolutely honorable toward you please don't answer this almost unreadable letter. Jean I want to thank you for the good time I had with you the little time I got to be with you. If I can come up to Enid Easter I certainly will. Because I'm afraid I met somebody I can't forget very soon. I could say a lot in this letter, but it will be a lot more fun telling it to you personally. You can tell Mona hello for me if you will, also Betty. We have an inspection the twenty-fourth and twenty-fifth. After this is over we can take it easy. Then maybe I'll have time to take care of my very neglected letter writing. Well Jean as my vocabulary is very limited I will have to close.*
>
> *Love*
> *Bob*

We didn't see much of Snip. Whenever Mama wanted to tell him something, she'd write him a letter.

Eve graduated from law school in the spring, and she and Haskell moved to Oklahoma City to be closer to his office at the state capitol building. Since he was now chief attorney of the School Land Commission, he no longer spent his time traveling. They bought a little bungalow in an area that was being cleared for the expansion of St. Anthony Hospital, and Haskell had it moved to a hill on Sixty-Third Street overlooking the city.

Since I was in summer school, I moved to Oklahoma City, too, and started commuting to the university in Norman, twenty miles away. Haskell would drop me off at the Interurban train station on his way to the capitol, and I'd ride the train to Norman. Then after class, I'd catch the Interurban back to the city, and walk the two or three miles to Haskell's office at the capitol building for him to take me back home.[1]

Now that Haskell didn't have to travel and Eve was finished with her education, they started to act more like a family. Haskell would come home in the evenings, and Eve even tried to cook a little. Haskell built a little pond out in the back yard, and he embedded pieces of colored glass in the concrete for decoration. It was kind of pretty. The neighbors told Haskell he wouldn't be able to find water up there, but he hired a diviner, and soon he had himself a well. Millwood School was just about half a mile down the road. Little Tom would be in the first grade in the fall.

Eve planted a little garden out in back, and one day when I got home from school, she and Little Tom were planting green onions. Eve came inside when I got there, and as she closed the door behind her, she called out to Little Tom to bring in the onions. Of course, she intended for him to bring in just the onions they had left over, but pretty soon Tom walked proudly through the door, his box full, having dug up all the onions they had planted. Eve didn't scold him. She just laughed about it. He was a smart little boy, but he took everything literally.

It only took a month or so for Haskell to get fed up with shuttling me back and forth to the train station, and the fare of twenty-five cents added up after a while, too, so he decided to give me an allowance of twenty-five dollars a month and let me live in Norman. It wasn't much to live on, but I was tickled to death. I was finally on my own.

I found a rooming house close to the campus and made a deal with the landlady, Mrs. Stacy, to rent a room there for ten dollars a month. Helen, who was about four inches taller than me, boiled one of her old dresses until it shrunk enough for me to wear. The hem was a little uneven, but it didn't look too bad. Eve also gave me one of her old dresses. I still lived on mostly toast and Cokes, with an occasional hot dog thrown in.

I had a roommate named Ruth, and we didn't hit it off, to say the least. I had to have quiet to study, so I stayed up late, and Ruth claimed that the light kept her awake. She didn't spend much time studying herself, and she had a greasy boyfriend she would invite up to our room. I couldn't stand him. Finally, I went to Mrs. Stacy and complained. I told her that one of us had to go. As it turned out, there was another girl living in the house named Maxine, who didn't have a roommate, so Mrs. Stacy moved me in with her. Maxine and I got along fine.

The classes got more interesting my junior year. My government teacher was French. He spoke with an accent and wore a beret to class. I took developmental psychology and used my new-found knowledge to analyze Little Tom. Probably my most interesting course was "Abnormal

Psychology." We studied about mental illness and mental retardation, and we made trips out to the state mental hospital to see examples of different syndromes. I remember one twenty-year-old girl who was simply beautiful. You would never have guessed that she was retarded, but she had to have help taking care of herself.

At the end of the spring semester I felt pretty good about myself. I was doing well in my classes and was living on my own. I visited my advisor and planned out my course schedule for summer school and for my senior year. I didn't want to risk making the same mistake I had in high school and fail to graduate with my class, so I stayed in Norman and went to summer school again.

About this time, a plan started to form in my mind. Once I got out of college and started earning a salary, I would help Oteka and Tom go to college. On the weekends I got to go back to Pauls Valley, I would take them aside and talk to them about the value of a college education. I probably started sounding like Haskell.

Oteka had just finished her sophomore year in high school, and she was blossoming. She was pretty and popular and busy in school activities. She was a singer like me, except I think her voice was prettier than mine. She sang in the glee club and in school musicals. When Helen invited her to sing for the Pauls Valley Music Club, Mama didn't stand in her way like she had when Helen invited me.

Teker met an interesting young man that summer—a young writer who was living with his parents in Choctaw, near Oklahoma City. He spoke to Mama's poetry club, and she invited Teker to come along with her to the meeting. Teker brought a friend of hers, Doris Moore. The young writer, "Duke" as he called himself, was impressed with Oteka. He wrote: "She is an attractive girl and has nice brown eyes and very pretty feet." Duke promised to write Doris an essay that she could use in school the next year, and he wrote a limerick for Teker:

> *There was a young lady named 'Teka*
> *Who came up to town for a week-a*
> *But when she got there*
> *She had a bad scare*
> *And headed for home like a streaka!*

Duke's real name was Louis LaMoore, which he changed to Louis L'Amour for a pen name. L'Amour went on write more poetry, short stories, and later novels. In a few years, he would become one of America's most famous and prolific Western writers.

Teker met another young man that summer from Wynnewood, a little town just about seven miles south of Pauls Valley. His name was Thurman McLean, and he was smitten with Teker from the first time he met her. Soon he was making regular trips to Pauls Valley to see her. Thurman was a couple of years older than Teker. He had just graduated from high school and was getting ready to attend OU the next year to study engineering. Thurman liked to fish, so Mama had plenty of catfish steaks to cook that summer.

Tom was still his same ornery self. I was worried about him. Mama was still spoiling him, and he wasn't doing well in school.

CHAPTER 29
- Haskell Loses His Marriage and His Job -

It was just before Christmas of 1934 when Haskell and Eve broke up. He had gotten the idea she was having an affair with one of her classmates in law school. I don't think she was, but Haskell was hard of hearing, and I think it made him paranoid. I had a friend like that, Mattie Elkins Baird. She was one of my best friends when I worked out at the state capitol, good-natured, generous—she became a teacher. But later in life she lost her hearing and became irritable and suspicious. Finally, when she couldn't hear well enough to talk on the phone, I lost track of her. Anyway, I think Haskell was a little like her.

When Haskell moved out, he left Eve and Little Tom in a bind. She had a law degree and had passed the state bar, but in that day and time, it was next to impossible for a woman to get a job as an attorney. She and Haskell weren't divorced—at least, not right away—so she had no alimony and no child support. She ended up working as a stenographer at St. Anthony Hospital while Haskell stayed with a friend.

About a week before Christmas, while Eve was visiting the neighbors, Haskell came back to the house, picked up Little Tom, and took him to Las Cruces, New Mexico. Eve must have known it was him, because she didn't file a missing person's report.

Haskell was doing some legal work in Las Cruces for Rufus Garland. He had gotten acquainted with Rufus through Snip, who had served in the legislature with him. Rufus had been voted out of office in 1932 when he opposed FDR's candidacy for president. After that, he and his wife Jenny moved to New Mexico, where Rufus opened a law practice.

Later, Little Tom recalled his experience:

> *Just before Christmas one night my dad woke me up and helped me dress. He had moved out of the house, and my mother must have been across the road at the Emricks'. I was too dumb to realize that she didn't know he was taking me.*
>
> *The next thing I remember was passing through Roswell, N.M. Dad pointed out the military institute and told me that Will Rogers Jr. was going to school there.*
>
> *We spent Christmas with Rufus and Jenny Garland in Las Cruces. This was before the Garlands had any children and they were very gracious and made us feel very welcome.*
>
> *Christmas morning, children were coming in pairs and in groups to the door, chanting, "Mis Christmas, Mis Christmas." Mrs. Garland let me tend to the door and hand out candy and fruit to the callers.*
>
> *On the way back to Oklahoma from Las Cruces, boredom inspired me to ask my dad if we could get the red wagon I'd just gotten for Christmas out of the trunk and tie it to the bumper so I could watch as we towed it. My dad wasn't irritated at all by the suggestion, and he gently explained how the wagon would not withstand highway speeds.*[1]

When Haskell returned to Oklahoma, he took Little Tom back to his mother, and then went back to work helping Snip prepare for his next attack on the School Land Commission. Oklahoma had a new governor in 1935—E. W. Marland, who was something of a legend in Oklahoma. A brilliant businessman with degrees in geology and law, Marland had amassed a fortune in the oil business and had devoted himself to philanthropy before going broke during the Depression. Marland's platform was to bring the New Deal to Oklahoma.

Marland was elected by a landslide, and once in office he began to unveil the specifics of his plan. He proposed the creation of five new agencies to administer his war on the Depression: a state planning board, a housing board, flood control board, new industries board, and highway board. His program would create jobs for the unemployed, and provide for welfare, homestead exemption, and an old age pension. He estimated the cost of his program at thirty-five million dollars, and to pay the bill he proposed increases in the sales tax, oil tax, and cigarette tax, as well as new taxes on insurance, salaries, and rent.

With such an overwhelming mandate, it was hard to imagine how Marland could fail, but he did. He just seemed to rub the legislators the wrong way. First of all, he thought he could run the state like a CEO. He arrogantly dispatched orders to the legislature, appointed his friends to important positions, and was impatient with criticism. The legislators didn't owe their jobs to him, and they didn't appreciate challenges to their entrenched patronage system.[2]

Snip took on Marland right away by opposing the first bill he proposed, an emergency education bill. I had been complaining to Snip about having to pay a mandatory fee for athletic tickets and about the smart aleck football players in my classes, and the first thing I knew, he had made a speech about it on the Senate floor:

> *Charging that professors down there "work an hour a week and spend the rest of their time writing books and playing golf," Senator Homer Paul, Pauls Valley, supported the Stewart amendment.*
>
> *"They charge for football, baseball and basketball, no matter if a student never has time to attend these games, before the student can even enroll," he declared.*
>
> *"They give fat jobs to football players to keep them on the team: now I am informed that they have just added an identification fee. Your students are being tagged like dogs, to show who they are, where they come from and to make public admission that they pay tribute to Caesar.*
>
> *"The regents have no more to do with running that institution than I do: it is run by Dr. W. B. Bizzell, another $10,000-a-year man, and two or three professors: all the regents do is to vote as Doctor Bizzell tells them."*
>
> *Paul charged that it is "the duty of this legislature to 'wise up' to what is going on and protect the boys and girls who really want an education."*
>
> *The Pauls Valley senator also launched an attack on the fraternities and sororities at the university and charged that Oklahoma University*

is *"run by the Urschels and other millionaires, with nothing but snobbery and abuse for the poor boys and girls who try to go there for an education."*[3] [He got this from Haskell.]

I sent the clipping to Teker with the note*:* "This clipping I'm sending has caused lots of comment on the campus so I'm keeping my mouth shut who I am so I can graduate without any prejudice." In Italian class, I scrunched down in my seat, hoping no one would recognize my name and connect me with Snip.

In the end, Snip co-authored the education bill, and it was actually more generous than Marland's proposal. The bill did prohibit mandatory fees for student athletic tickets, though. The penalty was a fine of ten to thirty dollars or a jail sentence of ten to thirty days. So even though the legislature complied with the governor's request, they made it seem like a rebuke.[4]

The governor's other proposals were all but ignored. Deficit spending was as controversial then as it is now, and the business community was solidly against new taxes. The only new boards created were a flood board and a state planning board. The latter was required in order for the state to receive federal New Deal funds.

After dispensing with the governor's proposals, the legislators went ahead with their own agenda: the investigation of the State Banking Commission and the School Land Commission, the state's largest agency,[5] where they could potentially find more revenue without raising taxes. Haskell knew there would be fireworks, so he asked me to save the newspaper clippings reporting on the hearings. I started buying copies of the *Oklahoma City Advertiser* and saving them for him.[6]

When brought before the committee, Haskell testified that he had found almost a million dollars worth of illegal loans made by the commission between 1919 and 1927, and that sometimes the state's own money was being used to pay off loans by means of a complicated legal shell game. There were several other charges being investigated as well: the unauthorized purchase of $750,000 worth of bonds by the commission, the failure of the commission to collect $150,000 from oil and gas leases, and the failure of the commission to collect delinquent payments on loans by state officials as required by the legislation written by Snip in 1933.[7]

The investigation took place in the House of Representatives, but the most spectacular event in the drama was a speech by Snip on the floor of the Senate. Snip accused three of the commissioners—Secretary of State Frank Carter, State Superintendent of Public Instruction John Vaughn, and State Auditor C. C. Childers—of personally sanctioning illegal acts. After Snip's speech, two things—well, really three things—happened in rapid succession: the secretary of state called for a grand jury investigation, the Senate instituted impeachment proceedings against the three commissioners, and Haskell was fired, along with his stenographer, Evelyn Moore.

Haskell responded in typical Paul fashion. He told the reporters, "I submitted my resignation as an easy way to end it. I felt that after what has happened, I could not work with the commissioners. Since this insult [his firing], I am going to stay here until I am ordered discharged by the secretary." But it was all over but the shouting. Haskell was suddenly unemployed.[8]

Snip's campaign against the commissioners petered out. The impeachment proceedings failed, as did a constitutional amendment that he proposed to reorganize the commission, but he was praised for his courage in attacking the commissioners, knowing they could take it out on his brother, and his prominence in state politics grew. He was a force to be reckoned with.

CHAPTER 30
- I Graduate from OU -

While Snip and Haskell were battling the School Land Commission, I was applying myself at OU. Even after testing out of junior English, I still had to take eighteen hours each of my last three semesters, and eight hours during summer school, in order to graduate, so I was exhausted most of the time. It was rough, but I kept telling myself that soon I would have a degree and a job with a salary. Finally, I would be able to help my family.

Snip and Haskell were too busy with their own problems to take me home for visits, and I didn't have enough money for a bus ticket, so I spent most of the school year in Norman. I still got letters from Teker, but toward the end of the first semester I was so busy I didn't have time to answer them. Finally, I had to write and reassure her that I wasn't mad at her.

Jan. 16, 1935
Dear Teker:

Got your letter today. Was pleased greatly to hear from you. Snip and Helen came by Sunday and Snip left me $6 to buy shoes and hose with. I think I'll go to the City between semesters. Our exams start Friday and last until next Wednesday.

The reason I haven't written was because I've been working so hard I had to get in two term papers. One I handed in had 104 pages in it. The other had 45 pages in it. That's what I've been doing. I've never had to work so hard in my whole college career. From last Sunday a week ago until Friday, 3:30 a.m. was the earliest I got to bed and Thursday nite I stayed up until 4:40 finishing it. I worked and used my eyes so much that I strained them and they are just getting now where things don't look so hazy to me as they did.

And now I'm studying for finals. I don't look forward to any good grades and if I hear anybody comment unfavorably about them I'm going to stop and tell the whole damn place to go to Hell. I'm simply worked down and if I flunk my Greek [I made a B] I'm certainly going to commit suicide or go to the asylum.

Yes, I knew Bob was in the City and I'm very proud of his appearance and rating [He was promoted to a higher rank], and I'm not mad at anybody, I've just been too busy to write....

Teker's boyfriend, Thurman, was in the engineering school at OU, and he was my other source of news. He told me that Mama had just made a trip down to Clarksville, Arkansas, to our old farm. She still owned the property. She went there to clean up the house to get it ready for Uncle Tom.

Uncle Tom had recently given up his farm on the Mississippi River. The farm work was getting to be too hard on him. He only had one leg, had been suffering from malaria for years, and was getting older. He was sixty-six. Mama had tried to get him to come and live with her, but he said he didn't want to be a burden. Finally, she hit on the idea of asking him to "take care" of her place near Clarksville. The climate was much better there than along the Mississippi River, where he had lived for so many years. Mama figured that he could keep himself busy managing the farm, and our old neighbors, the Selfs, could help him out if he got sick.

I was also corresponding with Bob and Kaliteyo. Bob was now in the advanced program at OMA, which meant he would graduate with a commission in the army and credits toward a college degree. He was planning to be a professional soldier.

Kaliteyo was still living with her two-timing husband, Richard, in Cement. She'd send me news about "Little L"—that's what we called her daughter Lahoma—and she also made clothes for me to wear at school.

During my senior year, I got my first real taste of social work. We were assigned to do "practicals," where we traveled twice a week to Oklahoma City to work at charity agencies with real clients. I'd ride the Interurban train back and forth from Norman.

The Depression was still in full swing in 1935, with an unemployment rate of around fifteen percent. Oklahoma City had several "Hoovervilles"— communities of the poor named after Herbert Hoover, the president everyone blamed for the Depression. The people there lived in squalid conditions, with no plumbing or electricity. There were two main sites. One was Walnut Grove on Reno Avenue near the downtown area, and the other was Community Camp, which was out by the stockyards on the banks of the South Canadian River. The most destitute lived there. They set up rude shacks made of scrap wood or tin, even cardboard. These poor people would be flooded out once or twice a year by the river, and then move right back in. They had no place else to go.

The government's poverty program hadn't gotten underway, so there was no welfare, no worker's compensation, no Social Security, no Medicare— only private charities. Variety, an organization of movie theaters, subsidized some medical care. There was also the Red Cross, the Sunbeam Home for crippled children, and some resources to provide glasses and dental care for children. While most people only had enough for themselves, a few churches had food programs. The United Provident Society was the biggest of the charities. It was a national organization and was supported by wealthy donors. We worked out of their office, which was on Reno Avenue near the downtown area.

The United Provident Society had a kitchen, and they operated a soup line providing one meal a day. They had a few cots out in back where people could come in to get out of the cold and a little garden where they grew vegetables during good weather. When people came in, the Provident Society would start a file on them and then try to hook them up with whatever services were available. They assigned me two families to visit.

My first family ended up in poverty after losing their farm. The husband was no good, but the wife was sweet. She had four children, and she was struggling to keep them clothed and fed. I somehow managed to get them an appointment with a loan officer at a bank to borrow money to lease another farm. They seemed so excited when I told them. The day after they were to apply for the loan, I went to their apartment and found the wife sitting in their tiny room, deep in despair. Her husband had gone out and gotten drunk, causing them to miss their appointment. There was nothing more I could do.

Wenonah, OU graduation, 1935

My other family made up for my frustration with the first one. They were poor, but they had found an apartment on California Street. The husband worked when he could, and they were scraping by. Their main problem was that their son had a heart defect. The little boy was well cared for, but he was so weak he could hardly move, and he was so pale he looked like a statue. I got him an appointment to see the heart surgeon at the medical school, and the doctor operated on him free of charge. After the surgery, that child literally came back to life. The color came back into his cheeks, and he started to smile and to move around. It was as if God had granted him a miracle.

Since my grades were better now—I even made a couple of A's—I applied for and got a student loan for the second semester. The loan was for one hundred dollars, a fortune to me. I was able to buy some clothes for myself and for Teker and Tom, and it got me to thinking about what I could do when I was out making my own money.

I guess it was unrealistic, but my hope at the time was that we could all return home to Pauls Valley and live as a family again. Haskell and I could support Mama and send Teker and Tom to college. We could fix up the old house so that Mama could be active in her clubs and entertain guests like she used to do. It would be almost the same as when Willie was alive. I told Teker about my dreams in a letter:

> …You just see when I come home for good I'm gonna do lots of things—I'm going to get things for _us_ and for the inside of the house so it'll be a pleasure for people to come to see us. I—we're—going to redo the kitchen and get some paper—oboy—I'm telling you I've planned so big I almost bust. It'll be too good to be true for me to get to live long enough to see the day that I'm out of this goldarned school and can really _do_ something. I sometimes wonder if God will let me. Wouldn't Willie be proud of me graduating from a university and making a keen salary every month. I can almost see him grinning. I wish the world was unreal and he could come back for just a little while…

Teker was always getting down on herself, so I used my letters to encourage her. First she worried that she wasn't good enough for Thurman. I set her straight on that subject:

...Thurman is quite honored to get to even go with you. Don't think he'd shower you with the attention he has if he wasn't proud of you. Where's that old conceit? Don't lose it—it's one of your best qualities—Where would your brothers be if they didn't have plenty of self assurance.

Teker was chosen to go to the district meet in singing like I had been, and when she told me she was worried about what kind of a showing she would make there, I wrote her again to encourage her:

Now I'm going to expound the old PV [Pauls Valley] sideline boost. Rah! Rah! You go over to Ada and do your dead level best. Try to win. But if you lose you've won in the long run. Experience—good sportsmanship, etc., etc. Don't think for a minute that people have gained anything in a day because they haven't, it takes a long time. In the case of a singer—years. I know, I've read many lives of artists in the field. Some of them had nothing but discouragement to live on...

I was also determined that Teker wouldn't be humiliated by having to wear old worn out clothes like I had been, so I continually tried to get nice clothes for her.

I'm sure sorry you can't wear my suit to Ada [It didn't fit]. Why didn't you write me sooner so I could have gotten you something in the City today? Will try to get something for you, Easter dress. Can you manage for some shoes? I'll go up and look for you something Thursday. I've got some money and there's no sense in you doing without—I had to and I know how it is—you just wait, we'll show those old PV girls something in a mighty short while. I'm gonna dress you up for once if it's the last thing I accomplish. You try to find some shoes, if you have to—charge them—and I'll pay for them next July when I get my first pay check and a pretty hat. Something with chic—that looks good on you and will go with white shoes.

Oteka was smart and talented and popular, and I just knew she would be successful in college. The next month she got a ride with Thurman's father and came to visit me in Norman. Teker was a big hit with my housemates and with Mrs. Stacy, too. They all joined me in encouraging her to go on to college. Even Ruth was on her good behavior. When Teker left, I just knew we had convinced her.

I didn't get to go home for Easter, but Snip took pity on me and invited me up to Oklahoma City to spend Easter with his family. Of course, I enjoyed visiting with Snip and Helen, and it was nice to spend some time with the little boys, but I really missed Mama.

We all worried about Haskell. He still visited me each month to give me my twenty-five dollar allowance, but he was usually in a bad mood, so I didn't dare ask him about Eve and Little Tom. Instead, I finally called Eve myself to find out how they were doing.

Haskell had continued to make headlines for a while after he was fired. Snip tried to get him appointed to a job with the state corporation commission, but the attorney general declared the appointment illegal since it wasn't provided for in the constitution. Haskell took private cases when he could get them. He sued the state on behalf of another attorney for the School Land Commission who hadn't been paid, and also for his former secretary, Evelyn Moore, but he couldn't find enough cases in Oklahoma City, so he moved back in with Mama in Pauls Valley and opened an office there.

He moped around the house for weeks, hardly speaking to anyone. He was unhappy about breaking up with Eve, I'm sure, and worried about Little Tom. Also, it was a long time before he started getting cases, so he had too much time on his hands.

He told me he was glad the state job fell through. He didn't want to be "beholden to anybody," was the way he put it. Actually, I think he felt like he had been sacrificed to Snip's ambition, and he didn't want to be put in that position again. To Haskell, it must have seemed like the end of the world, but I was ecstatic. Our family was coming back together again.

About a month before graduation, I came down with tonsillitis. There I was in bed, with nothing to relieve the pain but Argyrol.[1] All I wanted to do was to go home to Mama, but I stuck it out. Nothing was going to keep me from graduating this time. When I was better, I buckled down, caught up with my classwork and passed my final exams. No A's, this time, but I did well enough to win an award—a scholarship in medical social work to the New York School of Social Work. Of course, I couldn't afford to go, but it was a big honor.

My graduation from OU was one of the proudest moments of my life. I may have fluffed off the first two years, but once I had a goal, I worked hard and made good grades. It felt so good to walk across the stage in my cap and gown, and for once I wasn't ashamed of how I looked. I wore some pretty white buck shoes I had bought with my loan money, and Mama made me a dress out of some material Haskell had bought.

Everyone was there: Mama, Snip and Helen, Haskell, Kaliteyo, Bob, Oteka, and Tom. I only wish that Willie could have been there to see me graduate. They were all proud of me, even Kaliteyo. She called my education my "brain trust." Snip and Helen gave me a set of luggage as a graduation gift. It had been Snip's idea to give his sisters a college education, but I think it was Haskell who was proudest of me—in spite of all the trouble he put me through. And he deserved to be, too. He was the one who had really pushed me to keep going, and he was the one who understood best what I had gone through.

After graduation, Dr. Ryan, the chairman of our department, found me a job working on one of Roosevelt's FERA[2] projects in the Cookson Hills of northeastern Oklahoma, Cherokee country.

CHAPTER 31
- The Cookson Hills -

Oklahoma's Cookson Hills, the foothills of the Ozarks, aren't very spectacular. They say the Cookson Hills are among the oldest mountains in North America, and maybe they were something to see in their day, but over the millennia they have been worn down to nubbins. There aren't any breathtaking vistas like you see in Colorado, no towering firs, and no cascading waterfalls, just mile after mile of blackjack trees, a few cedars, and an occasional mountain stream.

The land in the Cookson Hills isn't really good for anything—it's too rocky—so it was one of the few areas in Oklahoma that was left to the Indians. It's Cherokee country, and although most of the full-bloods were cheated out of their allotments, many still lived back in the hills when I worked there. During the Depression, the Cherokees were joined by poor whites, many of them squatters, looking for a place to eke out a living. There was a lot of tuberculosis, malnutrition, and alcoholism, and since we still had Prohibition at that time, many of my clients had stills hidden back in the woods where they made moonshine.

I worked out of Tahlequah, the old Cherokee capital, and I lived with Judge R. H. Couch and his wife. Judge Couch had preceded Haskell as chief attorney for the School Land Commission, and he had been Haskell's mentor when he started with the department. Judge Couch was from Tahlequah, and after his stint with the commission, he had returned home.

As soon as he found out where I would be working, Haskell arranged for me to stay with the Couches. They were really nice. Mrs. Couch mothered me. Every day that I went out into the mountains, she would ask me where I was going and when she should expect me back. It made me feel good to have someone watching out for me.

I had to have a guide, at least at first, because none of the roads were marked, and an interpreter to help me communicate with the Cherokees. Every day I would go out and visit families to assess their needs. My supervisor warned me to honk my horn when I got within sight of a house, so if the family had a still out in back, they could see that it was me coming and not the revenuer. If I surprised someone, they might hide in the woods, or worse, take a shot at me.

After reading my first letter home, Mama started to worry:

> *Dear Jim*
>
> *we received your Letter and Haskell redd them both at Dinner yesterday. very interesting but sounds dangerous. You must be very careful and don't make any enemys. Be friendly whether you want to or not. Don't make those trips alone. Huckleberries & Blackberries sound good I have 9 qts of green beans and will put up some beets this next week out at Snips. I will go with you when you come if it causes a divorce in my famaly. we have been having lots of rain here next week I will take my washing over to Mrs Stevens and do it on her washing machine Bob still holds his Job it sure was a Godsend. he bought some prettie grey pants and some pretty white shoes. I have your crocheted dress finished do you want me to send it. Hellen wants one she thinks yours is so prettie. I will send it next week you can ware it some I am sure. Everything is OK so goodbye and good Luck*
>
> *Mother*

Both she and Haskell were afraid that my tendency to speak my mind might get me into trouble. Haskell had a slightly different take on it, though. He wasn't so much afraid for my safety as he was that I'd quit. He wanted me to succeed and not embarrass him, and frankly, I think he was a little envious. He wrote me a letter of encouragement and sent it along with Mama's letter:

> *Dear Jim:*
>
> *I received your very interesting letter yesterday. Mama is having*

your shoes fixed and mailed to you today.

All the disagreeable things that you write about is evidence that you have a good job. They would never have sent you to such a difficult territory to handle if they had not had supreme confidence that you could handle it. Get acquainted with the territory and the people in it and forget all about every thing else except what you are supposed to do—work hard at the job—don't pop off about anything at all to those people—and you will be a success. Those people are very suspicious of every one and especially any one with a quasi-official connection, and it is therefore of greatest importance that you assume an attitude that you are not experimenting either with them or yourself, and that you are not interested in anything but doing your job well.

There is one out-standing quality that those people have which should help you. They are used to taking people for exactly what they are, and as long as you impress them with the seriousness with which you take it, they will accept you as one of themselves. They realize the handicap you are under in getting to them and will appreciate it. Just be yourself and lean back to keep from putting on any "airs" and you will be O.K.

Make a success of this job and you have made a success of your life. The first job is like the first million—always the hardest, but the others and the better ones come easier.

Go ahead and use my car if you need it. I am looking for a good second-hand car to buy. If I find a good one I will buy it and drive it over there for you.

People will watch you closely. The social workers are always more talked of than any other class of people. If you are different from the rest and know what you are doing, and they can detect it, and attend to your own business, the hill-billies will take you into their hearts the same as did the negroes take in Livingstone. Personally I like those people. They are sufficiently independent to live unto themselves, as you say "to make their own laws," and that's "sumpin."

Will be over to see you before long. Give Judge and Mrs Couch my sincere good wishes.

H.

P.S. Tahlequah has 2 "hs".

The car Haskell found for me was an old Model A Ford. With my own car, I felt more independent. As Haskell said, the people did appreciate my visits, and I was never really afraid. I liked the people for the most part, and I enjoyed working in the mountains. After a while, I no longer needed a guide. The country was beautiful and peaceful. There were a lot of little streams coming down out of the mountains, and every day I'd pick me a spot next to one of them to have my lunch, usually a can of salmon and some vanilla wafers. I loved listening to the birds and watching the squirrels and rabbits. Sometimes a deer would come down to the stream to drink.

The only problem with my job was that it didn't fit into my plan for helping Mama, Teker, and Tom. It wasn't long before the car Haskell gave me had a flat tire, and it took a week's salary just to have it repaired, so right away I had nothing left over to send Mama. I wrote home again, expressing my frustration. Haskell didn't get it, though. He was just interested in strengthening my character, so he wrote me another letter to boost my morale:

Dear Jim:

Mama said Oteka had received a letter from you, and after so much talk and search it was produced for me to read. I was neither surprised nor disappointed that you appeared a little blue and dissatisfied. When one has the ordinary reactions to an unsatisfactory condition but the fortitude to go ahead in spite of them, they show good mettle.

I believe I have mentioned before that the extreme difficulty of your job over there is the main element of greater opportunity for you.

Do not worry about sending any money home. Everything is in good condition here. Save what money you can for your schooling this fall. [He was talking about my scholarship to the New York School of Social Work.] No doubt you will go, for you will if they have a vacancy for you which I judge they will.

While you are spending so much on the expenses of handling your job, just remember that you are now attending the greatest school, Hard Experience, where your best professor and most exacting professor is in charge, Yourself. Like Kipling said, "If you can keep your head when others all about you are losing theirs, and blaming it on you,"—you'll "pass" again with a satisfaction to yourself that more than compensates for the expense and the trying conditions that you work under.

In my opinion you are now possessed with your greatest opportunity. Sometimes we get so close to a situation that we cannot see it's true form. And sometimes the little things absorb so much of our attention, that we fail to recognize the bigger things. In your situation, I can easily see that you are confronted with a wonderful opportunity to work. Your assignment is in the remotest, most inaccessible territory in the United States, and among the most independent, stubborn people in the United States. The former will test your steel and build your character, while the latter will improve your ability.

Here is a thought I picked up:

Opportunity

"This I beheld
A craven hung along the battle edge,
And thought, "Had I a sword of keener steel—
That blue blade that the King's son bears— but this
Blunt thing—" he snapt and flung it from his hand,
And lowering crept away and left the field.
Then came the King's son, wounded, sore bestead,
And weaponless, and saw the broken sword,
Hilt-buried in the dry and trodden sand,
And ran and snatched it, and with battle-shout
Lifted afresh, he hewed his enemy down,
And saved a great cause that heroic day."

This well illustrates that the greater the difficulty, so is the opportunity correspondingly greater. It was once said to me, "Paul, what the world is interested in, is Results, not Excuses." I'll never forget those words. They made a great impression on me and I am a better man than I was before they were spoken.

In school they had us memorize Longfellow before we could appreciate him. But now if we will go back we can recognize a great lesson in:

"Let us then, be up and doing,
With a heart for any fate;
Still achieving, still pursuing,
Learn to labor and to wait."

If you will ignore the irony of ingratitude for the accomplishment of a hard job, and the lack of appreciation of the worth of it, and the hardships under which it was accomplished, you can succeed. And you will have learned a great lesson. That is politics and life too. Many go through life and do not learn it. Sometimes the learning of it costs many tears and much bitterness, but once that chapter is well mastered you are self sufficient. You do not expect anything from anyone but yourself. You are therefore in a very happy position. You can either make yourself a success or a failure as you may desire, for you will realize that it all depends upon no one but you.

Do not transfer to another place. It shows weakness. Every body else follows the line of least resistance. The road to oblivion and failure is always overcrowded with such people. Love your work, hard as it is. Give your clients an excuse to appreciate the job you hold. You took the assignment at least with a suspicion that there was a good reason why others could not succeed over there. You showed some courage in taking such an assignment, I would not disappoint either myself or the others involved by following the line of least resistance in asking for a transfer.

You do not realize it, but you are making your character either great or mediocre on this, your first and hardest job. You will prove to yourself that you can make a great success or none, right over there in those hills. You should master your part of that situation even if you worked for nothing. It is that important to you.

I ordinarily charge for these lectures, but since you are my sister I'll let the charges go.

Love,

Haskell

I think Haskell got a little carried away with himself on this one. Oh, did I mention that he loved poetry?

The people I worked with were in desperate need. I had a service day once a month when I delivered food and supplies provided by the department, and I also had a little extra money to spend on things for individual families like cooking utensils, a saw, a coat, or some shoes. The Indians were timid about asking for help. They didn't trust the government, but they were hungry and in need so they came anyway. The white families were always the first in line, so if I wasn't careful, I would run out of goods by the time the Indian families got their turn. I learned to ration my supplies so my Indians would get their share.

Not long after I moved in with the Couches, a full-blood Cherokee man, Jackson Standing Deer, was put on trial for murder. Judge Couch couldn't talk about it, but it was in the paper every day. Jackson Standing Deer was being represented by the famous Cherokee attorney, Houston Teehee[1]. Jackson lived with his wife on a small plot of land in the Cookson Hills, and like most people, they were barely getting by. He had a job "tie hacking," or splitting ties for the railroad, and his wife had a small garden where she grew a few vegetables. Some neighboring white squatters noticed that Jackson was gone during the day, so they started stealing food and supplies. Jackson's wife was helpless to stop them alone. The Standing Deers didn't complain, though, and they didn't go to the authorities, so the neighbors became bolder, openly trespassing and taking what they wanted. Still, Jackson held his peace. Then one day he returned home to find his cabin broken into, and his wife raped. Jackson went to the squatters' cabin and buried his axe in the rapist's head.

This was one time that public sentiment was on the side of the Indian, especially in Tahlequah, but in spite of Mr. Teehee's defense, Jackson Standing Deer was sent to prison.

Fortunately, I never had any trouble with my clients, but I did have some interesting experiences. The roads out in the mountains were terrible, with big rocks and deep ruts. One day, my car got stuck on a tree stump that was hidden by the tall grass. I couldn't go forward, and I couldn't go back. I walked to the nearest house and asked for help, and the family was very hospitable. The husband walked over to my car and tried to get it loose from the stump, but it was stuck fast. They had no phone, of course, so they offered to drive me back into Tahlequah. This is when my real adventure began. The family car apparently doubled as a truck, and the seats had been removed to make more room for cargo. The driver had a stool to sit on, but I had to sit on the floorboards. Even this wouldn't have been so bad, except that chickens had been roosting in there, so I rode all the way into town while sitting in chicken droppings. I didn't complain, though. It was all they had.

Tires were still my main problem. The rocky roads cut into them unmercifully, so it seemed I was always looking for someone to help me fix a flat. One day, as I was looking for help, I noticed a group of men nearby working on the road. As I walked toward them, I noticed that the workers were surrounded by men with rifles. By that time they had noticed me, and the man in charge was motioning for me to come over to where he was standing. He told me that they were a work gang from the prison at McAlester, which wasn't far away. He asked me why I was walking along the road out in the middle of nowhere, so I told him about my flat tire. He was very accommodating. He told me he would have some of the men change my tire for me. While they were working, he told me the men changing my tire were kind of celebrities at the prison. They had been members of Charles "Pretty Boy" Floyd's gang.

After I had been working in the hills for a while, I invited Teker to come up to visit me. She would be a senior in high school the next year, and I wanted to keep encouraging her to go to college. The Couches didn't mind an extra guest, and they made her feel welcome. She stayed with me for a week. We had a good time together. I showed her the little college in Tahlequah, the old Cherokee government buildings, and the Illinois River, which ran through town, and I took her along with me on my rounds. As we bumped along in my little Ford, I pointed out the scenery, and we stopped by my favorite streams for lunch. We were lucky one day to have a little deer fawn come right up to us. Teker fed it some of my vanilla wafers.

After showing Teker what a good time I was having with my job, I brought up the subject of her going to college. She gave me a "Mama" look, and then replied, "With what?"

I lied and told her that I had plenty of money left over from my salary to help her out. She said she didn't believe it, and then pointed out that Snip was already helping Bob at OMA, and Haskell had lost his job with the state and was struggling to get his law practice started in Pauls Valley, so there was no one who could help her.

That was it for me. I quit my job with the OERA,[2] moved back home with Mama, and returned Haskell's car. He was furious. He called me a quitter and a weakling. He said I had let him down and the family down after all they had done for me. He told me I would never be able to respect myself again. I told him I wasn't interested in proving anything to anybody. I just wanted to help Mama, and I couldn't do her any good by spending all my money fixing flat tires in Tahlequah. Haskell still didn't get it, though.

He just kept on ranting and raving. I let it go in one ear and out the other.

When Snip came home, we repeated the whole argument for him, and then I asked him to get me a job for the state. Actually, Snip was more sympathetic. He could see the reason behind my decision. He was angry, but it was only because he knew he'd have to find me another job.

After I quit, Haskell sulked. He was disappointed that I didn't share his enthusiasm for my job, but I think the main reason was that he missed hearing about my adventures.

After a month or so, Snip got me a job with the new state welfare program. We were a new department, and they had trouble finding space for us. Finally, they put us in a room right next to the governor's office. We had a typewriter, an adding machine, and an old-fashioned copier. Although the job was in the welfare department, it actually called for a clerical worker, so even though I had a college degree, I was fired. Governor Marland told Snip I wasn't qualified for the job, and back home I went, after working only two weeks. I didn't work for the welfare department again for another twenty-five years.

CHAPTER 32
- Three Come Home, One Leaves -

I spent the winter of 1935-36 at home with Mama. Haskell was taking cases anywhere he could get them, so he was actually gone most of the time. It was a joy to be around Teker. She was a senior in high school and busy with school activities and singing. She was in and out, usually with one of her friends, and she was in love, always looking forward to Thurman's occasional trips home from OU. Mama enjoyed Teker, too. She was always working on a new outfit for her.

Tom was enjoying himself a little too much. He was flunking half of his subjects in school, although you wouldn't know it by his mood. I helped Mama around the house, working with her in her garden and trying to help with the sewing, although I wasn't very good at it.

The legislature wasn't in session, so Snip and Helen were living out at the farm. We visited back and forth, at least Helen did, so I got to see my nephews, Little Willie and Little Homer, fairly often. Snip was busy politicking, of course, but I reminded him every time I got a chance that he needed to get me a job.

Kaliteyo came home in March. Her husband, Richard, had been picked up by the Pauls Valley police at one o'clock on a Sunday morning, with two of his brothers and three girls, all drunk, having driven their car off the road into a ditch. That was the last straw for Kaliteyo. She left him, and it was about time.

About a week after Kaliteyo came home, Richard came to the house looking for her. I'll never forget it. Mama met him at the door with the shotgun and said, "You get off my porch or I'll blow you off of it!" Kaliteyo was standing behind Mama, and as Richard retreated down the steps, she shouted, "Run, Richard, run!" The gun wasn't loaded, of course, but Richard didn't know that. He didn't try to come back.

It was nice to have Kaliteyo home. She, Teker, and I joked and teased each other and traded clothes. Kaliteyo's old friends came over to visit and to commiserate. She was so funny. She could tell a story as well as Mama, and boy, did she have some humdingers to tell about Richard and his brothers. We all enjoyed Little L, too. She was four and so cute, always cheerful, always singing. Teker and I did our best to spoil her.

Kaliteyo was obsessed with keeping Little L clean. She bathed her so much that Mama warned her she was going to scrub the color right out of her skin—she had the same pretty bronze complexion as her mother. Little L hadn't been living with us long before she got impetigo from scratching chigger bites. The doctor told Kaliteyo to pull off the infected crusts and to clean the raw sores with alcohol. Kaliteyo would make her stand on a chair while she worked on her sores. Little L would squirm and cry, and Kaliteyo would yell at her to be still. We all suffered with her.

About a month after Kaliteyo came home, Haskell brought his son Little Tom to live with us. Apparently Eve had told Haskell sometime before, that she couldn't afford to keep Little Tom. I think that Eve loved Tom, but she didn't want the responsibility of caring for him. Haskell probably felt the same way, because he didn't take Little Tom at first. Instead he stalled.

First, he talked to Mrs. Moore, his stenographer at the School Land Commission, about adopting Little Tom. Tom told me later his father took him out to see her several times. Little Tom didn't like Mrs. Moore because he thought Haskell and she were involved romantically. Of course, that wasn't true. Mrs. Moore was twenty years older than Haskell and had grown children, but to a seven-year-old it made sense, I suppose. Mrs. Moore must have considered taking Little Tom, though, because she once asked him if he'd like to be called Tom Moore. Little Tom told her in no uncertain terms that he didn't like her, and he certainly didn't want to be called Tom Moore, and that was that.

Finally, Eve forced Haskell's hand. She was just barely getting by on her salary as a stenographer when she got word that her sister in Santa Fe, New Mexico, was sick with tuberculosis. Eve called Haskell and told him she was going to Santa Fe, and that she couldn't take Little Tom with her, so Haskell picked up him and brought him home to Pauls Valley. That was just fine with Mama. She was happy to have another grandchild to spoil.

Once Little Tom was in Pauls Valley, Mama installed him in Haskell's old bedroom over the cistern, and then she took him down and enrolled him in Lee School, where all of us, from Willie on down, had gone to school. The principal, Miss Perry, who had been my kindergarten teacher, made him feel welcome. Soon after his arrival, she arranged to have him give the Bible reading at morning assembly. Later that day, Miss Perry came by Tom's class and casually remarked about what a good reading Tom Paul had given.

We all tried to make sure Little Tom was properly taken care of. After doing an inventory of his clothes, Teker marched up to Haskell and told him that she was going to need some money to take Tom shopping. I held my breath expecting Haskell to growl at her, but he gave her the money.

Having Lahoma and Little Tom around improved everyone's mood, even Haskell's. One day he decided to make some grape jam. From the start, I knew it would be a disaster. It was always a bad idea for any of my brothers to go near the kitchen. When he finished, there was syrupy goo all over everything. It took Mama and me days to clean it up, but Haskell was so proud. I'm just sure Mama dropped him on his head when he was a baby.

In spite of all our efforts to make him feel welcome, Little Tom missed his mother, and after he learned she had gone to Santa Fe, he decided to follow her there. Little seven-year-old Tom looked at the maps his father had collected on his travels, and he planned and memorized the route he would take to New Mexico. He figured he could hitchhike, and that the ten dollars he had saved should be enough to buy food.

When Little Tom was ready, he confided in my brother Tom, his fifteen-year-old uncle, who tried to talk him out of going. Tom told him that the family was happy to have him and that Mama would take good care of him, but Little Tom said he needed to be with his mother. Tom pointed out how far it was, and how many days it would take him to get there, but Little Tom was still determined to go, so Tom said, "Okay, then I'll go with you."

Tom helped his little nephew pack some clothes, along with some of Mama's biscuits, and then they headed out of town on foot toward Whitebead. There was no traffic on the road that evening, so no one picked them up, much to Tom's relief. As they walked along, they talked.

212

Tom kept asking questions, trying to inject doubt into Little Tom's mind. He'd say, "What if no one picks us up?" "What if we run out of money?" "What if we get stranded out in the country?" "What if it rains?" Little Tom dismissed all of these objections and maintained his opinion that someone would eventually pick them up, and they would be in Santa Fe the next evening.

A few cars passed by, but they were all coming into town, not going away. Then it started to get dark and cold. Finally Tom said, "Maybe we should give it up for today and try again tomorrow," so they walked back into town. I think Tom used pretty good psychology on Little Tom, but he underestimated his nephew's determination to be with his mother. To this day, Little Tom still claims the only reason he turned back was because he thought Tom was getting scared.

After their adventure together trying to hitchhike to Santa Fe, Tom decided it was his job to entertain Little Tom. He had him help with the chores, feeding the chickens and milking the cow. Mama's cow had a calf about that time, and she had bought special food for him, called Graham's Meal. Little Tom mentioned that it looked like breakfast cereal, so Tom said, "Okay, let's see what it tastes like." They each put some of the calf's feed into a bowl, added milk and sugar, and then tried to eat it. Little Tom told me about it later. He said it didn't have much taste, and it was hard to chew. They didn't eat much.

According to Little Tom, his uncle had lots of ideas for his entertainment. He taught him to roll cigarettes out of Bull Durham tobacco. He showed him how he could avoid having to go downstairs to the bathroom by just peeing through the window screen. He gave him boxing lessons, and they jumped out of the hayloft together. When the calf got a little bigger, Tom suggested they have a rodeo. He put the calf in a stall, tied a rope around its belly, and then had Little Tom jump on his back. Little Tom said he was sore for a week.

Mama tried to keep Tom from leading her little grandson astray, but he was getting too big to spank. When she caught him doing something ornery, she would take out after him with her broom, but Tom would just run away giggling.

Little Tom had another story about an adventure with his uncle that got them both into trouble with Haskell. One day, Tom came up to him and said, "How would you like to go driving?" Little Tom, who always liked cars, said yes. It just so happened that Haskell had walked downtown to his office that day instead of driving, and he had left his car in the driveway.

Tom had more sense than to mess with his brother Haskell, but I guess he figured that they could take a drive and be back before Haskell got home. But things didn't work out like he planned.

Tom and Little Tom took Haskell's keys and got into his car. I don't remember what kind it was—Little Tom would—but it was a pretty big car. Anyway, they got it started, backed it out of the driveway, and then headed west on the road to Whitebead. After a while, Tom turned off the main road and let Little Tom get into the driver's seat. As Tom concentrated on coaching, he forgot to watch the road. Before he knew it, they were headed for the ditch. Little Tom said they turned the wheel back toward the road, but once the car started sliding, it didn't stop until it had slid all the way down to the bottom of the ditch.

They got out and pushed. They tried backing up. They put grass and twigs under the wheels. But everything they did seemed to sink the car deeper into the ditch. After realizing their attempts were futile, they just sat down on the side of the road, wondering whether Haskell would beat them to death or just strangle them. Pretty soon, along came a car. It was Judge Ben T. Williams and his wife. They gave the unlucky pair a ride into town. Haskell must have been furious, but Little Tom was actually innocent, and "Big" Tom was under Mama's protection, so they both survived.

Meanwhile, it took a several months for Snip to get me another job. It was just in time, too, because Kaliteyo and I were getting on each others' nerves. She complained that I was always in a bad mood. I was, but it was because I didn't have a job and couldn't help Mama. Kaliteyo didn't have a job, either, but it didn't bother her. She was satisfied to just sit around the house.

The job Snip got me was with the state highway department in Oklahoma City. It was just clerical, filing and keeping records, but I didn't mind. It was work. I would be bringing in a regular paycheck, so I could buy things for the family. Snip even found me a room close to the capitol so I could walk to work. That part of it didn't work out because my landlady was a fussbudget. I wasn't allowed to have visitors, and she wanted me to be in by a certain time. She kept checking my room to make sure I hadn't made a mess. She didn't even want me to sit on the bed. I put up with that for about a month, and then I found a room in the same neighborhood renting from an Indian lady. We got along just fine. She was Sauk and Fox and a cousin of the great Olympian, Jim Thorpe.

After a while, Haskell started giving Kaliteyo trouble about being at home. Mama came home one day to find her bawling. He had told her he couldn't afford to support her, and she needed to go back to her husband. Maybe he was having second thoughts about ending his own marriage, but it was a bad idea for Kaliteyo. She was lucky to be rid of Richard. Mama comforted her, saying if anyone moved out, it should be Haskell, because a man could make it on his own better than a woman, but it pushed Kaliteyo into doing something. She decided to go to school to become a stenographer.

She enrolled in a six-month clerical course in Oklahoma City, so I invited her to stay with me. My room was big enough for the two of us, but she had to leave Lahoma at home with Mama. It must have been hard on Little L, being away from her mother, and since Kaliteyo was living with me, she blamed me for it. The first time Kaliteyo and I came home together for a visit, she walked over and kicked me on the shin.

Being away from Little L was hard on Kaliteyo, too. She was always in a bad mood. One day I came home to discover she had moved out on me. I found out later that she had gone to stay with our old neighbor, Mrs. Walter Hart. Mr. Hart had died, and she was living alone. I don't know where Kaliteyo got her nerve. I would never have been so presumptuous, but Kaliteyo had a warped sense of pride. She would rather take advantage of Mrs. Hart than be indebted to me.

After a while, Kaliteyo decided to quit school, and I tried to help her out again. I heard about a job opening at the state welfare department, and talked her into applying for it. She got the job—it was a good job, too— but Little L was still in Pauls Valley with Mama, and Kaliteyo missed her, so she gave up the job and moved back home. I was flabbergasted. During the Depression, you just didn't turn down a perfectly good job. She could have sent for Little L when she got settled. When I asked her why she quit, the only thing she would say was, "I didn't like it." It was that pride again. She just couldn't accept help from me.

In the spring, Oteka graduated from high school. Everyone was excited for her. Mama and Kaliteyo made her a pretty dress, and I bought her some shoes to match. We all came to see her graduate: Haskell, Little Tom, Kaliteyo, Little L, Tom, me, and of course, Mama. Snip and Helen were there, too, and Bob was home from OMA. Oteka sang a solo at the ceremony and got an award for the most "activity points." Her boyfriend, Thurman was there, of course, and they were so happy together.

I got Teker something personal for her graduation, which she appreciated:

Dear Jim:

I sure like the things—especially the B—thank you a lot. I don't have a stamp or I'd write—wish u & K—could come home this week end I want u to see all my things and also Mama is leaving for Ark.—No news at all. Write us a letter. You and Kal too—send me Harts address I can't find it out here. Got a perfectly Beautiful Negligea (or however u spell it)

Lots of Love,

Oteka

It was after Mama got back from visiting Uncle Tom in Arkansas that Teker let the bomb drop. She told us that she and Thurman had been secretly married for over a month. She didn't tell Mama until the very day that Thurman was coming to take her to Norman with him—he was going to summer school at OU. It was raining hard that day. Little Tom was there, and he told me about it later. Mama made Thurman wait out on the porch while she pleaded with Teker not to go.

After a while, Little Tom went out to keep Thurman company. He said they could hear Mama and Teker inside. Mama was telling Teker they should at least announce the wedding and let people know. She could still have a shower for her, even a church wedding. Why didn't she just wait until the fall, even another week or two? They needed more time to plan. Did she have everything she would need? Finally, in desperation, Mama told her that it was bad luck to leave in the rain.

Oteka didn't have a shotgun wedding like Kaliteyo's, but it still hurt Mama. She hadn't been there for Snip's, Haskell's, or Kaliteyo's weddings, and now Oteka had run off and got married. It hurt me, too. I was planning for Teker to go to college.

Well, there was still Tom.

CHAPTER 33
-Kaliteyo Spreads Her Wings -

Once Kaliteyo was safely back home with Mama, I began to relax. I was making a hundred dollars a month, so I felt like I had plenty of money to meet my needs and to help the family. Haskell wanted me to send my paycheck home to him so he could manage everyone's money, but I was through taking orders from him. I was going to spend my money however I wished. I bought my brother Tom some clothes, and I went to the doctor and got my tonsils out. They had been making me miserable off and on all my life, and now I could afford to get rid of them.

The other thing that had bothered me for a long time was my stomach. I had been having stomach cramps on a regular basis ever since I got into college, and there were times when I could hardly function. I met a girl out at the capitol named Ann Fannon, who had had the Saint Vitus' Dance. It caused her fingers to draw up so that she couldn't type, and she was a stenographer. She told me about a doctor named Phillip McNeil who taught at the medical school. He had given her an experimental treatment that had cured her spasms. The treatment was to inject her with typhoid extract. It would give her a fever that lasted for several hours. The fever made her miserable, but it must have burned out the poison that caused the Saint Vitus' Dance, because after a few treatments, her spasms went away, and she was able to keep her job. Ann suggested that I go to Dr. McNeil and see if he could cure my stomach cramps.

Dr. McNeil was nice. He examined me, checked my blood count, and fluoroscoped my stomach. His diagnosis was laxative abuse. He told me that living on Cokes and toast at the university had caused me to be constipated, and now I was addicted to laxatives. He said that if I got back on a normal diet, I would feel better. Specifically, I was to lay off the Cokes and toast and eat more meat and vegetables. I did, and pretty soon my stomach felt better.

After getting my health straightened out, I suddenly realized I was in over my head in debt. Not only did I have doctor bills, I hadn't paid off my student loan. I couldn't go to Snip. He had just gotten me a job and a place to stay, and I certainly wasn't going to admit to Haskell that I was broke. Finally I confided in Mrs. Moore, Haskell's secretary at the School Land Commission. She had been sweet to me when I was in school at OU, and her daughter Jeannette and I had become good friends. Jeannette was about my age, and we both worked at the capitol. I spent a lot of time at their house.

Mrs. Moore sat me down and gave me a lecture about living within my means, and then she took me to see a banker she knew who gave me a small loan and another lecture. It was about then I found out about the YWCA. Several of the girls who worked at the capitol lived at the Y. The rent was only ten dollars a month, and you could stay there for three years, so I packed up my things and moved over to the Y.

Back in Pauls Valley, Kaliteyo still didn't have a job, so Haskell decided to hire her as his secretary. That was a big mistake. When Haskell said, "Jump," he expected you to say, "How high?" Kaliteyo didn't put up with that for long.

All this time Mama was watching over and planning for Little Tom and Lahoma. Little Tom had done fine at Lee School the previous year, and he had gotten attached to Mama, so he didn't miss his mother as much as before. He had started following her around the house like we used to do, except for when my brother Tom was "entertaining" him, and Little L was getting to be the same way.

It was about this time that Kaliteyo decided to assert her independence. She thought that Mama was too bossy, making her stay home and take care of Little L instead of going out and having a good time. So when Kaliteyo got another job working as a secretary, she used her first month's salary to rent a garage apartment.

Soon after Kaliteyo and Little L moved out of the house, Uncle

Tom passed away—he didn't live long after moving to Mama's farm in Clarksville—so Mama had to make another trip to Arkansas for the funeral. She took my brother Tom along with her. Uncle Tom had been the same kind of brother to her that Willie had been to us, and she took his death hard. They buried him out on Stillwell Mountain, near the farm.

While Mama was gone, Bob, Haskell, and Little Tom were left at home to "bach." Little Tom told me about it. Bob was their cook. He cooked by heating jars of vegetables and fruit that Mama had put up and stored down in the cellar, and Haskell and Little Tom ate whatever he fixed. According to Little Tom, the highlight of the week was when Bob made pancakes, or rather *a* pancake. Bob just mixed up some batter, poured it all into a skillet and cooked it. They divided the pancake three ways and ate it with jam. They must have been glad when Mama got back home.

Kaliteyo's first attempt to strike out on her own didn't last long. Someone left a car running in the garage under her apartment, and the carbon monoxide fumes almost killed her. Luckily, Little L was with Mama at the time. Kaliteyo was so weak she was practically helpless, so Mama moved her back home. Fortunately, she didn't lose her job, and she agreed to stay home with Mama for the time being.

With Kaliteyo back home, Mama started to think about what she could do for Lahoma, so she decided to start a preschool in our house. She went into partnership with Dixie Noble, who had run a preschool when Kaliteyo was little. They got several children enrolled and started having classes. They met upstairs in Snip's old room.

It was a great idea. Not only would the school prepare Little L for kindergarten, it could provide Mama and Dixie with an extra source of income.

Dixie had the experience, and Mama was good with children. Mama was enthusiastic, and Little L was so excited, but the preschool was not to be. Before long, Mama and Dixie had a falling out. I suspect Dixie challenged Mama's authority. If Mama did anything, she had to be the one in charge, at least among other women. Men were a different matter.

Meanwhile, Snip had been wheeling and dealing. It was the year of the presidential election, and he had supported Roosevelt, who was easily re-elected because of his popular New Deal. Snip was up for re-election himself. During the summer he had successfully lobbied the highway department to pave over seventy miles of road in Garvin County, so he was also a shoo-in.[1] After the election, he became head of the Senate

219

Left to right: Mattie Elkins, Wenonah, and Ede Roberts

Committee on Committees, which decided committee assignments and chairmen.[2] Even Governor Marland, who had learned from his first two years to respect the power of the legislature, was vying for Snip's support.[3]

Since the legislature was in session that year, Snip and Helen had moved to Oklahoma City, so I got to see them fairly often. The little boys, Willie and Homer, were so cute. Little Willie was in the first grade, and he was very curious. Mama watched him for Helen one weekend while I was home. As she sat in her rocker sewing, he asked her question after question about her, about the house, and about her sewing. He would preface each question with, "Grandmother-rrr," with the accent on the last syllable. Mama patiently answered all his questions.

Helen knew I was trying to scrimp in order to send money home, so she made me an outfit. It was stylish then for women to wear suits that were cut like men's, so she took one of Snip's old suits and altered it to fit me. I wore that suit for two years, then I gave it to Teker, and she wore it for another two years.

Snip and Helen also got me involved in the Indian-Okla Club, an organization of Indian leaders that met regularly in Oklahoma City. It was exciting for me to go to the meetings. The membership list read like a "who's who" of Oklahoma Indians. There was the old Choctaw Chief Will Durant; Douglas Johnston Jr., son of the last Chickasaw Governor before statehood; and Dennis Bushyhead, a Cherokee and a state senator from Claremore—he asked me out a few times. Snip's friend Jim Nance, a Choctaw, senator, and newspaper editor from Purcell, was a member, and also Muriel Wright, historian and granddaughter of the Choctaw chief Allen Wright, an early advocate for an Indian state for which he suggested the name "Oklahoma," a Choctaw word meaning "Red People." My good friend Lula Pybas also belonged to the Indian-Okla Club. Lula was a full-blood Chickasaw from Purcell who worked out at the capitol, and lived at the Y like me.[4]

Haskell was as excited as I was about the Indian-Okla Club, but he lived too far away to go to meetings, so he grilled me about who I met there, what they talked about, and so forth.

My roommate at the Y was Mattie Elkins. Mattie had moved to Oklahoma from Dallas to find work, and like me, she had connections with a politician. Her French teacher in high school was married to Bill Holloway, the former governor of Oklahoma, and the same man who had referred Snip to Dr. O'Donahue, who saved Oteka's leg. Governor Holloway got Mattie a job as stenographer for the secretary of the School

Land Commission, Jess Larson. Jess had taken Haskell's place as chief attorney for the commission, and they had remained good friends in spite of Haskell's firing.

That fall, Mattie invited me to go down to Dallas with her for the OU-Texas football game. The game was a big deal then, just as it is now. I was, of course, too poor to go when I was in school at OU, but it sounded like fun to go with Mattie, and we could stay at her parents' house while we were there. The Texas State Fair is always timed to coincide with the game, so we went to the fair, too. We dressed in red and white to represent OU and got pins to wear and pennants to wave, but I think we enjoyed the fair more than the game. I got my portrait done in chalk by an artist on the midway.

Another friend of mine who lived at the Y was Ede Roberts. Her room was across the hall from ours. Ede also worked at the capitol, so she and Mattie and I all went to work together. Ede ran the Western Union telegraph office at the capitol, and she knitted all the time. She knitted at work, she knitted in the car, and she knitted in her room at night. She could knit and talk at the same time. She would even go to the movies with us, knitting in the dark, and never dropping a stitch. I think it calmed her nerves.

Ede had a radio, and when there was a special broadcast, we would all go into her room to listen. I can still remember crowding around her radio to hear King Edward's abdication speech. He gave up his throne to marry a commoner, Wallis Warfield Simpson. Not only was Mrs. Simpson a commoner, she was an American, and a divorcee at that. To the British, it was a big scandal. The Anglican Church and the British cabinet refused to accept the marriage. The prime minister even threatened to resign. I'll never forget listening to the little king's words: "…I have found it impossible to carry the heavy burden of responsibility and to discharge my duties as king as I would wish to do without the help and support of the woman I love." The other girls thought his sacrifice was so romantic, but to me it was disgusting—as if he had ever gone through hardships!

I had a lot of other friends, too. There was Eugenia Moseley. She worked as a typist for the highway department. She and her husband, J.L., had moved to Oklahoma from Texas because of hard times. Like Mattie, they had gotten their jobs from Governor Holloway—J. L. was Holloway's nephew. They had a son named Lewis. When Eugenia told Lewis that I was an Indian, he asked her, "Where are her feathers?"

Eugenia knew a woman who had gone to school with Mama back in "territory days." She told me how pretty and popular Mama was back then.

Another one of my friends at the capitol was Hattie del Trieves. She was older than the rest of us, so she became our unofficial chaperone.

That winter I got sick with the flu. On the day I returned to work, I passed out, and my supervisor called Snip. It was embarrassing. I was okay. I had just tried to come back to work too soon, but Snip bundled me up and took me home to Mama. It was a nice break. Ede sent me a postcard while I was recuperating. It seems I missed my flowers:

> *Dear Jim,*
>
> *Did you have to get sick and run off just when I had some home remedies to put on your chest? Hope your mother soon has you well and about. Some flowers came from "the gang." They sent them back. Come home.*
>
> *Ede*

Oklahoma was located in the dust bowl, and in 1937 was suffering from a severe drought, so Governor Marland, although he had lost much of his influence with the legislature, submitted a plan to give some relief to the state's struggling farmers. He proposed a modest appropriation to supplement those hurt worst by the drought and a homestead exemption to reduce taxes on their farms. To make up for the lost revenue for the counties, he proposed the legalization and taxation of beer.

Snip supported the governor's plan, but by doing so he put himself right in the middle of a firestorm of controversy. On the one hand, the powerful oil companies supported the beer tax in order to avoid a higher tax on oil, and on the other, there was still strong sentiment in favor of Prohibition. It was true that the state needed more revenue just to match federal New Deal funds, but this didn't matter to the influential Tulsa and Oklahoma City newspapers, which had opposed the New Deal all along. In order to defeat Governor Marland and his supporters, they labeled his plan the "oil-liquor deal," and accused him of buying the legislators' support by allowing them to dispense patronage. Snip was accused of being responsible for fifty to a hundred patronage jobs himself.[5]

Snip, characteristically unruffled by the accusations, retaliated by getting a bill passed prohibiting family members of newspaper reporters from working for the state.[6]

The beer tax failed, but the legislature passed a homestead exemption bill anyway, preventing many farmers from losing their farms. They also voted

223

to support federal New Deal projects that provided jobs for thousands. This put the state into debt[7] and helped to earn Snip the title "Robin Hood of Garvin County."[8]

Near the end of the session, Snip got sick. At first they thought it was the flu, like I had, but he just got sicker and sicker. He finally went to see one of his colleagues who was a physician, Louis Ritzhaupt, from Guthrie. Dr. Ritzhaupt examined Snip and diagnosed him with meningitis.[9]

I was terrified. Meningitis was what had killed my sister Victoria. They put Snip in St. Anthony Hospital in Oklahoma City, and I went there every day. Every time Snip saw me, he would yell at the nurses, "Get her out of here." At the time, it hurt my feelings. I didn't go there to chat with him. I only wanted to make sure he was still alive. Later, I figured out that he was only trying to protect me from catching what he had.

Mama was scared, too, and Haskell drove her up to Oklahoma City one weekend to visit Snip. Little Tom and I came along, too, but my brother Tom stayed at home. He was mad at Snip for not letting him go to OMA, like Bob. Mama had been working on Snip to send him. Tom must have felt bad about not visiting Snip, though, because when we got back home he had cleaned up the kitchen. That may not sound like a big deal, but for one of my brothers it was unheard of.

It was never clear how Snip got meningitis. Doctor Ritzhaupt thought he might have gotten it during a visit the week before to the state reform school that was in his district. Fortunately, though, Snip recovered quickly, and he got right back to work in the Senate. Within about a month of his release from the hospital, he was feeling well enough to slug a reporter in the jaw:

Senator Paul Hits Reporter in State House
Apology Is Accepted after Sudden Attack.

Homer Paul, Pauls Valley state senator, expressed regret Monday for a physical attack upon Otis Sullivant, reporter for the Daily Oklahoman, *on the Senate floor Tuesday during the noon recess of the last day's session of the legislature.*

The fistic encounter, in which the reporter was struck a glancing blow, occurred after Paul had sharply criticized newspapers in the morning Senate session for an article in another newspaper about a statement of Dr. J.S .Fulton, Atoka, that the Oklahoma Medical Association spent "a good deal of money" pushing legislation. Paul accused newspapers of causing the public to lose faith in public officials and said they "were helping to pull down the government."

Sorry says Paul

"I'm sorry I did it," said Paul to the reporter, and the apology was accepted. "I am sincere about my viewpoint."

Sullivant and Edward Burks, Tulsa World reporter, were seated at the Senate press table discussing the legislature with several senators.

Paul came into the chamber and sat down at the table. The discussion turned to his speech and the newspaper story. Paul had made a motion to call the reporter who wrote the article before the bar of the Senate and said Doctor Fulton would be called to explain what he meant.

Whippings threatened

"If any reporter writes a story about me saying anything like that about me, I'll whip him," said Paul. "I'll whip him every time I see him in the capitol, and I'll remember it for thirty years."

"I do not write stories I can not prove," answered Sullivant. "but if I get a story about anything I wouldn't be afraid to write it."

"All right, let's go," said Paul, starting around the table.

Burks steps in

Paul swung, the blow glancing off Sullivant's cheek. Paul was restrained from further activity by Burks, who received a light blow in the face. Joe B. Thompson, Ardmore, stepped in front of Sullivant, and W.O. Ray, Tishomingo, and Bower Broadus, Muskogee, intervened to prevent further encounter.[10]

I didn't pay much attention to Snip's antics at the capitol once I knew he was healthy again. I was more concerned about Teker. She and Thurman had been married for a year now, and she was pregnant, alone much of the time, and suffering from morning sickness. Thurman's parents had cut off his support after they learned of his marriage, and he was working nights and weekends as a roustabout in the oilfields. Kaliteyo and I would go down to Norman on weekends and stay with Teker. Thurman used to joke that he had slept with both of his wife's sisters. Actually, we slept on the floor.

Thurman did everything he could think of to make ends meet. In addition to working in the oil fields, he caught fish and shot rabbits on his way to and from work. He even sold ties to the professors at OU.

Oteka's condition went from bad to worse as she got further into her pregnancy. Her blood pressure went up, and her legs swelled. The doctor told her she had to go to bed, or she would lose the baby, or worse. Teker was miserable cooped up inside the house, so Thurman would sit her in a wheelbarrow and roll her down the sidewalk so she could get out. Mama came down to help during Teker's last month, and finally on May 8, 1937, she delivered a healthy baby boy. She named him Homer Dean, after our brother Homer, who had done so much for all of us since Willie died. Homer Dean was supposed to be Oteka's last baby, though. The doctor warned her that if she got pregnant again, she might not survive.

CHAPTER 34
- Haskell Goes to Jail, Little Tom Visits Arkansas -

The same spring that Teker had her baby, Bob graduated from OMA as the highest-ranking cadet.[1] He not only made good grades, he also played in the band and was captain of the polo team. On graduation, he received a commission as a second lieutenant in the army, with orders to report to Fort Bliss for further military training. We all went to Claremore for his graduation.

The graduation ceremonies were spectacular, with all the cadets dressed in their uniforms marching onto the stage and snapping to attention before the commandant as they received their diplomas. Bob was called up separately because of his special status. I don't know why, but someone decided he should wear spurs. Maybe it was because he was on the polo team. Anyway, it was a bad idea. When Bob clicked his heels together, his spurs locked, and he almost fell over! It was funny to me, but Bob was mortified. His face was as red as a beet when he made it back to his seat.

That evening there was a ball honoring the graduates. Of course, Bob was taking one of his many female admirers, and the senator from Claremore, Dennis Bushyhead, had invited me to go with him. I liked Dennis. We had been out together before, and I was starting to get excited about going when Bob threw a wet blanket on everything. He told me he wasn't happy about me going with Dennis. He acted like he was being protective, but I saw right through him. He didn't want me to go at all. He was ashamed to be seen with me, because I showed my Indian blood. I had always been darker than him, and if I showed up, especially with Dennis, who was a quarter Cherokee, it would be clear that our family had Indian blood. I called Dennis and told him I couldn't make it. When Bob left to go down to Fort Bliss, our parting was a little cool, but we hadn't been that close, anyway, since he was carted off to military school.

Things settled down after his graduation. Teker had bounced right back after her difficult pregnancy, and she was enjoying her new baby, Homer Dean. Kaliteyo and I still spent a lot of our weekends with her in Norman. Kaliteyo seemed happy with her new job, and she was acting more responsibly than at any other time that I could remember. She worked, counted her pennies, and stayed home in the evenings to take care of Lahoma. Mama was proud of her. When school started, Little Tom would walk Little L to kindergarten every day, and Mama would prepare a big meal for them when they got off for lunch, just like she had for us when we were little.

In her spare time, Mama was working on Snip to get him to send my brother Tom to OMA. After spending two years in the eighth grade, Tom was about to flunk the ninth grade, too. She had been lenient with Tom, her baby, letting him skip school and then having to tutor him at home. Mama had thought having Haskell at home would help, but Tom just ignored him and went about his business—"monkey business" would be a better way of describing it. I suppose he was a lot like Snip had been at his age. Mama pointed this out to Snip and begged him to send Tom to OMA. Now that Bob had graduated, he could just use the money he had been spending on Bob's expenses for Tom. It wouldn't cost him a penny more.

I'm sure Snip and Helen had been looking forward to some financial relief after Bob's graduation, but Snip was still true to the promise he had made to Mama after Willie's death, and he agreed to send Tom to OMA. It was a good plan, because Tom really wanted to go, to be like his brother Bob. Mama just knew that military school would snap Tom out of his lethargy, and he would do well.

While Mama was negotiating with Snip, I was still working at the capitol and living at the YWCA. It was really hot that summer, and it was especially hard to sleep at night, until someone got the idea of sleeping outside on the roof of the building. We'd take cots up there and moisten our sheets, so that every little breeze felt cool and refreshing. I enjoyed living at the Y, I liked my job, and I was being more careful with my money now. Between the Indian-Okla Club, the girls I worked with, and the YWCA gang, I had plenty of friends.

I also spent a lot of time at Mrs. Moore's house visiting with her daughter, Jeannette. She had grown up in Oklahoma City, and sometimes her high school friends would come to her house to visit. One of them, Bud Bickford, was a chemical engineer and worked at Peppers Oil Company's refinery. He had a roommate named Don Gunning, who also worked for Peppers, and they both lived with Bud's parents. I felt a little out of place with Jeannette's big-city friends, but I felt comfortable with Don. He was from a fairly large town, Enid, but growing up he had spent his summers with his mother's family in the small farming community of Fay. He never tired of telling me about the wonderful people there.

Haskell was in a pretty good mood that summer. He had decided to find himself a wife and had started dating. He had two prospects, a teacher named Madge Butler, and my high school friend, Carrie O'Harro, who was now working at the bank. Madge was Little Tom's favorite. She let him sit in her lap and "drive" her car. Going to the Baptist church was a drawback—she taught Sunday school there—but Tom was willing to overlook that in order to get to drive her car.

Little Tom spent most of that summer with his mother in Santa Fe. Eve's sister had died, and she had gotten a job as a clerk for a federal judge there. Little Tom had a wonderful summer with his mother, and he didn't want to come back to Pauls Valley, but neither he nor his mother had a choice. Haskell now had custody.

Haskell always had a soft spot in his heart for farmers. He had seen our brother Willie struggle to support us with his little farm, and he had spent the first part of his career representing the School Land Commission, loaning money to farmers to help them keep their land. So when he went into private practice, he took a lot of cases defending farmers from foreclosure. Often they couldn't afford to pay his fee, so they'd give him livestock, hay, or even chicken wire.

Once, a farmer promised to give Haskell a hog after it was slaughtered. When Haskell went out to get his hog, the farmer ambled over to the car and said, "Haskell, I hate to tell you this, but your hog died."

Like all of us, Haskell had a temper, and one time it got him into trouble in court. Kaliteyo, Lahoma, and Little Tom were sitting in the living room with Mama one day when my younger brother Tom burst through the door, out of breath and laughing so hard he could hardly talk. I wasn't there, but Little Tom told me all about it later. As soon as Tom caught his breath, he said, "Haskell's in jail. He slugged Joe Curtis!"

We got the full story later from the horse's mouth, so to speak; Haskell told us about it after he got out of jail. The incident had occurred at a tax sale, where property was being auctioned off for payment of delinquent taxes. These sales were presided over by a judge, and back then all the local attorneys would attend, sometimes representing clients, and sometimes bidding on the properties themselves.

As each piece of property was considered, the judge would give its size, location, a list of improvements, whether there were any liens, whether the mortgage payments were up to date, and the amount of taxes due. Then bids on the property were taken. The farmers were allowed to make bids on their own properties, and if a farmer's bid was the highest or only bid, he was allowed to keep his farm, giving him a little longer to save his home and his family's livelihood.

Before the sale, Haskell called each of the other attorneys aside and asked him not to bid against the farmers on their own land. For a while, things went well, and some of the farmers were allowed to keep their property. Then, after a particular farmer made a bid on his farm, Joe Curtis, one of the other attorneys, outbid him. Haskell, furious with Joe for going back on their agreement, stood up and confronted him about the bid. A verbal exchange followed, and Joe finally called Haskell a fool. That was it for Haskell. He made a little speech describing the plight of the farmers and the selfishness of someone who would take away another man's livelihood for his own personal gain. He finished by telling Joe that going back on his word was also a personal insult. Then he leaned over the table and slugged Joe, right in the mouth.

Haskell won a lot of respect by standing up for the farmers that day. Joe Curtis' own father-in-law and law partner, T. J. Blanton, commented when he heard about the incident that "Joe had it coming." Months later, Little Tom was with his father visiting a small rural community near Pauls Valley when a man came up to him and said, "Out here we're shore proud of what you done at court, Haskell."

Haskell regretted the conflict, though. He made up with Joe Curtis, and they remained friends for the rest of their lives. Many years later, I reminded Haskell of the incident, and he immediately picked up the phone, called Joe, and asked him how he was doing. Men are like that. They can have a big fight and then be best of friends. When women fight, they hold onto a grudge forever.

Before school started in the fall, Mama made a trip to her farm near Clarksville to make arrangements to lease it, and she took Little Tom along with her.

On the long bus trip to Fort Smith, she entertained him with stories about the Fort Smith of "territory days," where her father-in-law, Sam Paul, had been tried and sent to jail for manslaughter by the famous Judge Isaac Parker. That night, she took him to a Hopalong Cassidy movie, and the next morning they took another bus into Clarksville.

Mama's farm was at the base of Stillwell Mountain, in the Ozarks, and the "bus" that took them there was actually a one-and-a-half-ton truck with a canvas top and wooden benches on either side of the bed. The road up into the mountains was rough, and when they finally arrived at Mama's farm, Little Tom was sore from being bounced and jostled around in the back of the truck.

After making a brief inspection of her old house, Mama took Little Tom down the road to visit the Selfs, our old neighbors from 1922. The Selfs gave Mama and Little Tom a warm welcome and insisted they stay for supper.

The next day, as Mama busied herself cleaning up the house, Little Tom got acquainted with the local children. They warned him about that same panther their parents had warned us about fifteen years before, the one that prowled the neighborhood waiting to eat little children who ventured outside at night. On Sunday, they went to church and Sunday school at the same little church we had attended when we lived there.

After about a week, Little Tom woke up at the Selfs' house. He had developed a fever during the night, and Mama had gone to the Selfs for help. Mama and Mrs. Self were both experts on children's ailments, and after examining Tom's rash, they diagnosed it as scarlet fever. Mrs. Self sent her family away to stay with neighbors to keep them from catching Tom's infection, and then she gave Tom a bedroom by himself. She and Mama took turns nursing him. They treated him in the old-fashioned way, with mustard plasters, and with hot toddies made from lemonade and whiskey. As Tom said, "One cup would put any nine-year-old at peace with the world." After a few days of this treatment, Tom was feeling better, and so he and Mama said goodbye to the Selfs, and made the trip back home to Pauls Valley.

CHAPTER 35
- Tom Wins Respect, Bob Lies About His Age -

I met a man once who mentioned to me that he had attended OMA back in the 1930s. I told him that my brother had also gone to school there, so we got to talking about it. I asked him if they had hazing when he was there, and he said, "Oh yes, and it was terrible." He then went on about how mean the older boys were and how miserable they made the lives of the younger cadets, or "plebes." Under the "rabbit system," as they called it, the upperclassmen were allowed to order the younger boys to do menial tasks—things like polishing their shoes or cleaning their rooms—but some of the boys took advantage of the system to humiliate or even physically abuse the younger boys. After we had chatted for a while the man said, "By the way, what was your brother's name?"

"Robert Paul," I replied.

Suddenly, all the color went out of the man's face, and he stared at me, dumbfounded. Then he said, "He was the worst one."

Bob's abuse of the younger boys was still fresh on the older cadets' minds when Tom arrived at OMA, so Bob's former victims, now upperclassmen, went after Tom with a vengeance. They made him wash the bathroom, sweep the paths, and shine their shoes. Bob had graduated, so there was no one there to defend him. It was me he complained to. He wrote me letters, and I rode the bus up to see him once or twice. He said he was miserable. It was humiliating, and he was exhausted all the time. He had no time to sleep or to study. Tom had looked forward to going to OMA for so long, and now he was thinking about quitting.

One night, the upper classmen went too far. They came into Tom's room in a group and beat him with coat hangers until he jumped out of his window to get away from them. His window was on the second floor. It's a wonder that he didn't break his leg. After that, Tom decided to take action. He picked out the leader of his tormentors and challenged him to a grudge fight.

Grudge fights were tradition at OMA. According to the rules, any cadet, even a plebe, could challenge any other to a grudge fight. These fights were supervised boxing matches held on a hill behind the school. Finally, Tom was able to take advantage of the training Bob had given him out in the alley behind our house. He knew how to box, and his Paul blood was up. He gave the older boy a sound whipping. In one step, he ended his misery and earned himself a place on OMA's boxing team.

After that, Tom started enjoying OMA. He had earned the respect of the other boys, and he did well on the boxing team. He also went out for tennis—another skill he had learned from Bob. He found that a racket worked much better than the board he had learned with. Now that he had time to study, he started making good grades for the first time in his life, and he started looking forward to the next year, when he could get his turn at the "rabbits."

My other brothers were also busy during the fall of 1937. While Tom was fighting for his life at OMA, Snip was running for Congress, Bob was training at Fort Bliss, and Haskell was planning his wedding to Carrie O'Harro, my friend from high school.

Haskell's marriage to Carrie was tough on Little Tom. She hadn't been his pick among Haskell's girlfriends, and furthermore, he was perfectly happy living with Mama. Haskell had good intentions, I'm sure. He wanted to provide a home for his son, but he handled the situation in his usual fashion, with the tact of a pit bull. First he told Tom he would have to call Carrie "mother," which Tom would never do. Then he arranged for the three of them to go to a movie together.

The movie date turned into a disaster. Little Tom told me the story years later. On the way to pick up Carrie, Haskell lectured Tom about how he should act and warned him about what would happen if he showed Carrie any disrespect. By the time they arrived at the movie, Tom was trembling with fear. Forced to sit between Haskell and Carrie, the movie seemed to last forever. When it was finally over, Little Tom was so anxious to get out of the theater, he accidentally tripped over Carrie's foot, and Haskell, thinking he had done it on purpose, slapped Tom, hard, on the side of his head. Tom said that his ear rang for days.

After that it was war. Haskell was bound and determined to force Little Tom to accept Carrie and her family, and Tom was determined to remain loyal to his mother. Haskell was brutal. He whipped Tom for any sign of rebellion, real or imagined. Once Mama tried to intervene, and Haskell accidentally hit her.

Mama was always Little Tom's refuge. He told me that when his father married Carrie, the hardest part for him was leaving Mama.

Apparently Little Tom wasn't the only one unhappy about the marriage. Carrie's parents didn't like the idea of their daughter marrying an Indian, and a divorced Indian, at that.

I was worried about Little Tom, so I went to see Carrie before the wedding. She told me she thought Tom was a wonderful child, and she intended to love him and take care of him as her own. That made me feel better. Carrie had always been my friend, and I trusted her. At the time, I didn't know about the beatings Little Tom had been getting, but she did.

The wedding took place at the O'Harro home. Jess Larson, secretary of the School Land Commission, was Haskell's best man. I didn't go. Our lives were just too confused at the time. Mama went, and Teker sang a song. She was always a peacemaker.

Haskell and Carrie went to Mexico on their honeymoon. Haskell had learned to speak a little Spanish while he was staying with Papa in San Antonio, so he could make himself understood. Carrie sent me a post card:

Miss Jimmie Paul, YWCA, Oklahoma City, Okla.

Dear Jim:

Having a grand time. Everything seems lovely to me, even if the weather is cool. Almost cold enough for real heavy coats. Drove though sleet yesterday from Temple, where we spent Sunday nite. Shall try to drop you another card later on the trip. See you when we get back, if you like. Be sweet.

Love

C. & H.

Haskell had saved enough money to make a down payment on a little house on Pine Street, just a few blocks from Mama, so when the newlyweds got back to Pauls Valley, they moved into their own home. Little Tom moved in with them, but he still spent most of his time with Mama.

During the last few weeks of the legislative session, Snip had introduced an unusual bill. It would permit any legislator who had served as many as three terms to be made an attorney by the Oklahoma Supreme Court.[1] It didn't pass, and the newspaper treated it as a joke, but I'm not so sure that it was, because the next fall Snip entered the Cumberland Law School in Lebanon, Tennessee.

I suppose he got the idea from his friend ex-governor Holloway, who had gotten his law degree at Cumberland. Snip's farm didn't bring in much money, so the income from a law practice would help during the years between sessions of the legislature. Haskell told Snip that if he passed the bar, he'd be happy to make him a partner in his growing practice. It would be good for both of them. Haskell could show Snip the ropes, and Snip's political notoriety would attract more clients.

Snip's plan to become an attorney was interrupted by an unexpected event. R. P. Hill, the representative to Congress from the Fifth District, died, leaving his seat vacant. Garvin County was included in the district, so Snip placed his name into the hat. There were fifteen candidates in all. The list included a former senator, T. P. Gore; a former governor, William H. Murray; a former federal district attorney, W. C. Lewis; and a former congressman, F. B. Swank. In spite of this formidable competition, Snip became the front-runner in Garvin County and a strong contender in the overall race. An article in the *Daily Oklahoman* described his chances:

Paul First in Home Area, Swank Second

Homer Paul, state senator, is in command of the field in Garvin County in the Democratic race for congressman and his chances in the district depend upon his rolling up a big vote in his home county.

Realizing that, F. B. Swank, Norman, former congressman, who used to have the county in the bag, is fighting for a sizable vote. Gomer Smith, Townsend plan candidate for United States senate last year, also has a hold in the county which has a large so-called radical vote.[2]

The race to finish out R. P. Hill's term was actually considered a practice run for the governor's race. The leaders of the state legislature, who had taken control of the state government from Governor Marland, hoped to take over the state's congressional delegation and the governor's mansion as well. *The Daily Oklahoman* referred them to as the oligarchy:

> [T]he Senate oligarchy will either be weaker or much stronger politically as a result of the Fifth District election.
>
> For the oligarchy, not content with dominating the state executive, as well as the legislature, has now sought to reach out and dominate the state's congressional delegation. This, it is declared at the capitol, is the reason the senators have gone to bat, in their effort to elect Homer Paul, one of their number, to Congress from the Fifth District.[3]

Snip's chances were considered good if there was a light turnout in the Oklahoma City area, but in the end, the Garvin County votes weren't enough to get him into the runoff. Ironically, the law firm of Blanton and Curtis—yes, the same Joe Curtis that Haskell had slugged in court—came out openly for Swank.[4] Snip lost in the primary election, but the effort did make him better known around the state, and by the time of the next session of the legislature, he was considered a contender for president of the Senate.[5]

As soon as the election was over, he moved his family to Tennessee and entered the Cumberland Law School. He and Helen enjoyed their stay in Tennessee. Little Willie started the first grade there, and even though he wasn't quite five yet, Little Homer started to kindergarten. Snip found time to take them all to the Kentucky Derby while they were there, but he must have found time to study, too, because the next spring, after only two semesters' work, he passed the Oklahoma state bar exam.

Meanwhile, Bob was excelling in his training at Fort Bliss, near El Paso. He wrote Mama a letter in November:

> *Saturday 6th,*
>
> *Dear Mama,*
>
> *If I'm not badly mistaken you owe me a letter or two but I shall write just to make sure. I am in the midst of a preparation for an exam Monday morning. I'm glad Tom is getting along fine at school. Yesterday I sent him some money as much as I could spare. I suppose*

on your way back from Arkansas you stopped by to see him. I'm getting along fairly well considering everything. By now I guess Lahoma is teaching in her school. [Mama must have written to Bob bragging about how smart Lahoma was] How is Oteka and her family getting along? Is Jim well? How is Snip getting along with his law? Are our love birds still cooing as rapturously as they were when I left? [Haskell and Carrie—this was before their wedding] I think it's a good idea for you to put that old man on your Arkansas farm. [Mama's renter] I believe he has the real stuff. Well don't work too hard and write whenever you have the time.

Love,

Bob Paul

We had a good Christmas that year. Bob was home from Fort Bliss, and Tom from OMA. The newlyweds, Haskell and Carrie, were still in a state of rapture. Kaliteyo, Teker, and I helped Mama with the cooking. We fixed a fat goose with all the trimmings, sweet potatoes, cranberries, ambrosia, biscuits, and gravy. Mama served eggnog, and we all sat around laughing and talking and making a fuss over Teker's new baby, Homer Dean. Snip and Helen weren't there, but we were happy that Snip was planning to go into partnership with Haskell.

During Bob's visit home, he told Mama that he had conceived a plan to go to West Point. He had chosen to make the military his career, and he realized that a degree from West Point would give him an advantage, so he went for it. He was just as ambitious as Snip and Haskell.

During Bob's leave, he spent all his spare time studying for the West Point exams. He was as nervous as a cat. He'd fidget and pace the floor. After a while, he convinced himself that he had high blood pressure. Then he tried to sit still and relax, which only made things worse.

The first requirement for getting into West Point was being appointed by a member of Congress, but that was the easy part for Bob. Snip asked Gomer Smith to appoint him. Smith had won the election the previous fall to finish out R.P. Hill's term in Congress.

The next hurdle that Bob faced was his age. He would be twenty-three years old before the next class of cadets entered West Point, which was over the age limit, so he decided to lie about it. He wrote to Mama, carefully instructing her on the "correct" date of birth to put on his application forms:

Mar 4, 1938

Fort Bliss, Texas

Dear Mama,

I want to apologize for not having written, but I have been in somewhat of a dither getting ready to go to West Point. Because of my fine record at OMA I was exempt from all mental and all I have to take is the physical. I have already taken the physical and appeared before the West Point Board. I made a hit with the Board and they gave me a waver on my teeth so July 1ˢᵗ your son will be off for West Point. Gomer Smith appointed me. My birth day is, I was born August 6, 1916. [His real date of birth was May 20, 1915.] I am going ahead and take these exams but fear I can't pass them so I shall go to West Point. I am well and everybody down here likes me very well so don't worry about me. On my papers sign where it says signature of parent or guardian and send it to the adjutant General, War Dept., Washington, D. C.. Send it at once. Write me and keep me posted about Jim's condition, [I had started seeing Dr. McNeil about my stomach trouble.] Also how you, Haskell and all the rest are coming along.

Love,

Bob Paul

PS Write soon.

Bob passed the entrance exams and was actually accepted to West Point, but someone there discovered the age discrepancy on his OMA records, and he was sent home. I guess it's a wonder he wasn't court-martialed, but he had impressed his superior officers at Fort Bliss and got by with a reprimand. In the end, he kept his commission, and the Army sent him to law school at OU, according to the original plan.

CHAPTER 36
- Helen Leaves Snip, I Take a Vacation -

Many people out at the capitol owed their jobs to Snip. Although the newspaper railed against it, political patronage was a fact of life in those days, on both the local and the federal level, and with the Great Depression in full swing, politicians practiced it openly. It's not an exaggeration to say that without Snip's help we would have lived in poverty, and none of us, except maybe for Haskell, would have gone to college. Snip got jobs for other people, too—for old friends in need of help, and sometimes, I'm sure, for those he owed political favors. One of our friends that Snip helped was Dixie Taylor, the little neighbor girl who used to keep him company when he had polio. Dixie had married a man named Anderson who had gambled away all their money and left her and their little son penniless, so Snip got her a job working for the state.

When Helen found out about this, she hit the ceiling. Mama tried to explain to her that Dixie was just a good friend, that she was like a member of our family, and any of us would have helped her if we could. She also pointed out that Dixie was a lot older than Snip, so there couldn't have been any romance between them. Anyway, I think Helen finally accepted Mama's explanation, but her suspicions had been aroused.

Snip was always outgoing and cheerful. He was a lot like Papa in that way. He was always joking and teasing people, and sometimes women got the wrong idea. One of the women who had her eye on Snip worked with me. Her name was Fanny, and she thought that she could use me to get close to him. Well, when I found out what she was up to, I put her in her place. She left me alone after that, but there were still rumors from time to time that Snip was having affairs. I never believed them, but then, he was my brother.

There was a period of time when Snip drank too much. He got that from Papa, too, but it kind of went with the territory. He had become a successful politician by making deals in smoke-filled rooms, and there wasn't just smoke in there, but also liquor, Prohibition notwithstanding.

The daughter of a preacher, Helen had strong principles, and she wasn't about to put up with Snip drinking, whether or not the rumors about him being unfaithful were true, so when he came home drunk one night, that was the last straw. She packed her bags, took the boys, and went to California to stay with her sister Juliette.

Snip was devastated. He put on a tough front, but deep down, he was tenderhearted. He'd get so sentimental sometimes he'd almost melt and run down into his shoes. I went out to the farm with him one day after Helen had taken the boys to California. When he saw one of their toys lying on the ground, he picked it up and started to cry.

In the end, it all worked out for the best. Snip begged Helen to come back. He told her how much she meant to him, and he promised to stop drinking and whatever else he had been doing. Actually, I don't know what he said. He certainly didn't confide in me, but Helen did come back, and Snip straightened up. If Helen hadn't taken a firm stand when she did, who knows what would have happened. Helen was the making of Snip. He was lucky he married such a fine woman.

My brother Bob spent the summer of 1938 at home after his appointment to West Point was rejected. Tom pestered him all summer, telling him about his first year at OMA and asking him about Fort Bliss, and after Little Tom got back from Santa Fe, he followed Bob around, too. Little Tom was having a hard time getting used to the idea of his father getting married again, so it was nice for him that Bob was there.

Snip had hired Bob to do some work for him out at the farm, and Bob took Little Tom along when he went out there. Bob seemed to enjoy Little Tom's company. They worked together tearing down the old house where Shorty used to live, salvaging the lumber and nails. Also, Snip had a yearling mare that needed to be broken to the saddle, and he asked Bob to do it for him, so Little Tom learned to break a horse the army way.

Every day when Bob and Little Tom went out to the farm, Bob would put the mare into the corral and have Tom go in there with her. He taught Tom to always have some kind of treat for the horse—some meal, sugar, or carrots. After a few days, when the mare was used to Tom and expecting a treat from him, Bob told Tom to hold back the treat until she let him put his hand on her neck. Pretty soon, the mare would let him touch her neck and back and even brush her coat. Then came the bridle, a blanket, and finally the saddle, the horse earning a treat with each new step. When the day came that he climbed into the saddle, the mare didn't bat an eye. He told me proudly, "I was the first person to sit on her back." At the end of the summer, Bob gave Little Tom a .22 rifle as payment for helping him.

While I was working at the capitol, I joined a businesswomen's sorority, Beta Sigma Phi. Jeanette Moore was a member, as well as a lot of my other friends. Our meetings were fun. One of the silly things we did was to write our own lyrics to the tune of popular songs of the day. Here is one written to the tune of "Smiles":

> *There are girls in California*
> *There are girls in China too*
> *There are girls in far away Australia*
> *Girls in France and India, too*
> *There are girls all over this great nation*
> *And wherever you may chance to roam*
> *You will never find an equal*
> *To our girls right here at home.*

Beta Sigma Phi also sponsored charity events, and we put on social functions. I usually arranged to get Don Gunning, the young man from Enid, invited, although we weren't exactly dating.

During the summer of 1938, I took my first paid vacation. One of the girls I knew from Beta Sig, Juanita Bowman, was dating a young man who organized tours to New Orleans. She was helping him sign up girls for a tour that summer, and she asked me if I'd like to go. The cost of the ten-day trip was eighty-nine dollars, and that included transportation, lodging, meals, and tours of Biloxi, New Orleans, and Baton Rouge, as well as boat trips into the Gulf and along the Mississippi River. The tour sponsors, a family named Lanza, owned an old Biloxi mansion they had named "Oklahoma Manor" for our benefit. Eighty-nine dollars was two-thirds of my monthly salary, but I had a little money saved up, so I was tempted. Jeanette and Juanita kept nagging at me to go, and it sounded like such fun, I finally said yes.

The Lanzas were Louisiana natives, and they were French, in spite of their Italian name. Mama Lanza would fix us a big breakfast every morning and a regular banquet of seafood every evening. She was really a good cook. The manor was right next to the shore. Each morning we would walk down to the beach to watch the ships come in, and some of the girls would go crabbing. Mama Lanza cooked their crabs for them in the evening. I wasn't used to seafood, but she was a good cook.

We got well acquainted with the Lanzas during our stay. Ruby, their oldest daughter, went on our tours with us, and she took a liking to me. The French are very superstitious, and the Lanzas told us stories about ghosts and witches and evil spells that had been cast on some of their unlucky neighbors. They reminded me of Mama. She was superstitious, too, and her mother's family was from Mobile, Alabama, just a little farther up the coast.

Ruby's older sister was engaged to a young man named Falkenstein, whose family owned a casino and a bowling alley in New Orleans. We got to know him and his family, too, and we went to his casino several times. I tried bowling, and some of the girls gambled.

The Lanzas had a sailboat, and one morning they took us to an island they called Deer Island. The island was a tropical paradise covered by big, beautiful trees with Spanish moss hanging from the branches and countless birds. The only trouble was the mosquitoes. The air was thick with them. One of the girls got so many bites she got sick and had to be sent to the hospital to have the poison boiled out of her. The island wasn't unhealthy for everyone, though. The Lanzas told us they took their teenage son over there every year for his asthma. It must have been before the mosquitoes hatched.

We toured Biloxi while we were there and also Baton Rouge, the state capital. We also took a boat tour down the Gulf coast and out onto Lake Pontchartrain, but the place we enjoyed most was New Orleans.

It was thirty or forty miles into New Orleans from where we stayed in Biloxi, but we spent as much time there as we could. I bought a bottle of French perfume in one of the fancy stores along Canal Street, which was once actually a canal. We took the streetcar out into the garden district and

Wenonah, 1938

saw the beautiful old mansions and Spanish moss hanging from the trees, and in the evenings we went to the nightclubs along Canal Street. I even got asked to dance a few times.

I loved the *Vieux Carre,* or French Quarter, with its narrow streets and overhanging balconies. Only a few years before our visit it had been a slum, but the city had renovated it, and by the time we were there it had become the city's main attraction. It was like going back in time. We sat in the Café du Monde on the Mississippi River next to the old French Market, drank chicory coffee, and ate the famous French doughnuts, or *beignets*. We toured the St. Louis Cathedral where, we were told, bodies had been stacked on top of each other to meet the demand for burial space. We strolled through Jackson Square, named for Andrew Jackson, one of history's greatest tyrants as far as the American Indians are concerned, and we learned that the *Vieux Carre* had first been laid out by the French Governor Bienville, who had tried twice to annihilate the Chickasaws.

The highlight of the trip for me, though, was seeing an exhibit of gowns worn by the French royalty before the revolution. They were on loan from the French government in honor of the renovation of the French Quarter and were being displayed in the *Cabildo*, the old Spanish courthouse. It was hard to imagine the nobility living in such luxury in a country were the common people languished in poverty, but I guess that's why the peasants cut off their heads.

When the week was over, we all returned home with wonderful memories, and a dream started to form in my mind. The next summer, I was going back to New Orleans, and I was going to take Mama.

CHAPTER 37
- Haskell Almost Dies, I Take Mama to New Orleans -

When I got back from my wonderful vacation in New Orleans, there was a notice waiting for me at the YWCA saying very politely that since I had lived there for the maximum time of three years, I would have to move out. I had known my time was coming, but it was still a big blow to me. The girls at the Y were like family, and I hated to leave them, but most of my friends were leaving, too, so it wouldn't be the same, anyway. My roommate Mattie Elkins had already moved out, and Ede and Hattie were looking for another place to stay, like I was. My Chickasaw friend Lula Pybas was moving back in with her parents in Purcell.

One weekend, Lula invited me to come home with her for a visit. We had a good time together, and while I was there I met her sister Daisy, who lived in the house next door to her parents. A week or so later, Daisy invited me to come and stay with her—she had an extra bedroom—so I moved to Purcell. I paid her a little rent money, and we got along fine.

Every morning, Lula and I would get up at the crack of dawn to make the thirty-mile drive to the state capitol in time for work. We rode with George Schwartz, who owned a business in Oklahoma City. Mr. Schwartz was an older man, and he had known Papa back in his ranching days. He knew about our family's tragedy, of course, but he had the tact not to talk about it.

As I was moving out of the Y, my brothers and sisters were making changes of their own. Tom was off to OMA, and Bob to the OU law school. Oteka and Thurman were living in Norman. Teker was busy with her baby, Homer Dean, and Thurman was working part-time and trying to finish his engineering degree by the end of the year. Kaliteyo was the only one of us left at home with Mama. Snip had gotten her a good job as head of the food stamp program in Pauls Valley, and Little L was starting first grade.

And then, just when I thought everything was going well, we were faced with another crisis. Haskell came down with Bright's Disease. It came on gradually. First he lost his appetite, then his energy, and then his body began to swell. His kidneys were failing. The doctor told him it was serious, and that he might not survive. It seemed that our family could hardly get through a single year without a crisis. I don't know how Mama stood it.

Carrie, now six months pregnant, was worried about how she was going to support her baby if Haskell left her a widow. Snip came back to Pauls Valley and tried to handle a few of Haskell's cases. We were all worried, but Haskell slowly improved. After about a month, he was able to go in to his office part-time, and so Snip went back to Oklahoma City to get ready for the next session of the legislature.

In December, Carrie delivered a baby girl named Vickie June, named after Mama, but the celebration was short and sweet. Vickie June turned out to be a "blue baby," a common term then for babies with a specific heart defect.[1] Haskell and Carrie took her to a heart specialist who said there was nothing that could be done to save her. It was just a matter of time.

While everyone was worried about Haskell, I was keeping track of my little brother Tom. When he arrived at OMA that year, he received a shock. They had banned hazing. Tom was so mad that he actually cried. "They've ruined the school!" he wailed. After all, he had suffered as a "rabbit," and he had been looking forward to getting his turn at lording it over the plebes. I just laughed.

Actually, Tom was happy at OMA that year. He was doing well in his studies, and was involved in tennis and boxing. He was so proud of himself. We corresponded regularly and I looked forward to getting his cute letters:

> Dear Jim,
> We get out the 16, at eleven O'Clock: I don't want you to send me the money to come home on because you have spent to much money

246

on me as it is. All I want you to do is to get it from Kaliteyo or ask her for me if she won't why just let it go. There is a Capt. That is going to take four boys to the City for $2.50 in his car and then I could catch a bus from there and it will be a lot faster and you just [ask] Kaliteyo for it and tell her to send me $.35 extery for a haircut. Because I need one very bad I have been in the hospital for 9 days but I got out today. I guess it was the flue or something because I had a rattle in my chest and the Doc said that it might have turned into Pneumonia if I hadn't come to the hospital when I did. But I am out, and feeling fine. I would have written Kaliteyo myself But she won't answer me when I do write her. Well I have just got to close.

Love

T M Paul

P S How do you like that Signature? [Tom wrote everything with a flourish and eventually developed a very artistic style of handwriting. In 1938, though, he was still working to perfect it.] Did Thurman ever get a job? [Thurman must have lost his job in the oilfield]

Write Soon

I spelled your name right for the first time. [He's talking about "Wenonah." This was about the time I changed the spelling of my name.]

I can't print worth a dam can I,

Tom

Tom was still signing his name as "T M Paul." The "M" was for "Merle." Mama had always told him that his name was Thomas Merle Paul, after Papa's cousin in San Antonio. Actually, Papa had put Thomas Smith Paul on Tom's birth certificate, but he didn't find out about it until much later. He was overjoyed when he found out that his middle name was Smith. He hated the name Merle.

I tried to make sure Tom got everything he needed. He didn't like to ask for money, but Snip didn't give him spending money like he had Bob. There was a loan company in Oklahoma City called the Morris Plan. They would make small loans of five or ten dollars for a month or two. It wasn't a very good deal. The interest amounted to as much as the loan, but when Tom needed money and I didn't have anything left from my salary, I would borrow a few dollars and give it to him. He eventually got a little job after school and on weekends, so he could have his own money.

Bob borrowed money from me, too, but he never paid me back. That was the difference between the two. Even when Tom didn't have any money, he would try and repay me in some way, by sending me an OMA patch or some stationery, but if you loaned something to Bob, you could kiss it goodbye.

The army only paid for Bob's tuition at OU, so he did need money, at least at first, and he needed a cheap place to stay. It was Kaliteyo who came up with a job for him working at the state mental hospital in Norman. The job came with free room and board, so it was an ideal arrangement, but I didn't approve of the way she got it for him. She had a friend who was the hospital administrator's mistress, and the friend had used her "influence" to get Bob his job. Kaliteyo had such lovely friends.

Meanwhile, back in Pauls Valley, Lahoma wasn't doing well in school. For a while there, we thought she was a little slow, but finally her teacher, my good friend Marguerite Baker, figured out that she couldn't see. We were so relieved. I bought her glasses myself, and she never made another bad grade.

Back in Norman, Teker was devoting most of her considerable energy toward raising Homer Dean. I went down to see her as often as I could. Homer was a sickly baby, so he kept her busy. He had a lot of allergies, and there were times when he had trouble breathing, but Teker stayed on top of it. Meanwhile she had gotten acquainted with all her neighbors. She was always so outgoing.

It just so happened that Teker and Thurman lived next door to Thurman's geology professor, and of course Teker and the professor's wife became good friends. She helped out during Teker's difficult pregnancy, and she knew how hard Thurman was working to make ends meet, spending nights and weekends working in the oilfields, fishing and shooting rabbits for food, and selling ties on the side.

Thurman studied hard in geology, but when he went in for his final exam, he was totally surprised. The professor gave each student a map and asked them to name all the geologic formations, from the west coast to the east. Thurman hadn't bothered to memorize them. He didn't think it was important, so he flunked the test and the course. He and Teker were devastated. He would have to take the course over again, and he wouldn't have enough credits to graduate by the end of the spring semester. They were just barely getting by, and they were counting on Thurman graduating in the spring so that he could go to work full-time.

Well, when the professor's wife found out about their dilemma, she told Teker not to worry, that she would talk to her husband, and sure enough, the next week, Thurman got a neighborly visit from the professor, wanting to discuss his test results. The professor said that he had thought about it, and maybe it wasn't quite fair to expect Thurman to memorize the names of all those formations. After all, it was more important to understand how they developed than to just memorize the names, so he had decided to try to make it up to him. It was too late to offer another test, so Thurman would still have to retake the course, but the professor promised him a passing grade so that he wouldn't have to worry about studying. That way Thurman could concentrate on his other classes and still graduate in the spring.

The state legislature was in session during the winter of 1939, so Snip and Helen rented a house in Oklahoma City in the fall so the boys wouldn't have to change schools in the middle of the year. That's the way they did it. Since the legislature was only in session every other year, the boys would go to school in Pauls Valley one year and in Oklahoma City the next. That fall, Little Willie was starting into the second grade, and Little Homer was in the first, the same as Little L, even though Homer was only five.

Little Homer was precocious, so Helen had enrolled him in kindergarten the previous year to give him an early start. She used to ride the streetcar when she went shopping downtown, and she would take the boys along with her. Children under five could ride for free on the streetcar, and Little Homer could pass for four, so when someone asked him how old he was, he would say, "I'm five at home, six at school, and four on the streetcar."

As soon as the Senate committees started meeting, I started to see Snip's name in the paper again. He was chosen as chairman of the Senate Highway Committee for the coming session of the legislature. There was a new governor in 1939, Leon "Red" Phillips. He was an outspoken opponent of the New Deal, and as Speaker of the House in 1935, he had been instrumental in blocking Governor Marland's version of the federal program.[2]

As an experienced power broker, Phillips personally met with the legislative committees to make sure they complied with his policy of cutting government spending and raising taxes. He even hired a team of investigators to dig up dirt on those legislators who opposed him.

Phillips moved fast to get as many departments under his control as possible, and the powerful highway department was one of the first on his list. Snip supported the governor's reorganization plan for the highway department, but he did push back on other issues. He managed to block Phillips' attempt to put all the state's legal staff under his control,[3] and he attempted to get relief for the state's poor by exempting necessary food items from Phillips' sales tax.[4] This amendment failed, but it won Snip political points.

As a highway department employee, I was personally affected by Governor Phillips' budget cuts. One day, I came into work to find my fellow clerks all in a stir about an article in the newspaper reporting that Bonnie Brinn and I—Bonnie was Jim Nance's sister—were making twenty dollars per month more than the other clerks, $145 instead of $125.[5] The scandal rolled off Snip like water off a duck's back, but it embarrassed me. I never knew if it was Snip who got us the raise, or just somebody trying to get on his good side, but Bonnie and I never saw any of the money we were supposed to be getting.

I soon got tired of commuting back and forth from Purcell, so after a couple of months I moved back to Oklahoma City. Hattie, one of my friends from the capitol, was living in a boarding house across the street from the medical school, and I moved in with her. We roomed together until I got married.

It was a good year for me. The girls I knew from work and from the Y went out together, and there were also functions put on by the Beta Sigs and by the Indian-Okla Club—I was their program chairman. I also met some guys. We'd usually go out in a group, not necessarily as couples, and just have a good time, but after a while I started pairing up with Don Gunning. We went to movies and we went dancing. In the summers, big-name bands like Tommy Dorsey and Guy Lombardo performed at Springlake Pavilion. We also went bowling and roller skating, and in the wintertime, when Shepherd's Pond froze over, we even went ice skating.

When spring came, I talked Mama into going to New Orleans with me. It wasn't easy, but Kaliteyo helped out by finding a daycare center where Little L could stay for a couple of weeks. Haskell was over his kidney problems, and Little Tom had gone to Santa Fe for the summer, so Mama had no excuse.

I had a two-week vacation with pay, and I had saved a little besides to pay for our trip. We rode the train down. For the first night, I splurged and put us up at the Monteleone Hotel on Canal Street. That evening, we ate in the hotel restaurant and listened to music in the lounge. The next morning, we moved over to the YWCA to save money. It was my friend Ede Roberts who gave me the idea of staying at the Y. It was nice there—and cheap. Ede told me she had traveled to a lot of places staying at Y's. The food there was good. It was Southern cooking and Gulf Coast cuisine. I especially liked the crab cakes. We also ate out sometimes. One afternoon, I took Mama to the Court of the Two Sisters, a famous restaurant in the French Quarter of New Orleans that was originally built in 1832 as the home of a wealthy banker.

We visited the Falkensteins while we were there, the family who owned the casino. They all fell in love with Mama. One evening, Mrs. Falkenstein fixed us a seafood feast. It was a perfect evening, except for when I choked on a fish bone. It scared Mama, but Mrs. Falkenstein took it in stride. "You're supposed to chew those bones up," she said.

Juanita, Mrs. Falkenstein's fifteen-year-old daughter, was our tour guide, and she went along with us to describe the places we visited. We visited the same places I had seen the year before, but having her there to explain things made it much more interesting.

I got better acquainted with the Falkensteins while we were there. They were deeply religious, and Juanita showed us several churches and religious shrines. Her mother had a serious eye disease, and she told us about how she had once crawled on her knees to the shrine of St. Lucy to ask for her mother's eyes to be healed.

Just like me, Mama was enchanted by New Orleans. She loved the Spanish moss and the gardens, the old houses and the people. Mama never met a stranger, anyway, and these were her people. The only thing missing was her shovel to dig up plants. She did manage to take home some flower seeds, though.

Mama and I were exhausted but happy when we finally boarded the train for Pauls Valley. It made me feel good to be able to do something for her after all she had done for us. Mama had worked so hard all those years trying to make a home for us, while putting up with Papa's drinking, seeing our prosperity evaporate, and finally losing my dear brother Willie. I felt like I was able to give her a little happiness by helping her connect with her roots.

CHAPTER 38
- Snip Goes Back on His Word -

It was early summer when Teker, Thurman, and little Homer Dean took off in Thurman's old Packard sedan. The car was stuffed so full there was hardly room to sit, but they were so excited. Thurman had high hopes, bolstered by his new degree in engineering and news of an oil boom in Illinois, but I had a bad feeling from the start. They had no friends, no job, hardly any money, and Salem, Illinois, where they were headed, couldn't have been a worse place to live.

The trip took several days. It was summertime and warm, so they slept outside to save money on hotels. When they got to St. Louis, they slept in the park. During the night they were awakened by growls, roars, and shrieks—the noise sounded close, too. Teker said she would have made Thurman pack up their stuff and drive on if she hadn't been so tired, but they eventually fell asleep. The next morning the mystery was solved. They had parked next to the zoo.

When they got to Salem, Teker and Thurman looked around for a place to rent. Finally, they located a trailer park with a vacancy and put down a month's rent for a small trailer. According to Teker, it was pretty basic. The sink was hooked up to water, and there was a gas stove, but the toilet was an outhouse. Teker was so neat and tidy, though, I'm sure she had everything shining in no time at all.

Thurman had used most of their money to pay the rent, so he needed to get a job, and fast. The national unemployment rate was still at fifteen percent, and there were a lot of people there looking for work, so it wasn't easy. The first thing he did was to ask where he could find work. A man in the trailer park advised him to go stand on the corner of Fourth and Main Street at seven the next morning. That's where the trucks stopped to pick up men to work in the oil fields.

The next morning there must have been twenty-five or thirty men waiting at the corner. A couple of trucks came by and picked up five or ten men each, and then left. Thurman wasn't one of the ones chosen. This went on for two or three days until finally, Thurman, a big man at six-feet-three and nearly two hundred pounds, pushed himself to the front and got the attention of a crew chief.

Thurman knew his first day would be critical. The job was laying pipe, and there were only two wrenches for the whole crew to use. As soon as Thurman's turn came to use the wrench, he kept it, refusing to take a break for the rest of the day. He wanted to convince the boss that he was a hard worker. Thurman had been doing hard work in the oilfields in Oklahoma for two years, so he was in good shape, but after that first day's work in Salem, he was so tired he didn't even take off his clothes when he got home. He just lay down on the floor of the trailer and passed out.

After Thurman had proven himself, he was chosen regularly for work crews, but the pay was low, and he and Teker were still struggling to pay for food, clothes, medicine, and rent. Homer Dean's allergies were acting up, too. Thurman kept them supplied with fish like he had in Oklahoma, and he sold minnows and worms on weekends for extra money.

Teker didn't like the people in Illinois. They were Yankees, and they assumed that anyone from Oklahoma must be a hick. She quickly informed them that she had never in her life used an outhouse until she came to Salem.

Back in Pauls Valley, Mama got a shock. Snip came by the house one day and informed her that he was going to stop paying for Tom to go to OMA! Tom had been so happy there. For the first time in his life, he was interested in school, and he was doing well, too. Mama was crushed. We all were, and angry. We felt betrayed. Snip had taken our farm, and then he had gone back on his promise to help the family. There he was, living high on the hog, wining and dining big shots in the state capital, and he couldn't spare enough money to give his little brother a chance for a decent education.

Looking back now, I can understand why Snip did what he did. It had been ten years since Willie's death, when he had promised Mama he would take Willie's place, and now he had his own family to support. He did have an important position politically, but his only real income was his salary from the legislature. He hadn't had a chance to build up a law practice, the farm didn't bring in much, and he had the extra expense of spending a year in Tennessee attending law school. But our relations with Snip were strained after that. Mama stopped confiding in him, and he stopped coming to family get-togethers.

The summer of 1939, Snip joined Haskell in law practice, and their business really took off. Snip's contacts and reputation helped the practice, and Haskell bought a real estate abstracting business from one of our Waite cousins, Corinne Lassater, which brought in more income as well.

Nineteen thirty-nine was also a significant year in Chickasaw history. It was the year that Douglas Johnston passed away. Johnston had been the last Chickasaw governor elected by the tribe. Ever since the passage of the Curtis Act, the tribal governor had been an appointed position, and he had been automatically reappointed since then.

With his death, the position was now open, and knowing about Haskell's pride in our Chickasaw heritage, Snip managed to have him nominated as Johnston's replacement. An appointment was set up for Haskell to be interviewed by the secretary of the interior.[1]

I don't know how many people were nominated for the governor's position, but one of them was our cousin, Floyd Maytubby. Floyd was the grandson of our great-grandmother Ela-Teecha's sister. After the interview, Haskell was told that the committee considered him too "provincial," whatever they meant by that. I guess they thought he was a hick. Anyway, if they had said it to his face, they might have found out just how provincial he was. I found out later that there was a requirement that the governor have a quarter degree of Indian blood, so Haskell wouldn't have qualified, anyway. He was only an eighth.

So Floyd Maytubby was appointed Chickasaw governor, and Haskell went back to Pauls Valley disappointed. It did give him an amusing story to tell, though, and he didn't mind all that much, because he liked Floyd. Haskell used to stop by to visit him when he was in Oklahoma City. At that time, the Chickasaw governor had no real influence and not much of a salary, either. Floyd's real job was selling insurance.

I kept encouraging Tom, now back at Pauls Valley High School, to continue with his education, reminding him how hard his brother Haskell had to work to get his degree. "If Haskell can do it, so can you," I said, and I bought him a nice suede jacket to wear to school so he wouldn't feel ashamed of the way he looked.

Tom cheered up for a while. He even decided to go out for basketball. He was strong and athletic. I'm sure he would have been a good player, but one day he came back to the locker room, and his new suede jacket was gone. He found it later in a trash can out behind the school, torn and stained. Tom quit the team, right then and there.

Bob wasn't doing very well at OU. He flunked over half his courses the first year. I don't know what his problem was. Whether it was disappointment over failing to be admitted to West Point, or if he was just having too much fun, he certainly wasted the year. He laid out of school for the first semester of his second year, but kept his job at the asylum. By the time the second semester rolled around, he was ready to start back to school and to apply himself.

During the summer, Kaliteyo and Lahoma moved to Purcell. Kaliteyo had been transferred to the welfare office there. It was a promotion. It seemed to make her happy to have an excuse to move out of Mama's house. She just couldn't stand to have Mama looking over her shoulder. She sent Little L to St. Elizabeth's day school there, and like her mother before her, Lahoma loved it.

I went to an open house at St. Elizabeth's one weekend with Little L. She excitedly showed me around the school and introduced me to some of her teachers. As she was telling me about a nun she especially liked, she suddenly cried out, "There she is!" and ran over to one of them. When the nun turned around, Little L looked disappointed and said, "Oh, this is the wrong one." The nun just laughed. They do kind of look alike in their habits.

I was still working at the capitol in Oklahoma City. Hattie and I had moved out of the rooming house and were renting a small house in the same neighborhood. I made another trip in October, this time to Chicago. OU was playing Northwestern in football, and several of us got a good deal on tickets.

Up in Salem, Illinois, Thurman had been promoted to pumper, a position with more responsibility. He was assigned three or four wells to supervise over an area of several square miles, and he was given the use of a pickup truck to make his rounds. His experience working in the oilfields

255

was actually doing him more good than his engineering degree. The work was still hard, and when the ground was muddy, the truck would get stuck, and he'd end up having to walk between wells. He was feeling more secure, though, even if he couldn't afford to move them into a house.

Meanwhile, Teker was getting fed up with life in a trailer park. It was now wintertime, and it got so cold during the day that she would get into bed with Homer Dean and pull up the covers just to stay warm. Water condensed on the linoleum floor and froze, and she slipped and fell several times. We cringed when we read Teker's letters. Mama's comment was, "It's like they're living in a fruit jar that's been thrown out in the yard."

The toughest thing for Teker, though, was Homer Dean. His asthma was bad, and he kept getting pneumonia. After his third bout, she had had enough. She packed him up, caught a train, and came home to Mama. We were all relieved.

Teker was like a mother bear after she got back. She was in a bad mood all the time. None of us could talk to her. She kept ruminating about Thurman, "Taking me and my baby to that God-forsaken place. It's not fit for a polar bear."

Thurman followed Oteka just as soon as he could pack up their things and drive back to Oklahoma. When he got to Pauls Valley, he came to the house to make up with her. "Teka, Teka, I didn't know it would be so cold there. I'm sorry I took you so far away from home." They were in Mama's room, where Teker was sleeping with Homer Dean. Thurman had kicked off his shoes and was sitting on the bed. Teker was so mad she couldn't see straight. She told him what she thought of him, and then picked up one of his shoes and hit him on the head.

I wasn't there, but Mama swore Teker knocked Thurman out. Anyway, he decided not to try to spend the night and drove on to his parents' house in Wynnewood. The next day, Mr. and Mrs. McLean made a visit to Haskell's office to ask him if he could do something to control that wild sister of his. It must have been hard for Haskell to keep from laughing, being asked to protect six-feet-three, two-hundred-pound Thurman from his little, skinny sister, but he contained himself and promised he would talk to her.

Thurman eventually won Oteka over. She couldn't stay mad at him for long. Then he found a job in the oilfields in the same area where he had worked while he was in school, and they moved back to Norman.

CHAPTER 39
- I Start Thinking About Myself -

It was sometime during the fall of 1940 that Don Gunning first asked me to marry him. At the time I wasn't even thinking about getting married, though. My goal ever since graduating from college—well, actually, ever since Willie had died—was to help my family, and I still had Tom to put through college, so I turned down Don's marriage proposal, but it did get me to thinking.

Don was a quiet and easygoing man, not at all like my brothers. Actually, I wasn't attracted to him at first. There was another man who liked me, too. He worked in the state auditor's office. He was funny, and he had a forceful, outgoing personality, a lot like my brother Snip. I liked him, but after a while I started to realize he was a little too much like my brothers. If we had gotten together, we'd have probably ended up killing each other.

I went out with several men while I was working at the state capitol, but I always came back to Don. He was considerate and thoughtful and, above all, persistent. I couldn't seem to run him off. I was always shooting my mouth off about something, but Don never contradicted me, never argued. He'd give his opinion, but always in a tactful way. I used to say derogatory things about athletes because of the smart-aleck football players I had met in my education class. It was only later that one of Don's friends told me that he had been a star basketball player at OU.

So Don kept asking me out, in spite of everything, and I continued to focus on my family, but he dropped the marriage conversation, at least for the time being.

Meanwhile, I was worried about Tom. After he had found his nice suede coat in the trash, I told him, "Just forget it. You'll be out of school soon." He just laughed, but I'm sure it bothered him.

Tom had friends, of course. He still hung out with Vic Swinney, although Vic was now in the class ahead of him. He played tennis with Jack Snodgrass, who was older, but no match for him on the tennis court. And then there was Imy Alvis. Her mother was a friend of Mama's, and the owner of the Alvis Hotel downtown. Like Vic and Tom, Imy and Tom had been friends since grade school.

Tom's way of dealing with problems was to laugh them off. He was a lot like Kaliteyo in that way. He always seemed happy and carefree, entertaining us at home with his stories and observations. And he was becoming a ladies' man, too, like his brothers Snip and Bob. Haskell was too serious for romance—and too practical. That was one way Haskell and I were alike.

Tom got himself a job in the evenings and on weekends and used his little bit of money on girls. He'd slick down his stiff, black hair with grease, put on some "smell-um-good," as he called it, and go out. I lectured him about his future, but he just laughed and teased me about worrying too much. It was hard to be serious with Tom.

Things weren't going as I had planned. It seemed like my brothers and sisters were going their own separate ways.

Teker and Thurman were now living in Norman. Thurman was working as a pumper, and Teker was busy with Homer Dean. I saw them less and less.

Kaliteyo still had her job with the welfare department in Purcell, and she had started giving Little L dancing lessons. I was on the program committee for the Indian-Okla club, so I scheduled Little L to dance at one of our meetings. She performed on the same program with a young Potawatomi girl, Yvonne Chouteau, who later became a famous ballerina.

Haskell's law business was growing, especially since Snip had joined him, and Carrie was working as his secretary, leaving poor little Vickie June in the care of a maid. The doctor had told Carrie that Vickie June could go at any time, and to go on with her life. I don't know how she could leave her baby, though. Mama could hardly stand it. She loved babies so much. Finally, in November, Vickie June died.

Meanwhile, the oil boom had hit Pauls Valley. Oil derricks were sprouting up all over the place, and there were a lot of workers in town looking for a place to stay. With all of us gone except for Tom, Mama got the idea of renting out rooms. Pretty soon she was making a little income for herself, and she no longer had to ask Snip and Haskell for money.

Even my friends were going their separate ways. Jeannette Moore married a salesman named Bill Beard. My roommate at the Y, Mattie Elkins, married a pharmacist from Dallas—Don and I drove down to their wedding. Ede Roberts joined the Navy.

The world was changing, too. In September of 1939, Germany invaded Poland, starting World War II. President Roosevelt had promised in his re-election campaign, "Your boys are not going to be sent to any foreign wars," and after his re-election, Congress renewed the neutrality law passed after World War I. No one thought that we would be involved, but Roosevelt started building up the military, anyway.

Don's brother Everett graduated from high school that year. Everett was really smart in a practical way, but he had always had trouble in school. Nowadays he would probably have been given the help he needed, but as it was, he couldn't get a job and was in a quandary over what to do next. Don advised him to join the military, so that's what he did. He chose the Navy.

About the same time, one of Tom's friends, Billie Stevens, joined the Army and wrote Tom a letter from boot camp:

Sunday

Dear Tom

This is the God-damdest thing I ever got into. I got here Thurs. and the next morning they shot me in the ass and both arms and then clipped my head. There are 9000 other silly bastards here and we all look like convicts.

I am assigned to the 63rd platoon but we don't start drilling until a week from Monday.

I saw Claud Scog. yesterday and he is already Private First Class in his platoon. Of course he drops that rank at the end of boot camp (7 weeks) but it helps his record. So you can imagine how you would rank out here. If he could make a PFC you should make a sgt.

Hell I can't even leave the dam gate of this camp for 7 weeks

259

and its sure going to be hell. They don't have a rabbit system but the officers sure rack your ass. A member of one platoon can't speak to a member of another. I had to talk to Scog. on the sly. He said if you see Austin to tell him to keep his ass out of here and thats my advice for you too. Because if you came out now you would be in a different platoon and I would never see you in Boot-camp and afterwards we would be stationed in different places. I don't know a damed thing about this place. All I've seen is the barricks and mess hall. I'm damed sure going to stick these 7 weeks out. There has been a lot of guys going over the hill and they are getting there ass stuck.

Now God-dam it be sure and write.

Bill

Private William A Stevens Jr

63rd Platoon

Recruit Depot MCB

San Diego, Calif[1]

That fall, Snip was busy with politics again. Helen moved to Oklahoma City to get the boys started in school, while Snip stayed in Pauls Valley and campaigned. The county attorney for Garvin County, S. J. Goodwin, was running against him. Goodwin argued that the tax exemption for food and clothing that Snip had proposed during the previous session would have led to a cut in old-age pensions. Snip accused Goodwin of failing to prosecute bootleggers and gamblers. Snip won.

After being in the state legislature for fourteen years Snip was no longer considered a young firebrand, but rather a seasoned veteran, and Helen had become prominent in social circles. She was president of the Ohohoma Club, an organization of legislators' wives.

We didn't see Snip and Helen much while the legislature was in session, but they did come down to Pauls Valley for Christmas. Everyone spent Christmas at Mama's house that year, and I invited Don down to meet my family. I think he was a little overwhelmed by my brother the senator, and by Haskell, too, but everyone liked him. Tom and Bob were interested in his athletic exploits, of course.

After the Christmas break, Tom disappeared. He turned up a couple of weeks later with news that would change my world. He had gotten married!

The previous summer he met a girl named Catherine Etheridge, who was visiting her grandmother in Pauls Valley, and they had fallen in love. They had been corresponding and getting together on the sly all during the first semester of school. By the time I found out about their affair, they were already married. Mama was hurt, and I was furious. Tom, in his charming, cheerful way, promised me that he would finish high school and then go to college, but I was finished. I told him that he could expect no more help from me.

Tom and Catherine got an apartment in Pauls Valley, and she started working as a secretary to support them. Tom did finish high school, and then went on to college, but by that time I had stopped worrying about him. I decided that it was time for me to worry about myself.

Tom's marriage got me thinking about Don's marriage proposal again. I realized that Don was special, and I knew that I would probably never find another man like him. I also started to think about having my own family, and my own children, a situation that I could control.

It all came together for me one weekend when we went down to Norman to visit Teker and Thurman. Teker's baby, Homer Dean, was having an asthma attack. Teker couldn't calm him down and neither could I. We were both too high strung. Finally, Don picked up the baby. Homer Dean must have sensed Don's gentle nature, and he settled right down.

On the way back to Oklahoma City, I told Don I'd marry him.

CHAPTER 40
- *Don* -

Don Gunning was a big, strong man, six feet, four inches tall, with broad shoulders. He was quiet and unassuming, but he carried himself with confidence, and when he said something, people paid attention. Everyone liked Don—everyone who knew him—and they respected him, too. He could be funny, especially when he was telling stories about his adventures, but for the most part, he was serious, hardworking, and dependable.

Don's father, Robert B. Gunning, had come to Oklahoma from Illinois about 1910. He worked for the railroad operating a pile driver, and as he was building a bridge across the North Canadian River, his pile driver collapsed on him, crushing his leg. After a long period of recuperation, Mr. Gunning was able to get around again, but he realized he wouldn't be able to return to doing heavy labor, so he learned to cut hair. He settled in the nearby community of Fay, where he met and married Don's mother, Jesse Boyd. They moved to Enid when Don was three or four, but Don spent his summers in Fay, and those times were some of his fondest memories.

Don's people were Yankees and Republican, and I don't think Mrs. Gunning thought much of Indians, either. The area around Fay had belonged to the Cheyenne and Arapaho before it was opened for settlement, and she had gone to school with some of them. The Indian families were poor and often asked for charity from her father.

The Gunnings and the Boyds were warm and accepting of me, though, and they were too polite to say anything openly critical of Indians. I liked them. They were good people, down-to-earth and hardworking. Later, after Don and I were married, we would spend the night with the Gunnings, and Don's mother would have the house cleaned up and breakfast cooked before we even got out of bed. They sure weren't like my family. Why, by the time my brothers finished thinking of excuses to get out of doing something, they could have had it done. Don's family was different from us in another way, too. They didn't fight with each other. That seemed a little boring to me at first, but in time I learned to appreciate it.

Don certainly didn't think his kinfolks were boring. In fact, he could talk for hours about his adventures in Fay. As a boy, his hero had been his uncle, Lester Morse. Uncle Les had been a carnival strongman before he married Don's Aunt Imo. According to Don, Les was so strong that he could load a five-hundred-pound bale of cotton onto a truck single-handedly. He operated the town's only gas station, post office, icehouse, and also a little store.

Don worked with his uncle at the filling station, and he also helped him with his chores. I think Don's favorite story was about one day when he went with Uncle Les to deliver ice. Les had an old Ford truck, and on this particular day, it was fully loaded with big blocks of ice as they headed down the hill out of town. At the bottom of the long hill, the road turned sharply to the left, so Les started applying the brake right away in order to keep the truck from accelerating. He couldn't take a chance on missing the turn, because straight ahead was the North Canadian River.

From the start, Les could tell that something was wrong, because when he pulled on the brake lever, it didn't budge. As the heavy truck picked up speed, Les pulled harder, but still nothing happened. As they neared the bottom of the hill, and Les was yanking and pulling on the brake lever with all his considerable strength, it suddenly broke loose in his hand. Les yelled, "Hang on!" as he turned the steering wheel. The truck skidded and leaned to one side as they turned the corner, but they didn't go into the river.

Don was from a family of four boys. J. E. was still in grade school when Don went to college, and Everett, the brother he advised to join the Navy, was also quite a bit younger. Don was closer to his brother Boyd, who was just two years older than him. Whereas Don excelled in sports, Boyd excelled in schoolwork and in social skills. He was president of the debate team and vice president of his senior class in high school, and after graduating, he went to OU and started working his way through law school like my brother Haskell.

Uncle Les may have been Don's hero as a boy, but as he grew older, it was his brother Boyd's example that guided him. When Don was a senior in high school, his football coach came to Mr. Gunning with a plan to have Don flunk a class or two so that he would have to repeat his senior year. That way, the coach could have him on the team for another year. When they presented the plan to Don, he would have none of it. He was determined to follow his brother to college.

After Don got to OU, the two brothers roomed together, and Don started helping Boyd in the business he had started the year before, a laundry delivery service for sorority girls. They would pick up the girls' dirty clothes, take them to the laundry, and then deliver them when they were ready, for a fee. They also worked in the kitchen of the Kappa Kappa Gamma house for a little money and all they could eat. The Kappa girls all sat together and rooted for Don at basketball games. They were some of his biggest fans.

College was a struggle for Don. There were no athletic scholarships, and he had to work to support himself, in addition to studying and spending long hours practicing basketball. I think his coach did help him get a loan his senior year. And after all that, Don couldn't get a job when he graduated. His degree was in business management, and nobody wanted to hire a supervisor with no experience. Finally, Mr. Gunning got him a job working at Peppers Oil Company—he was Mr. Peppers' barber. Then Don went back to OU for a degree in accounting.

That's when I met him. He was working for Peppers, commuting to OU, and playing Amateur Athletic Union (AAU) basketball. I don't know how he managed to fit it all in. Oh, and he was playing and coaching for Peppers' softball team, too. I didn't care much about sports, but I did go to one of Don's softball games. During the game, he was a different person from the calm, mild-mannered man I had gotten to know. He was running around, yelling at the other players. He seemed to be making most of the scores too.

When we went out, I noticed that Don seemed to be a kind of hero to the other men. I remember one time when we were out together dancing, someone tried to start a fight with one of Don's friends—I think it was Tom Pierce, who worked with Don out at Peppers. The man was mad at Tom because he had accidentally tripped him. Anyway, as the man was heading over to our table, muttering curses, Tom calmly turned to Don and said, "Don, stand up." It was really funny to watch the man's face as

Wenonah and Don

he watched Don slowly rise up to his full six feet, four inches. That doesn't sound so big nowadays, but back then, Don seemed like a giant next to most people. Anyway, the man just kind of wilted. All the aggression went out of his face. Then he backed up, turned around, and walked back to his own table.

The work at Peppers was hard and dangerous. Don had to inspect and clean the big oil tanks. The fumes were not only poisonous, they could explode at any time. He had nightmares about it after we were married. He told me a story about one night when a big tanker was delivering oil to the plant in a rainstorm. The power lines were too low for the truck to pass under, so one of the men on Don's shift stood on top of the tanker to lift up the wires. As Don watched, the man inched his way along the top of the truck, holding the wire up with a tree branch. Suddenly, his feet slipped on the wet metal, the wire fell on him, and he was electrocuted.

Actually, Don had been offered other jobs. His basketball coach at OU had tried to get him to stay and be an assistant coach, but Don had turned him down. He had also been offered a job working for Park's clothing store, because he played on their basketball team. It was customary for companies who sponsored AAU teams to give their players jobs, but Don decided to keep working at the refinery instead, because Mr. Peppers had promised to give him a job as an accountant when he got his degree.

Don knew what I had gone through, and he was considerate of my feelings. When we started dating, he used to drink a little, but when I told him about how my father's drinking had ruined our lives, he stopped and never drank again. One time, after we had been going out together for a while, Don started to give me a hard time about talking to other men, so I told him that I wasn't going to let him tell me who I could talk to and who I couldn't. I told him about Papa, and that he was so jealous of Mama she couldn't even go to church, so Don backed off.

Don was a blessing to me. I always spoke my mind, but he never contradicted me. He would give his opinion, but he wouldn't argue, and he never went back on his word. He had a gift of making the right decisions and sticking to them, and Don really loved me. Throughout my whole life, he's the only person who was always on my side.

CHAPTER 41
- Our Wedding -

Everyone seemed surprised when I told them Don and I were getting married. Mama was surprised, too, but happy. She loved parties and celebrations, and she hadn't been able to celebrate any of her children's weddings. Snip didn't invite anyone to his, and all the rest had gotten married in secret. Mama at least got to go to Haskell's second wedding, but it wasn't much of a celebration.

Truthfully, I would just as soon have run off, too. I told Mama that I wanted a small wedding, with just the family and maybe Mrs. Garvin and Mrs. Ashurst, but she wouldn't hear of it. The first person she told was Snip, and after that, the affair was totally out of my hands.

Snip started planning immediately. He set the date for the wedding, and then he arranged to have it at the First Presbyterian Church. Actually, we hadn't gone to any church on a regular basis since the bishop decided to sell our little Episcopal Church, but the First Presbyterian was the biggest church in town, and Snip was planning for my wedding to be the social event of the year. After choosing the church, Snip proceeded to invite everybody in the county and then some. When I threatened to back out, he told me, "You're going down that aisle if I have to drag you by the hair of your head." My brothers were so tactful.

In retrospect, it was probably a good thing for our family. We had had enough tragedies, and it was time we celebrated something. It made Mama happy, and it was good politics.

Right away, Helen took me under her wing. We went to Wacker's together and picked out everything I would need to set up housekeeping: dishes, silverware, cooking utensils. I still use some of those things. I bought my own dress for twenty-five dollars. It had a full, white, floor-length skirt and a green bodice. I also got a heart-shaped tiara with a train attached for fifteen dollars—it cost almost as much as the dress. Helen worried about it not being all white, but I like green.

Snip was to give me away, and he tried to play the fatherly role. One day, he picked me up as I was walking home from the bus stop and proceeded to give me a lecture on how to toady to Don. I listened politely, but I thought to myself, "If there's going to be any toadying, it's certainly not going to be me."

On another occasion when Don and I were in Pauls Valley together, Haskell mentioned that Snip wanted to talk to us. That evening, I got Don to drive me out to the farm. We visited for a while, and Helen served refreshments. Snip was his usual charming self. He welcomed Don to the family, but he didn't hint at what it was he wanted.

Pretty soon we left, and I told Don to drive me by Haskell's house. Carrie answered the door, and when I asked for Haskell, she showed us back to the bedroom. Haskell was lying on the bed, chewing on a cigar and reading. He had taken his shirt off, and his undershirt had a big hole in it. I said, "Haskell, what was it that Snip wanted to talk to us about?" Haskell cleared his throat and then said, "He wants you to quit your job."

Later, Don told me that Snip and Haskell took him aside after the wedding and asked him if I was planning to continue working. I guess asking Don—all six-foot-four of him—was easier than confronting me. Don said, no, of course not. It was a matter of pride with him to be the man of the house and to support me. Snip would have been embarrassed if I hadn't quit, because he had gotten me my job. Back during the Depression, it was considered a privilege to have a job, and I would have been criticized for taking a job from someone who needed it more.

Everyone had a part to play at my wedding. As I said, Snip gave me away, and Kaliteyo was my matron of honor. Teker sang a solo. My bridesmaids were my roommate Hattie; Clara Paul, a friend from work and no relation; and Uncle Buck's daughter, Elizabeth Paul. Little L and Joe McClure's daughter Lacquanna carried candles in the procession. Mary Jane Williams, the daughter of one of my high school classmates, was my flower girl. Four-year-old Homer Dean was the trainbearer. Haskell, Tom, Thurman, Little Tom, and Little Willie were ushers. Helen and Carrie served the cake. Don's brother Boyd was his best man.

The only member of my family who wasn't there was Bob. He had already left for active duty at Fort Bliss.

Not everything went smoothly. Kaliteyo threw a fit because the family was going to so much trouble for my wedding. Mama told her they would have done the same for her if she hadn't run off, but she was inconsolable. Finally, Snip told her to settle down or he would get her fired.

As the day for the wedding approached, it began to rain. It rained, and it rained, a real frog-strangler, and then it began to flood. The skies cleared up the day before the wedding, but it took most of the day to pump the water out of the church basement where my reception was being held.

Don had to work the night before our wedding, but he had two full weeks of vacation after that for our honeymoon. We were planning to drive down to Mexico City. The morning of the wedding, he went back to our new apartment, got cleaned up, and drove over to Brown's Bakery to get our wedding cake. The cake was a big one. It had three tiers and a little bride-and-groom figurine on top. Don put the cake in the back seat of his car and started out on the sixty-mile trip to Pauls Valley. Just as he rounded the first corner, the top layer slid off the cake. Don carefully picked up the damaged cake and took it back to the bakery. After it was repaired, he set out again. This time, he was more careful and reached the highway before the cake slid apart again. He turned around and went back to the bakery for a second time. This time, the ladies gave him a bag of icing and showed him how to repair the cake himself.

It was a beautiful day in Pauls Valley. The skies had cleared, and the church was filled to overflowing. When everyone had been seated, Oteka sang her solo. Then they watched as Mary Jane Williams started down the aisle strewing rose petals. Suddenly, little four-year-old Homer Dean rushed up to her and said, "Don't do that. You're making a mess," and he started trying to pick up the petals. Everyone laughed as they continued down the aisle together arguing. Finally, Teker retrieved Homer Dean so that he could go back and hold my train.

The rest of the wedding went pretty smoothly. Snip gave me away. We said our "I do's," kissed, and walked out to the familiar refrains of the wedding march. Pictures were taken. Don cut the cake. It was a little smudged in spots, but there was plenty of icing.

After the wedding, our job was over. Snip was busy shaking hands. Mama was lost in a crowd of her friends. Even Kaliteyo was having a good time. Everyone ignored me. I felt like an actress who had played her role and was no longer needed. Finally, Don and I changed our clothes and got our luggage. I had to hunt just to find Mama to tell her goodbye. Snip did hunt me down to remind me that I had three hundred thank-you notes to write when we got back from our honeymoon.

Then, Don and I took off for Mexico City with only twenty-five dollars, but that's another story.

- Epilogue -

In 1962, after Mamma died, I found the following poem and letter among her things:

Willie

The things he used to play with are in the closet here
and on the shelf his books he loved to read
His shoes and gloves are covered with mud
His clothes are packed away
His picture and his violin his loving hands have played

The labor of the day is over
His tasks on earth were hard
He sleeps beneath the shadows
Strange silence broods oer all

Dear Willie:
A few lines to let you know that all the family are well at present
time. Tom, Oteka, Jim, and Kaliteyo are grown. Aside from that,

there isent much to tell, except it is Spring time and we miss you so! You ought to see the changes that have been made. Some you would like and some would make you sad. Mack has grown old and stiff and deff I hear. Maggie is the same but still we know she's old. Bob dog has passed away and left a space no other dog can fill!

The cows are sold, no others to take their place. Yesterday I took your papers, books, and maps and dusted them and placed them in boxes away from dust and prying fingers of those who may not care as much as you and I.

The house is quiet and I am alone, but for my memories. Some make me sad, some make me glad. Remember how you used to joke when things went bad, you always smiled, I know your heart was sad.

My room is never strange, never empty. There my father sat with Jim and his newspaper. I see you children all buisy doing different things. You Willie, Snip, Haskell, Kaliteyo, Jim, Bob, and Tom, and yes Victoria I always see, and little Samuel, so sweet, and with us so short a while. Victoria so sweet and kind to everyone. I see you boys troop upstairs to bed and hear your goodbyes as you troop off to school. Those memories are more to me than great Riches. They are myne I've lived them with you.

Your loving mother

Victoria Paul

Mama standing by Willie's grave

- Conclusion -

Wenonah's Story ends as my mother, Wenonah, and her brothers and sisters start out in life, having overcome the hardship and tragedy of their childhoods. There is more to their story, of course, much more than I can include in this book. Like any family, they had successes, failures, joys, and disappointments, but as their lives unfolded, they continued to rely on each other, just like they always had.

Mama, Victoria May Rosser Paul

The family was closest while Mama was still alive. "Mama was our anchor," Wenonah used to say. She was her children's refuge, and her house was always their home. The Paul clan gathered there on holidays and on special occasions.

Wenonah never forgot her promise to Willie to take care of Mama, and even though we didn't have much money, we drove down to Pauls Valley to see her every other Saturday all through my childhood. Wenonah would clean up the house, buy groceries, and take Mama out to the cemetery to tend the graves of Little Samuel, Victoria, and of course, Willie.

Mama always loved children, and she helped raise her grandkids. We all slid down her bannister, climbed her trees, and read her books. She sent us out to feed the chickens and weed the garden, and as a reward, she'd fix us cornbread, eggs scrambled with green onions, and okra fried down into crisp little kernels. Then she'd sit with us on the porch swing, telling us stories about "territory days," and greeting people as they walked by on the sidewalk.

Snip, Homer Paul

Snip began to take responsibility for the family as soon as he got his first job. He used his first year's salary to have gas installed in Mama's house. After he was elected to the state legislature, he got Willie a job as game warden, and when Teker fell into the hay mower, he used his connections to get her the best surgeon in the state.

After Willie died, Snip made a promise to Mama to take Willie's place, and he kept it. He got jobs for both Haskell and for Kaliteyo's husband Richard. He supported Mama, he sent Bob and Tom to OMA, and he convinced Haskell to support Kaliteyo and Wenonah in college, all in the middle of the Depression.

Snip was probably the most accomplished of my uncles. He served in the Oklahoma State Legislature for seventeen years, and from the start of his career, he was a man to be reckoned with. Snip always spoke his mind, regardless of the consequences, and he managed to thrive among the movers and shakers of his time. Jim Nance, Bill Holloway, Bill Murray, Leon Phillips, Robert S. Kerr, and Roy Turner all became his allies. In 1944, at the peak of his influence, Snip was elected president pro-tempore of the Senate, beating out Governor Kerr's pick for the job. During the session, Snip didn't always support the governor's policies, but he won his respect. When the 20th Legislature adjourned, Kerr declared it the most productive in state history.[1]

Snip's career in the legislature came to an end in 1948 when he lost his Senate seat to Herbert Hope, a returning veteran of World War II. He died the next year of complications from a fall in his barn. Wenonah always loved Snip for guiding and supporting the family through difficult times. One of the few times I ever saw her cry was when I asked her to tell me about him.

Haskell, Haskell Paul

Haskell, unlike his older brothers Willie and Snip, lived a long, full life, and he continued to display the same drive and curiosity that characterized him as a boy. He was one of the most fascinating people I've ever known.

He was well-read and enjoyed poetry and literature. He was a naturalist and a member of the American Forestry Association. He did research into the genealogy of our family, making trips to North Carolina, California, and even Scotland, searching for relatives and for family documents, and he could tell a story almost as well as Mama.

Haskell served his community as an attorney, a judge, and as one of Pauls Valley's most ardent supporters. He was an authority on the history of the region, a charter member of the Lions Club, president of the Garvin County Historical Society, and like his father, a 32nd degree Mason.

Haskell represented the Chickasaw Nation on the Intertribal Council for twenty years, and like Wenonah, he served on the board of directors of the Chickasaw Historical Society. After his retirement, he was elected and served for three years as a tribal judge, and after his death, he was inducted into the Chickasaw Hall of Fame.

Kaliteyo, Kaliteyo Mahota Paul Willingham

For twenty years, Kaliteyo worked as a cashier in the coffee shop of the ritzy Skirvin Hotel in downtown Oklahoma City. She loved people, and she spent her days listening to the trials and tribulations of the waitresses she worked with. Then she'd come over to our house and discuss their problems with Wenonah over leftover cornbread—she loved Wenonah's cornbread.

She and Wenonah continued to argue and fight, just like they had as children. Kaliteyo would storm out of our house one day and be back the next, raiding our refrigerator. And Wenonah continued to worry about her, inviting her over to our house every week to feed her a good meal.

I had wonderful times with Aunt Kaliteyo. Often she'd be with Wenonah when I got home from school, and we'd have cookies and milk together while I told her about my day. She played Old Maid and Canasta with me. She taught me to sit up straight, to use good manners, and because Wenonah was afraid of the water, she taught me to swim.

Kaliteyo enjoyed being with Teker. They went on trips together, and when Kaliteyo could no longer work, Teker sent her money so she could remain independent. Kaliteyo eventually became senile, and Wenonah moved her into our house where she lived until she required nursing care.

Bob, Robert Edward Lee Paul

None of Wenonah's brothers left home with greater potential than

Bob. He entered military service after graduating at the top of his class at OMA and passing the state bar exam. Soon after the United States entered World War II, he was promoted to the staff of General Kreuger, who would become one of the principal generals in the Pacific Theater. But a quirk of fate changed his life.

While stationed at Camp Bullis, Texas, Bob married Georgia Miers, whose father owned a large cattle ranch. When Mr. Miers offered Bob a job on his ranch with the promise of someday owning his own spread, Bob jumped at the chance. He had always loved horses. Since the Miers ranch was a major supplier of beef for the US military, he was given a deferment and released from active duty. It was just in the nick of time, too. As it turned out, the plane that was to carry him to the front went down over the Pacific.

Bob's life after that was a series of disappointments. His marriage failed, and he became estranged from his children. His ventures into ranching and law also failed, and then Bob disappeared. Wenonah didn't hear from him for ten years. She thought he was dead. Then one day in 1970 she got a call from him. He was living in Fort Worth, Texas, managing a filling station and raising racehorses.

Bob and Wenonah visited frequently after that, and for a while, they were able to relive their childhoods together through their memories of fighting, climbing Mama's trees, and riding Mack and Maggie. Bob's other siblings also got together with him, and his children, so he finally achieved some peace. He died about ten years later, while feeding his horses.

Teker, Oteka Paul McLean

All through her life, Aunt Oteka had the same cheerful enthusiasm she had as a girl. She was a Paul—assertive, strong, and the center of attention in any group—but there was something else that set her apart, even among her siblings. She had a way of concentrating her energy on others. She was always the peacemaker in the family, and we all looked forward to being with her. As my mother said, "everyone loved Oteka."

Like Wenonah, Teker believed that it was her duty to stay at home to take care of her children, and she did a great job of it. Her house was always spotless. Wenonah said it seemed like her washing machine was always running. She encouraged and supported her two sons in their activities, and she became as good a grandmother as Mama had been.

Teker always lived in Texas, but she still managed to be part of the family.

Every summer she came up to Pauls Valley and spent a month with Mama. When Tom's daughter needed a home, Teker kept her. When Haskell's son got in trouble, she kept him. When Kaliteyo's daughter was sick, Teker stayed with her, and when Bob was broke, she lent him money.

My cousin Steve told me a story about his mother that illustrates how involved she was with the family. She had called Wenonah long-distance during one of our family crises and lost track of time. We had to pay a premium in those days for long distance calls over three minutes. Teker ran her phone bill up so high she had to pawn her wedding ring to pay the bill.

Tom, Thomas Smith Paul

Out of all Wenonah's brothers and sisters, Tom had to be her favorite. She watched him as a child wrestle with Victor Swinney, and she listened to him make excuses to get out of going to school. She consoled him when he was a plebe at OMA, and she put her own future on hold to help him go to college. When Tom got married, Wenonah told him that she was washing her hands of him, but she didn't really mean it.

Tom's marriage was short lived. He couldn't make enough money to support his wife and go to college, so he volunteered to work on the Alaskan highway. When he returned a year later, his marriage was broken, and he was soon divorced.

Tom spent most of the next fifteen years doing construction work overseas. While he was gone, Wenonah made sure his child support was paid, and his taxes were filed. He worked in exotic places—Alaska, Guam, Morocco, and Iceland—and sent Wenonah and my aunts beautiful scarves, jewelry, and figurines. When he came home, the whole family would gather at Mama's house to hear about his adventures.

Uncle Tom was like a big brother to me. He taught me to box and to ride a horse, and he played tricks on me like he did Little Tom. Wenonah treated him like another child. One time, she caught him holding one of my hands behind my back while another boy tried to hit me. He tried to explain to her that I needed to learn how to dodge punches, but she grabbed a broom and took out after him like Mama had when he was little.

Tom was killed in a car crash when he was forty-three. It was the first time that I had lost someone close to me, and I felt like a hole had been cut out of my heart. Wenonah was hysterical. My cousin Steve told me Aunt Oteka cried for days.

James Wenonah Paul Gunning

Marriage wasn't the end of Wenonah's struggles or her accomplishments. Heading off on their honeymoon with only twenty-five dollars was one of my parents' few miscalculations. Don and Wenonah were frugal, and they never took chances. We never went out to eat, and we drove our cars until they wore out.

My father was the perfect complement for Wenonah. While she was volatile, he was calm, and while she was intuitive, he was patient and thoughtful. He never brought his work home. When he got home in the evening, he helped with the cooking. He was a wonderful father, strong and gentle at the same time. He made Wenonah, and me, feel safe and secure. He was our "Rock of Gibraltar," as she used to say.

Wenonah believed what Mama had taught her, that children are like clay, to be molded by their parents. So for the first twenty years of her marriage, she devoted most of her considerable energy to raising me. She took part in my every activity. When I had trouble reading, she taught me at home. When I entered Cub Scouts, she became a den mother. When I graduated from grade school, she organized a youth group at our church that hosted parties and taught ballroom dancing so that we would learn social skills. When I wanted to play the violin, she used her grocery money to pay for lessons. I didn't realize until years later that her brother Willie had also played the violin.

Wenonah never forgot her promise to Willie. She always did her best to help Mama and her brothers and sisters, and she also gave them advice, though they rarely appreciated it. She was always plainspoken. She said what she thought, without any attempt to be tactful. She told me once she thought it was dishonest not to say what you think.

For example, in 1956, Aunt Kaliteyo remarried to a rancher from Texas who used to stay at the Skirvin Hotel where she worked. On the day of her wedding, Wenonah stopped her on the church steps and said, "Kaliteyo, you're going to be miserable living out there on the ranch. Tell Hugh to build you a house in town so you can be around people."

I don't think Kaliteyo spoke to Wenonah any more that day, even though her reception was at our house, but about six months later there was a knock on our door. It was Kaliteyo. She had left Hugh. "I couldn't spend another night in that house," she said. "I was alone all day, and when Hugh came home at night, he wouldn't say five words to me."

The year before I graduated from college, my grandmother died. Unable to bear her grief at home alone, Wenonah went back to work as a social worker. She started at the bottom, but over the next fifteen years, she worked her way up to a position in the state director's office. After she retired, she devoted herself to preserving our family's history. She compiled the pictures, letters, and other documents she had collected over the years into scrapbooks and donated items to the Chickasaw Archives, as well as to the Five Civilized Tribes Museum at Muskogee, and the local museums at Pauls Valley and Wynnewood. She also served on the board of directors of the Chickasaw Historical Society, like Haskell before her.

I didn't hear about the details of Willie's death until Wenonah was telling me her story for this book. When I realized what an effect his death must have had on her, I asked her how much she thought about him, through the years.

She replied, "Every day of my life."

When Wenonah was dying, she held onto my hand almost until the end. Then suddenly she dropped it, looked up, and cried, "Willie take me, Willie, Willie, Willie…"

Those were her last words.

- *Endnotes* -

CHAPTER 1

[1]Excerpt from *The Song of Hiawatha* by Henry Wadsworth Longfellow.

[2] Confederate military records, Muster rolls, 1862, from Oklahoma Board of Pension Commissioners, 1915. Several entries list James, and later J. T. Rosser, in Company D, Phillips Legion, Georgia State Guards in 1862. Entry in May of 1862 documents his enlistment as a private. An entry for May-June states that his enlistment was for "3 years or the war," and that he was "sick in hospital." An entry for September-October 1862 states, "not stand."

[3] Ancestry.com has a record of the marriage of James Rosser and Emily Bass on "4 Sept 1863, in Barbour Co, Ala. Alabama Marriages, 1809-1920, (selected counties)." It must have been a quick trip, because the Confederate military records have him in the army between August and December 1863.

[4] Confederate military records, Muster rolls, 1863-64. The roll lists James T. Rosser as a volunteer mustered in with rank of sergeant to Captain Wimberly's Company, Floyd Legion, Georgia, Aug. 4, 1863, at Cedartown, Ga. Another record shows that he resigned in December 1863.

[5] United States Federal Census, 1870. James Rosser's age is listed as 25; Emily, 24; Cora, 6; Thomas, 3; and Luther, 1. James' occupation is listed

as "farm hand," and Emily as, "keeping house." Birthplace for James and Emily is listed as Virginia, Georgia for Cora, and Alabama for Thomas and Luther.

[6] Ibid.

[7] Family records include a handwritten note that states: "Kittie Bun Rosser was born near Benalla, Alabama, June 1874. Victoria May Rosser was born in Mississippi, Pittsburgh, Calhoun Co., March 31, 1877. Ada Edward was born Palmer, Arkansas, 1880. Eula Lee born Palmer, May 1882, Philip Co. Lutha Rosser born in Alabama. Died in Mississippi in 1877. Eula died Palmer Station, 1882. Lutha was born in Alabama died in Mississippi. Lutha was 7 years, 7 months and 27 days old when he died." Mama's notes didn't include Sister Lillie, but she was between Sister Kittie and Mama in age so she would have been born in either 1875 or 1876. Victoria May Rosser Paul, undated, handwritten note. Original in personal files.

[8] Family records include the following handwritten note: "I was born in Pittsboro, Calhoun County. 3 miles of yellow bushy swamps. Ada was born on the Mils place Munroe county. 2 year 3 year Rushen (?) Eula was born in 82." There is a river and a county in Mississippi near Pittsboro named "Yalobusha," a Chickasaw word meaning tadpole place. In her memory, Mama probably converted the name into words she was familiar with. Victoria May Rosser Paul, undated, handwritten note. Original in personal files.

[9] Ibid.

[10] Ibid. From this note the family would have come to Arkansas between 1877, when Mama was born in Mississippi, and 1880 when Sister Ada was born in Arkansas.

[11] Ibid.

[12] Arkansas, County Marriages Index, 1837-1947. Record of marriage of Cora L. Rosser to H. B. Morris, 4 April 1883.

[13] According to Haskell Paul's research notes: "Sam Paul was a Progressive. He went into North Texas and also Arkansas and urged whites to move into Smith Pauls Valley." I'm not really sure whether it was Sam Paul who convinced Grandpa to come to Indian Territory, but it's certainly plausible. Haskell Paul, notebook, undated, transcription, p 5. Original in Nora Sparks Warren Memorial Library, Pauls Valley, Oklahoma. Copy in personal files.

[14] The town was originally called Smith Paul's Valley, but when the Santa Fe Railroad located a depot there they put "Pauls Valley" on the sign, and after

that the town became known as simply Pauls Valley. The story was told that the name was shortened because the longer name was too long to go on the sign. Haskell Paul, notebook, undated. Copy in personal files.

[15] Mrs. Victoria Paul, Interview #8492 by Maurice R. Anderson, *Indian Pioneer History Project for Oklahoma*, September 14, 1937. OkGenWeb. org/pioneer papers. "It cost five dollars a year permit for a family to live in the Indian territory and two dollars and fifty cents for a single man. There would be collectors come around and collect this fee and if the collectors did not turn in all that he had collected then he would be tried under Indian law and given so many lashes across the back. They had a whipping post at the place where the court was held."

[16] Arrell M. Gibson, *The Chickasaws* (Norman: University of Oklahoma Press, 1971), 251-52. Gibson discusses the building of railroads across the Chickasaw Nation.

[17] Mrs. Victoria Paul, Interview #8492 by Maurice R. Anderson, *Indian Pioneer History Project for Oklahoma,* September 14, 1937. OkGenWeb. org/pioneer papers.

[18] John Bartlett Meserve, "Governor William Leander Byrd," *Chronicles of Oklahoma* 12, no. 4, (December 1934) 439.

[19] Brief prepared by O. W. Patchell for Sarah J. Paul, applicant for enrollment as intermarried Chickasaw citizen before the Commission of the United States to the Five Civilized Tribes, Dept. of the Interior, 17 July 1903, Chickasaw Nation Archives, 2. The brief states, "when her boy William H. Paul was but two days old her husband (Sam Paul) went off with an Indian girl and was gone a month on a love feast."

[20] From testimony of Sarah J. Paul before the Commission of the United States to the Five Civilized Tribes, Dept. of the Interior, 8 May 1903. Chickasaw Nation Archives, 1.

[21] From testimony of Sarah J. Paul before the Commission of the United States to the Five Civilized Tribes, Dept. of the Interior. May 8, 1903. Chickasaw Nation Archives, 2.

[22] Subscription schools were the same as private schools today. The parents paid a tuition for their children to attend.

[23] From a biographical sketch of Sam Paul in Harry F. O'Bierne, *Leaders and Leading Men of the Indian Territory: Choctaws and Chickasaws* (Chicago: American Publishers' Association, 1891), 282.

[24] "Paul and Burk, Attorneys at Law," *Chickasaw Chieftain* (Indian

Territory), October 22, 1891. Courtesy of Jim Phillips.

[25] Haskell Paul, notebook, undated, 1. Original in Nora Sparks Warren Memorial Library, Pauls Valley, Oklahoma. Copy in personal files.

CHAPTER 2

[1] "Paul-McClure Wedding," Name of newspaper unknown, May 2, 1875. Original at Depot Museum, Pauls Valley, Oklahoma.

[2] Moman Pruiett, *Moman Pruiett, Criminal Lawyer* (Oklahoma City, Harlow Publishing Corp. 1945), 84 – 86.

CHAPTER 4

[1] Haskell Paul, notebook, undated, 7. Original in Nora Sparks Warren Memorial Library, Pauls Valley, Oklahoma. Copy in personal files. "Sam Paul gave lots to Grant and Martin, Wm. G. Kimberlin, and Sam Garvin to help get the new town started. The town was built entirely on Sam Paul's Farm. When Sam Paul died in Dec. 1891, Joe received 2 lots, one where Menefee is & the other where Burns is. Papa and Uncle Buck received 30 or 40 lots together. Most of it had been disposed of before they reached the majority age."

CHAPTER 5

[1] *Garvin County History: From Bluestem to Golden Trend* (Fort Worth: University Supply & Equipment Company, 1957), 155.

[2] "Convention of Mock Heroics, Muskogee Affair Is in Control of Enemies of Statehood," *Daily Oklahoman*, August 22, 1905. This article, ridiculing the efforts of Indian Territory to become a separate state, lists the officers of the convention: chairman, Pleasant Porter (Creek Chief); vice-chairman, Charles Haskell (first governor of Oklahoma); secretary, Alex Posey (Creek poet and writer; acknowledged as editor of first Indian published daily newspaper); assistant secretary, William H. Paul.

CHAPTER 6

[1] Mrs. Moore was a remarkable woman. She studied law and was admitted to the bar; she organized the emergency relief effort for Oklahoma City during the depression, and for thirty-five years she was a member of the board of directors for the Oklahoma State Historical Society. From Muriel H. Wright, "Jessie Elizabeth Randolph Moore of the Chickasaw Nation," *Chronicles of Oklahoma* 34, no. 4, (1956), 392-96. Article reprinted in *The Journal of Chickasaw History* 6, no. 3, (2000): 4-8.

CHAPTER 9

[1] S.C. Cornwall, "The Ferns," in *The Heath Readers: Second Reader* (Boston: D. H. Heath and Co., 1907), 108.

CHAPTER 11

[1] Pauls Valley's original site was on land controlled by Papa's uncle, Tecumseh McClure. Tecumseh refused to give up land for a railroad depot, so Sam Paul offered some of his land and the town was moved. Sam's land was nearer to Rush Creek, and the town has been prone to flooding ever since. Haskell Paul, notebook, undated, 5. Original in Nora Sparks Warren Memorial Library, Pauls Valley, Oklahoma.

CHAPTER 14

[1] Dr. Laird not only provided dental care to small communities, he also put on "medicine shows" in which his daughter Mignon played her harp and danced. Donavan L. Hofsommer, *Katy Northwest: The Story of a Branch Line Railroad* (Bloomington, Indiana University Press, 1999), 44. Mignon went on to become a featured performer with the Ziegfeld Follies. Laura Haywood, "The Ziegfeld Club," *seniorwomen.com*.

[2] "From a Faulty System," *Daily Oklahoman*, April 14, 1935.

CHAPTER 15

[1] *Garvin County History: From Bluestem to Golden Trend* (Fort Worth: University Supply & Equipment Company, 1957).

CHAPTER 17

[1] A Methodist missionary named John Carr founded Bloomfield in 1852. Reverend Carr and his wife located their school in a meadow covered by wild flowers, hence the name "Bloomfield." The Chickasaw Nation started supporting Carr's project when the tribal government was established in 1856, and except for a brief period during the Civil War, the school continued to operate until 1948. With the demise of the Chickasaw government in 1906, control of the school passed to the federal government, but it was still supported by Chickasaw funds, and when Wenonah was a student there, many of the teachers and other staff members were Chickasaw or Choctaw. Amanda J. Cobb, *Listening to Our Grandmothers' Stories, The Bloomfield Academy for Chickasaw Females, 1852-1949*, (Lincoln and London: University of Nebraska Press, 1970).

CHAPTER 18

[1] Fictitious name.

CHAPTER 20

[1] "Funeral Address," date and name of newspaper unknown. Original in Paul Family Bible. Courtesy of Homer McLean.

CHAPTER 21

[1] "W. H. Paul Guilty Of Manslaughter," *Pauls Valley Democrat*, December 6, 1928.

CHAPTER 22

[1] "Homer Paul Becomes a Benedict, Garvin County Solon Weds Claremore Girl In Oklahoma City," *Pauls Valley Democrat*, January 10, 1929.

[2] "Investigating Committee Pledged to Secrecy After Night Session," *Daily Oklahoman*, January 18, 1929.

[3] Information about Governor Johnston and the 12th Oklahoma Legislature obtained from James R. Scales and Danney Goble, *Oklahoma Politics: A History* (Norman: University of Oklahoma Press, 1982), Chapter 8.

CHAPTER 23

[1] R. E. Wood, "History of the Acquisition of the Different Classes of State and School Lands of Oklahoma," *Chronicles of Oklahoma,* 13, no. 4, (Dec 1935): 381-85.

[2] Robert Perry, *Uprising! Woody Crumbo's Indian Art* (Ada, Oklahoma: Chickasaw Press, 2009), 83.

[3] "Home Stands Firm 68 Years," *Pauls Valley Democrat,* December 9, 1973. Mama is quoted as saying: "You don't know what a depression is, unless you've had prosperity and the pioneers don't know anything about depressions because they've never been prosperous."

[4] I realize that this is a contradiction. The antics of Oteka and Tom that Wenonah describes are similar to those of Bob and herself, and Tom's truancy was hardly worse than Snip's. Also, Mama's punishments described later to me by Uncle Tom are the same. Still, Wenonah always maintained that Mama was easier on her younger children.

CHAPTER 24

[1] "W. H. Paul Passes Away Here Monday," *Pauls Valley Enterprise*, September 25, 1930. The article gives Uncle Buck's first name incorrectly as Sam instead of Smith, and of course, they misspelled Wenonah's and Kaliteyo's names.

[2] Sam Walter Foss, *The House by the Side of the Road*, in *One Hundred and One Famous Poems*, compiled by Roy J. Cook (Chicago: Reilly and Lee Co., 1958).

CHAPTER 25

[1] *Garvin County History: From Bluestem to Golden Trend* (Fort Worth: University Supply and Equipment Company, 1957), 184. Bennie Owen was OU's football coach from 1905-26, and he also coached the basketball and baseball teams.

[2] "Paul to Seek Speaker Post," *Daily Oklahoman*, September 10, 1930.

[3] Story of William H. Murray taken from James R. Scales and Danney Goble, *Oklahoma Politics: A History* (Norman: University of Oklahoma Press, 1982), Chapter 9.

[4] Ibid., 165.

[5] "Shower of Gifts Fetes Recent Bride," name of newspaper and date of article unknown. Copy of clipping in family Bible.

CHAPTER 26

[1] "Wacker's" was one of the original "Five and Dime" stores. It was started in 1922 in Pauls Valley by George and Mona Wacker. Wacker's was successful and grew into a chain of seventy-eight stores before it was bought in 1980. The Wackers made their home in Pauls Valley, and Mr. Wacker served on the city council and as mayor. Mary Anne Lynn, *Home: A Pictorial History of Garvin County*, (Marceline, Mo.: D-Books Publishing, 1995), 79.

[2] Susan Garvin was an old friend of Mama's, and she was like a grandmother to us. She was full blood Choctaw and her parents had been neighbors of Smith Paul before the Civil War. Her husband Sam was a prosperous farmer, and Garvin County was named for him. Wenonah's oldest brother Samuel was also named after him, and her oldest sister Victoria Sue was named after Mrs. Garvin. Mama and Papa were married in the Garvins' house.

CHAPTER 27

[1] "Frying the Political Fat," *Daily Oklahoman*, May 15, 1932.

[2] "Session 'Youngsters' Talk It Over," *Daily Oklahoman*, January 8, 1933.

[3] "Farmers Wait While Few Get Favors, Beckett Hints on Stand," *Daily Oklahoman*, June 6, 1933.

[4] "Long Inquiry Predicted as Group 'Digs In,'" *Daily Oklahoman*, June 2, 1933.

[5] "Paul Chosen Head of Group to Write Bill," *Daily Oklahoman*, July 9, 1933.

[6] "School Land Probe Faces Opening Test," *Daily Oklahoman*, May 26, 1933.

CHAPTER 28

[1] The Interurban was an extension of the Oklahoma City streetcar system that connected the downtown area with the suburbs and surrounding towns. It ran on electricity and therefore didn't contaminate the city with soot. The Interurban stayed in operation until after World War II, when the automobile put it out of business.

CHAPTER 29

[1] Thomas H. Paul, "Genesis: Part Two" (unpublished manuscript, undated) 56-57. Copy in personal files.

[2] Ibid., 186-87.

[3] "Senators Rap Student Fees at University, Bizzell Runs School as Regents Obey Orders, Paul Asserts," *Daily Oklahoman*, February 6, 1935.

[4] "Senate Votes Ban on Forced Ticket Sales, Measure is Passed Providing Penalties for Violations By State Schools," *Daily Oklahoman*, April 20, 1935.

[5] "From a Faulty System," *Daily Oklahoman*, April 14, 1935.

[6] James R. Scales and Danney Goble, *Oklahoma Politics: A History* (Norman: University of Oklahoma Press, 1982). Chapter 10 provides overview of E. W. Marland's term as governor.

[7] "Heavy State Losses Cited By Attorney," *Daily Oklahoman*, April 3, 1935; and "House Asked to Authorize Land Inquiry," *Daily Oklahoman*, Febuary 8, 1935.

[8] "House Probers to Question Trio of Dismissal of Paul," *Daily Oklahoman*, April 18, 1935.

CHAPTER 30

[1] Argyrol is a patent medicine used to swab the throat to relieve pain. It is rarely used now for this purpose because antibiotics are available.

[2] The Federal Emergency Relief Administration was created in 1932 by President Herbert Hoover as the Emergency Relief Administration (ERA). It provided loans to states to create relief programs during the Depression. It was later replaced by the Works Progress Administration. In Oklahoma the

loans were used to create the Oklahoma Emergency Relief Administration (OERA.)

CHAPTER 31

[1] Houston Teehee, a five-eighths Cherokee Indian born in Indian Territory in 1874, became an attorney and held many public offices including registrar of the United States treasury and assistant attorney general of the state of Oklahoma. He returned to the private practice of law in 1931, during which time he defended Mr. Standing Deer. Through the years he rendered great service to the leaders of the Cherokee Nation, acting as counselor and advisor in matters affecting individuals as well as families and communities. He was inducted into the Oklahoma Hall of Fame in 1942, and he passed away in 1953. "Famed Cherokee Leader Is Dead," *Daily Oklahoman*, November 20, 1953.

[2] The Oklahoma Emergency Relief Administration was Oklahoma's version of the Federal Emergency Relief Administration.

CHAPTER 33

[1] "State Senate Candidate Hopes to Ride in on Paving," *Daily Oklahoman*, July 24, 1936.

[2] "Legislative Mill Will Start Rolling Today With Gavel's Bang," *Daily Oklahoman,* November 24, 1936.

[3] "State Politics," *Daily Oklahoman*, December 13, 1936.

[4] "India-Okla Club Banquet Will Be Given Thursday, Indians From Over State to Attend," *Daily Oklahoman,* February 16, 1936.

[5] "Session Studies Measures Calling for Expenditures of $8,490,069," *Daily Oklahoman*, December 13, 1936.

[6] "Senate Votes Bill to Halt Kinfolk Evils, Action Is Aimed at Hiring Each Other's Relatives," *Daily Oklahoman,* January 27, 1937.

[7] James R. Scales and Danney Goble, *Oklahoma Politics: A History* (Norman: University of Oklahoma Press, 1982), 198-200.

[8] "Pauls Valley Robin Hood Dies," *The Tulsa Tribune*, January 10, 1949.

[9] "Senator Paul Ill; Sent to Hospital," *Daily Oklahoman*, March 20, 1937.

[10] "Senator Paul Hits Reporter in State House, Apology Is Accepted After Sudden Attack," *Daily Oklahoman*, May 12, 1937.

CHAPTER 34

[1] "Senator's Brother Promoted to Highest Cadet Post at Academy, Robert Paul Made Lieutenant Colonel at Claremore," name and date of newspaper unknown. Original in Paul family Bible.

CHAPTER 35

[1] "Legislators Vote That They Can Become Lawyers," *Daily Oklahoman*, May 9, 1937.

[2] "Paul First in Home Area, Swank Second," *Daily Oklahoman*, November 17, 1937.

[3] R. M. McClintock, "State Politics," *Daily Oklahoman*, November 22, 1937.

[4] "Paul Is First in Home Area," *Daily Oklahoman*, November 17, 1937.

[5] "Rinehart and Curnutt Seek Power," *Daily Oklahoman*, July 22, 1938.

CHAPTER 37

[1] Lay term referring to a child with a congenital heart defect that causes blood to bypass the lungs, so that it contains less oxygen, giving it a blue color.

[2] James R. Scales and Danney Goble, *Oklahoma Politics: A History* (Norman: University of Oklahoma Press, 1982). Chapter 11 describes Leon Phillips' term as governor.

[3] "Senate Trims Bill to Give Attorney General Added Help in Office," *Daily Oklahoman*, March 9, 1939.

[4] "Big Beer Levy Voted Out by Upper House," *Daily Oklahoman*, March 29, 1939.

[5] "Senator's Kin Given Pay Cut, Salaries Reduced to Bring Them Into Line," *Daily Oklahoman*, June 7, 1939.

CHAPTER 38

[1] "Monroney to Back Paul As Tribe Head, Brother of State Senator In Crowded Race," *Daily Oklahoman*, July 8, 1939.

CHAPTER 39

[1] Private William A. Stevens Jr. to Tom Paul, San Diego, California, July 22, 1940. Original in personal files. Billie Stevens was killed in World War II.

CHAPTER 43

[1] "Session's End Likely Today," *Daily Oklahoman*, April 26, 1945.